OXFORD REFERENCE

THE CONCISE
OXFORD DICTIONARY OF
MATHEMATICS

THE CONCISE
OXFORD DICTIONARY OF
MATHEMATICS

CHRISTOPHER CLAPHAM

Oxford   New York

OXFORD UNIVERSITY PRESS

Oxford University Press, Walton Street, Oxford OX2 6DP

Oxford New York Toronto
Delhi Bombay Calcutta Madras Karachi
Petaling Jaya Singapore Hong Kong Tokyo
Nairobi Dar es Salaam Cape Town
Melbourne Auckland

and associated companies in
Berlin Ibadan

Oxford is a trade mark of Oxford University Press

First published as an Oxford University Press paperback 1990
Reprinted 1990, 1991 (twice)

British Library Cataloguing in Publication Data
Clapham, Christopher
A concise Oxford dictionary of mathematics.
1. Mathematics
I. Title
510
ISBN 0-19-866156-8
ISBN 0-19-286103-4 pbk

Library of Congress Cataloging in Publication Data
Clapham, Christopher
A concise Oxford dictionary of mathematics/Christopher Clapham.
p. cm.
1. Mathematics—Dictionaries. I. Title
510'.3—dc20 QA5.C53 1990 89-39359
ISBN 0-19-866156-8
ISBN 0-19-286103-4 pbk

Printed in Great Britain by
Clays Ltd.
Bungay, Suffolk

PREFACE

This dictionary is intended to be a reference book that gives reliable definitions or clear and precise explanations of mathematical terms. The level is such that it will suit, among others, sixth-form pupils, college students and first-year university students who are taking mathematics as one of their courses. Such students will be able to look up any term they may meet and be led on to other entries by following up cross-references or by browsing more generally.

Statistics, computing and applied mathematics are not included. However, the concepts and terminology of all those topics that feature in pure mathematics courses at this level today are covered. There are also entries on major mathematicians and important mathematics of more general interest. The reader's attention is drawn to the appendices which give useful tables for ready reference.

One detail may need explanation. Within its own entry, a keyword appears in bold type at the point where it is defined or explained. Occasionally within an entry, other keywords, in bold type, may appear if this is the most appropriate context in which to define or explain them. Slanting type is used to indicate words with their own entry, to which cross-reference can be made if required.

I am most grateful to John Pulham, a colleague at the University of Aberdeen, for writing the short biographical sketches of the mathematicians. It has been impossible, of course, to be comprehensive; the intention has been to make mention of the greatest mathematicians and others that are important and about whom there is something of interest to say. Those included may perhaps serve to arouse an interest in the casual reader.

My thanks also go to Ivor Grattan-Guinness and Robin Wilson, who read and commented on some of the material, and to Roger Wheeler, who took much trouble and made valuable suggestions.

Christopher Clapham

A

Abel, Niels Henrik (1802–1829)   Abel was born a pastor's son in Norway. At the age of 19, he proved that the general polynomial of degree greater than 4 cannot be solved by 'extraction of roots'. In other words, there can be no formula for the roots of such equations similar to the familiar formula for quadratics. Abel was also responsible for fundamental developments in the theory of algebraic functions. This was his most significant work. His name gives us the term *abelian*. He died in some poverty at the age of 26, just a few days before he would have received a letter announcing his appointment to a professorship in Berlin.

abelian group   Suppose that G is a *group* with the operation ∘. Then G is **abelian** if the operation ∘ is commutative; that is, if, for all elements a and b in G, $a \circ b = b \circ a$.

abscissa   The **abscissa** is the x-coordinate in a Cartesian coordinate system in the plane.

absolute error   See *error*.

absolute value   For any real number a, the **absolute value** (also called the *modulus*) of a, denoted by $|a|$, is a itself if $a \geq 0$, and $-a$ if $a < 0$. Thus $|a|$ is positive except when $a = 0$. The following properties hold:

   (i) $|ab| = |a||b|$.
   (ii) $|a + b| \leq |a| + |b|$.
   (iii) $|a - b| \geq ||a| - |b||$.
   (iv) For $a > 0$, $|x| \leq a$ if and only if $-a \leq x \leq a$.

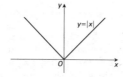

absorption laws   For all sets A and B (subsets of some *universal set*), $A \cap (A \cup B) = A$ and $A \cup (A \cap B) = A$. These are the **absorption laws**.

abstract algebra   The subject of **abstract algebra** is concerned with the many different algebraic structures, such as *groups*, *rings* and *fields*, involving sets of elements with particular operations satisfying certain axioms. The purpose is to derive, from the set of axioms, general results that are then applicable to any particular example of the algebraic structure in question. The theory of certain algebraic structures is highly developed; in particular, the theory of vector spaces is so extensive that its study, known as *linear algebra*, would probably no longer be classified as abstract algebra.

acceleration   Suppose that a particle is moving in a straight line with a point O on the line taken as origin and one direction taken as positive. Let x be the *displacement* of the particle at time t. The **acceleration** of the particle is equal to $\ddot{x}$ or d^2x/dt^2, the *rate of change* of the *velocity* with respect to t. If the velocity is positive (that is, the particle is moving in the positive direction), the acceleration is positive when the particle is speeding up and negative when it is slowing down. However, if the velocity is negative, a positive acceleration means that the particle is slowing down and a negative acceleration means that it is speeding up.

acute angle   An angle is **acute** if it is less than a *right angle*. An **acute-angled** triangle is one all of whose angles are acute.

addition modulo n See *modulo n, addition and multiplication*.

addition (of complex numbers)   Let the complex numbers z_1 and z_2, where $z_1 = a + bi$ and $z_2 = c + di$, be represented by the points P_1 and P_2 in the *complex plane*. Then $z_1 + z_2 = (a+c) + (b+d)i$, and $z_1 + z_2$ is represented in the complex plane by the point Q such that OP_1QP_2 is a parallelogram; that is, such that $\overrightarrow{OQ} = \overrightarrow{OP_1} + \overrightarrow{OP_2}$. Thus, if the complex number z is associated with the *directed line-segment* $\overrightarrow{OP}$, where P represents z, addition of complex numbers corresponds exactly to the addition of the directed line-segments.

addition (of directed line-segments)   See *addition* (of vectors).

addition (of matrices)   Let $\mathbf{A}$ and $\mathbf{B}$ be $m \times n$ matrices, with $\mathbf{A} = [a_{ij}]$ and $\mathbf{B} = [b_{ij}]$. The operation of **addition** is defined by taking the **sum** $\mathbf{A} + \mathbf{B}$ to be the $m \times n$ matrix $\mathbf{C}$, where $\mathbf{C} = [c_{ij}]$ and $c_{ij} = a_{ij} + b_{ij}$. The sum $\mathbf{A} + \mathbf{B}$ is not defined if $\mathbf{A}$ and $\mathbf{B}$ are not of the same order. This operation $+$ of addition on the set of all $m \times n$ matrices is *associative* and *commutative*.

addition (of vectors)   Given vectors $\mathbf{a}$ and $\mathbf{b}$, let $\overrightarrow{OA}$ and $\overrightarrow{OB}$ be *directed line-segments* that represent $\mathbf{a}$ and $\mathbf{b}$, with the same initial point O. The sum of $\overrightarrow{OA}$ and $\overrightarrow{OB}$ is the directed line-segment $\overrightarrow{OC}$, where $OACB$ is a parallelogram, and the **sum** $\mathbf{a} + \mathbf{b}$ is defined to be the vector $\mathbf{c}$ represented by $\overrightarrow{OC}$. This

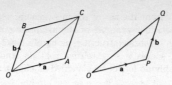

The parallelogram law   The triangle law

is called the **parallelogram law**. Alternatively, the sum of vectors **a** and **b** can be defined by representing **a** by a directed line-segment $\overrightarrow{OP}$ and **b** by $\overrightarrow{PQ}$, where the final point of the first directed line-segment is the initial point of the second. Then $\mathbf{a} + \mathbf{b}$ is the vector represented by $\overrightarrow{OQ}$. This is called the **triangle law**. Addition of vectors has the following properties, which hold for all **a**, **b** and **c**:

   (i) $\mathbf{a} + \mathbf{b} = \mathbf{b} + \mathbf{a}$, the commutative law.
  (ii) $\mathbf{a} + (\mathbf{b} + \mathbf{c}) = (\mathbf{a} + \mathbf{b}) + \mathbf{c}$, the associative law.
 (iii) $\mathbf{a} + \mathbf{0} = \mathbf{0} + \mathbf{a} = \mathbf{a}$, where **0** is the zero vector.
 (iv) $\mathbf{a} + (-\mathbf{a}) = (-\mathbf{a}) + \mathbf{a} = \mathbf{0}$, where $-\mathbf{a}$ is the negative of **a**.

additive group   A *group* with the operation $+$, called addition, may be called an **additive group**. The operation in a group is normally denoted by addition only if it is *commutative*, so an additive group is usually *abelian*.

additive inverse   See *inverse element*.

adjacency matrix   For a *simple graph* G, with n vertices $v_1, v_2, \ldots, v_n$, the **adjacency matrix** **A** is the $n \times n$ matrix $[a_{ij}]$ with $a_{ij} = 1$, if v_i is joined to v_j, and $a_{ij} = 0$, otherwise. The matrix **A** is *symmetric* and the diagonal entries are zero. The number of ones in any row (or column) is equal to the *degree* of the corresponding vertex. For example, a graph and its adjacency matrix **A** are shown below.

$$\mathbf{A} = \begin{bmatrix} 0 & 1 & 1 & 0 \\ 1 & 0 & 1 & 0 \\ 1 & 1 & 0 & 1 \\ 0 & 0 & 1 & 0 \end{bmatrix}$$

adjoint   The **adjoint** of a square matrix **A**, denoted by adj **A**, is the transpose of the matrix of cofactors of **A**. For $\mathbf{A} = [a_{ij}]$, let A_{ij} denote the *cofactor* of the entry a_{ij}. Then the matrix of cofactors is the matrix $[A_{ij}]$ and adj $\mathbf{A} = [A_{ij}]^T$. For example, a 3×3 matrix **A** and its adjoint can be written

$$\mathbf{A} = \begin{bmatrix} a_{11} & a_{12} & a_{13} \\ a_{21} & a_{22} & a_{23} \\ a_{31} & a_{32} & a_{33} \end{bmatrix}, \quad \mathrm{adj}\,\mathbf{A} = \begin{bmatrix} A_{11} & A_{21} & A_{31} \\ A_{12} & A_{22} & A_{32} \\ A_{13} & A_{23} & A_{33} \end{bmatrix}$$

In the 2×2 case, a matrix **A** and its adjoint have the form

$$\mathbf{A} = \begin{bmatrix} a & b \\ c & d \end{bmatrix}, \qquad \text{adj } \mathbf{A} = \begin{bmatrix} d & -b \\ -c & a \end{bmatrix}.$$

The adjoint is important because it can be used to find the *inverse* of a matrix. From the properties of cofactors, it can be shown that $\mathbf{A} \text{ adj } \mathbf{A} = (\det \mathbf{A})\mathbf{I}$. It follows that, when $\det \mathbf{A} \neq 0$, the inverse of **A** is $(1/\det \mathbf{A}) \text{ adj } \mathbf{A}$.

adjugate = *adjoint*.

Algebra, Fundamental Theorem of See *Fundamental Theorem of Algebra*.

algebra of sets The set of all subsets of a *universal set* E is closed under the binary operations $\cup$ (*union*) and $\cap$ (*intersection*) and the unary operation $'$ (*complementation*). The following are some of the properties, or laws, that hold for subsets A, B and C of E:

(i) $A \cup (B \cup C) = (A \cup B) \cup C$ and $A \cap (B \cap C) = (A \cap B) \cap C$, the associative properties.

(ii) $A \cup B = B \cup A$ and $A \cap B = B \cap A$, the commutative properties.

(iii) $A \cup \emptyset = A$ and $A \cap \emptyset = \emptyset$.

(iv) $A \cup E = E$ and $A \cap E = A$.

(v) $A \cup A = A$ and $A \cap A = A$.

(vi) $A \cap (B \cup C) = (A \cap B) \cup (A \cap C)$ and $A \cup (B \cap C) = (A \cup B) \cap (A \cup C)$, the distributive properties.

(vii) $A \cup A' = E$ and $A \cap A' = \emptyset$.

(viii) $E' = \emptyset$ and $\emptyset' = E$.

(ix) $(A')' = A$.

(x) $(A \cup B)' = A' \cap B'$ and $(A \cap B)' = A' \cup B'$, de Morgan's laws.

The application of these laws to subsets of E is known as the **algebra of sets**. Despite some similarities with the algebra of numbers, there are important and striking differences.

algebraic number An **algebraic number** is a real number that is the root of a *polynomial equation* with integer coefficients. All *rational numbers* are algebraic, since a/b is the root of the equation $bx - a = 0$. Some *irrational numbers* are algebraic; for example, $\sqrt{2}$ is the root of the equation $x^2 - 2 = 0$. An irrational number that is not algebraic (such as π) is called a *transcendental number*.

algebraic structure The term **algebraic structure** is used to describe an abstract concept defined as consisting of certain elements with operations satisfying given axioms. Thus, a *group* or a *ring* or a *field* is an algebraic structure. The purpose of the definition is to recognize similarities that appear in different contexts within mathematics and to encapsulate these by means of a set of axioms.

algorithm   An **algorithm** is a precisely described routine procedure that can be applied and systematically followed through to a conclusion.

altitude   An **altitude** of a triangle is a line through one vertex and perpendicular to the opposite side. The three altitudes of a triangle are concurrent at the *orthocentre*.

amplitude   Suppose that $x = A\sin(\omega t + \alpha)$, where A (> 0), ω and α are constants. This may, for example, give the displacement x of a particle, moving in a straight line, at time t. The particle is thus oscillating about the origin O. The constant A is the **amplitude** and gives the maximum distance in each direction from O that the particle attains.

analysis   The subject of **analysis**, or **mathematical analysis**, is generally taken to include those mathematical topics that involve the use of limiting processes. Thus *differential calculus* and *integral calculus* certainly come under this heading. Besides these, there are other topics, such as the summation of infinite series, which involve 'infinite' processes of this sort. The *Binomial Theorem*, a theorem of algebra, leads on into analysis when the index is no longer a positive integer, and the study of sine and cosine, which begins as trigonometry, becomes analysis when the power series for the functions are derived. The term 'analysis' has also come to be used to indicate a rather more rigorous approach to the topics of calculus, and to the foundations of the real number system.

angle (between lines in space)   Given two lines in space, let $\mathbf{u}_1$ and $\mathbf{u}_2$ be vectors with directions along the lines. Then the **angle** between the lines, even if they do not meet, is equal to the angle between the vectors $\mathbf{u}_1$ and $\mathbf{u}_2$ (see *angle* (between vectors)), with the directions of $\mathbf{u}_1$ and $\mathbf{u}_2$ chosen so that the angle θ satisfies $0 \leq \theta \leq \pi/2$ (θ in radians), or $0 \leq \theta \leq 90$ (θ in degrees). If l_1, m_1, n_1 and l_2, m_2, n_2 are direction ratios for directions along the lines, the angle θ between the lines is given by

$$\cos\theta = \frac{|l_1 l_2 + m_1 m_2 + n_1 n_2|}{\sqrt{l_1^2 + m_1^2 + n_1^2}\sqrt{l_2^2 + m_2^2 + n_2^2}}.$$

angle (between lines in the plane)   In coordinate geometry of the plane, the angle α between two lines with gradients m_1 and m_2 is given by

$$\tan\alpha = \frac{m_1 - m_2}{1 + m_1 m_2}.$$

This is obtained from the formula for $\tan(A - B)$. In the special cases when $m_1 m_2 = -1$ or when m_1 or m_2 is infinite, it has to be interpreted appropriately.

angle (between planes)   Given two planes, let $\mathbf{n}_1$ and $\mathbf{n}_2$ be vectors *normal* to the two planes. Then a method of obtaining the **angle** between the planes is to take the angle between $\mathbf{n}_1$ and $\mathbf{n}_2$ (see *angle* (between vectors)), with the directions of $\mathbf{n}_1$ and $\mathbf{n}_2$ chosen so that the angle θ satisfies $0 \leq \theta \leq \pi/2$ (θ in radians), or $0 \leq \theta \leq 90$ (θ in degrees).

angle (between vectors)   Given vectors $\mathbf{a}$ and $\mathbf{b}$, let $\overrightarrow{OA}$ and $\overrightarrow{OB}$ be *directed line-segments* representing $\mathbf{a}$ and $\mathbf{b}$. Then the **angle** θ between the vectors $\mathbf{a}$ and $\mathbf{b}$ is the angle $\angle AOB$, where θ is taken to satisfy $0 \leq \theta \leq \pi$ (θ in radians), or $0 \leq \theta \leq 180$ (θ in degrees). It is given by

$$\cos \theta = \frac{\mathbf{a} \cdot \mathbf{b}}{|\mathbf{a}||\mathbf{b}|}.$$

angular measure   There are two principal ways of measuring angles: by using *degrees*, in more elementary work, and by using *radians*, essential in more advanced work.

annulus (plural: annuli)   An **annulus** is the region between two concentric circles. If the circles have radii r and $r + w$, the area of the annulus is equal to $\pi(r + w)^2 - \pi r^2$, which equals $w \times 2\pi(r + \frac{1}{2}w)$. It is therefore the same as the area of a rectangle of width w and length equal to the circumference of the circle midway in size between the two original circles.

antiderivative   Given a *real function* f, any function ϕ such that $\phi'(x) = f(x)$, for all x (in the domain of f), is an **antiderivative** of f. If ϕ_1 and ϕ_2 are both antiderivatives of a *continuous function* f, then $\phi_1(x)$ and $\phi_2(x)$ differ by a constant. In that case, the notation

$$\int f(x)\, dx$$

may be used for an antiderivative of f, with the understanding that an arbitrary constant can be added to any antiderivative. Thus,

$$\int f(x)\, dx + c,$$

where c is an arbitrary constant, is an expression that gives all the antiderivatives.

antilogarithm   The **antilogarithm** of x, denoted by antilog x, is the number whose *logarithm* is equal to x. For example, suppose that common logarithm tables are used to calculate $2{\cdot}75 \times 3{\cdot}12$. Then, approximately,

$\log 2.75 = 0.4393$ and $\log 3.12 = 0.4942$ and $0.4393 + 0.4942 = 0.9335$. Now antilog 0.9335 is required and, from tables, the answer 8.58 is obtained. Now that logarithm tables have been superseded by calculators, the term 'antilog' is little used. If y is the number whose logarithm is x, then $\log_a y = x$. This is equivalent to $y = a^x$ from the definition of logarithm. So, if base a is being used, antilog$_a x$ is identical with a^x; for common logarithms, antilog$_{10} x$ is just 10^x, and this notation is preferable.

antisymmetric matrix   = *skew-symmetric matrix*.

antisymmetric relation   A *binary relation* $\sim$ on a set S is **antisymmetric** if, for all a and b in S, whenever $a \sim b$ then $b \not\sim a$. For example, $<$ is an antisymmetric relation on the set of integers.

Apollonius of Perga (about 262–190 BC)   Apollonius worked during the Golden Age of Greek mathematics and was more or less contemporary with Archimedes. He emphasized the idea of epicyclic motion for the planets. His most famous work is *The Conics*, which was, until modern times, the definitive work on the conic sections: ellipse, parabola and hyperbola.

Apollonius' circle   Given two points A and B in the plane and a constant k, the locus of all points P such that $AP/PB = k$ is a circle. A circle obtained like this is an **Apollonius' circle**. Taking $k = 1$ gives a straight line, so either this value must be excluded or, in this context, a straight line must be considered to be a special case of a circle. In the figure, $k = 2$.

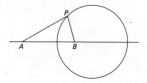

approximation   When two quantities X and x are approximately equal, written $X \approx x$, one of them may be used in suitable circumstances in place of, or as an **approximation** for, the other. For example, $\pi \approx \frac{22}{7}$ and $\sqrt{2} \approx 1.414$.

arc   An **arc** is the part of a curve between two given points on the curve. If A and B are two points on a circle, there are two arcs AB. When A and B are not at opposite ends of a diameter, it is possible to distinguish between the longer and shorter arcs by referring to the **major arc** AB and the **minor arc** AB.

arc (of a digraph)   See *digraph*.

arccos, arccosec, arccot, arcsin, arcsec, arctan   See *inverse trigonometric function*.

arccosh, arccosech, arccoth, arcsinh, arcsech, arctanh   See *inverse hyperbolic function*.

arc length   Let $y = f(x)$ be the graph of a function f such that f' is *continuous* on $[a, b]$. The length of the arc, or **arc length**, of the curve $y = f(x)$ between $x = a$ and $x = b$ equals

$$\int_a^b \sqrt{1 + (f'(x))^2}\, dx.$$

PARAMETRIC FORM. For the curve $x = x(t)$, $y = y(t)$ ($t \in [\alpha, \beta]$), the arc length equals

$$\int_\alpha^\beta \sqrt{\left(\frac{dx}{dt}\right)^2 + \left(\frac{dy}{dt}\right)^2}\, dt.$$

POLAR FORM. For the curve $r = r(\theta)$ ($\alpha \le \theta \le \beta$), the arc length equals

$$\int_\alpha^\beta \sqrt{r^2 + \left(\frac{dr}{d\theta}\right)^2}\, d\theta.$$

Archimedean spiral   An **Archimedean spiral** is a curve whose equation in polar coordinates is $r = a\theta$, where a (> 0) is a constant. In the figure, $OA = a\pi$, $OB = 2a\pi$, and so $OB = 2OA$.

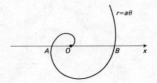

Archimedes (287–212 BC)   Archimedes was one of the greatest of all mathematicians. He made fundamental contributions to geometry and the theories of hydrostatics and equilibrium. In pure mathematics, he is best remembered for Archimedes' axiom in the theory of the real number system. His style is remarkably modern and the geometrical problems that he handled are very sophisticated. It is work like this that led Littlewood to declare that the ancient Greek mathematicians were 'not clever schoolboys but fellows of another college'. His most fascinating work, *The Method*, was rediscovered only in 1906. Archimedes may or may not have shouted 'Eureka' and run naked through the streets of Syracuse. He was certainly murdered by a Roman soldier, an event which marks the end of an era in mathematics.

area of a surface of revolution   Let $y = f(x)$ be the graph of a function f such that f' is *continuous* on $[a, b]$ and $f(x) \ge 0$ for all x in $[a, b]$. The **area of**

the surface obtained by rotating, through one revolution about the x-axis, the arc of the curve $y = f(x)$ between $x = a$ and $x = b$, equals

$$2\pi \int_a^b y\sqrt{1 + \left(\frac{dy}{dx}\right)^2}\, dx, \quad \text{or} \quad 2\pi \int_a^b f(x)\sqrt{1 + (f'(x))^2}\, dx.$$

PARAMETRIC FORM. For the curve $x = x(t)$, $y = y(t)$ $(t \in [\alpha, \beta])$, the surface area equals

$$2\pi \int_\alpha^\beta y\sqrt{\left(\frac{dx}{dt}\right)^2 + \left(\frac{dy}{dt}\right)^2}\, dt.$$

POLAR FORM. For the curve $r = r(\theta)$ $(\alpha \le \theta \le \beta)$, the surface area equals

$$2\pi \int_\alpha^\beta r\sin\theta\sqrt{r^2 + \left(\frac{dr}{d\theta}\right)^2}\, d\theta.$$

area under a curve   Suppose that the curve $y = f(x)$ lies above the x-axis, so that $f(x) \ge 0$ for all x in $[a, b]$. The **area under the curve**, that is, the area of the region bounded by the curve, the x-axis and the lines $x = a$ and $x = b$, equals

$$\int_a^b f(x)\, dx.$$

The definition of *integral* is made precisely in order to achieve this result.

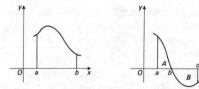

If $f(x) \le 0$ for all x in $[a, b]$, the integral above is negative. However, it is still the case that its absolute value is equal to the area of the region bounded by the curve, the x-axis and the lines $x = a$ and $x = b$. If $y = f(x)$ crosses the x-axis, appropriate results hold. For example, if the regions A and B are as shown in the figure:

$$\text{area of region } A = \int_a^b f(x)\, dx, \quad \text{area of region } B = -\int_b^c f(x)\, dx.$$

It follows that

$$\int_a^c f(x)\, dx = \int_a^b f(x)\, dx + \int_b^c f(x)\, dx$$

$$= \text{area of region } A - \text{area of region } B.$$

Similarly, to find the area of the region bounded by a suitable curve, the y-axis and lines $y = c$ and $y = d$, an equation $x = g(y)$ for the curve must be found. Then the required area equals

$$\int_c^d g(y)\, dy,$$

assuming that the curve is to the right of the y-axis, so that $g(y) \geq 0$ for all y in $[c, d]$. As before, the value of the integral is negative if $g(y) \leq 0$.

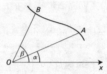

POLAR AREAS. If a curve has an equation $r = r(\theta)$ in polar coordinates, there is an integral that gives the area of the region bounded by an arc AB of the curve and the two radial lines OA and OB. Suppose that $\angle xOA = \alpha$ and $\angle xOB = \beta$. The area of the region described equals

$$\int_\alpha^\beta \tfrac{1}{2} r^2 \, d\theta.$$

Argand diagram   Another (less preferable) name for the *complex plane*.

Argand, Jean Robert (1768–1822)   Argand was a Swiss mathematician who was one of several people who invented a geometrical representation for complex numbers, the others including Gauss and Wessel. This explains the name *Argand diagram*.

argument   Suppose that the *complex number* z is represented by the point P in the *complex plane*. The **argument** of z, denoted by $\arg z$, is the angle θ (in radians) that OP makes with the positive real axis Ox, with the angle given a positive sense anti-clockwise from Ox. As with polar coordinates, the angle θ may be taken so that $0 \leq \arg z < 2\pi$. Usually however, the angle θ is chosen so that $-\pi < \arg z \leq \pi$. Sometimes, $\arg z$ is used to denote any of the values $\theta + 2n\pi$, where n is an integer. In that case, the particular value that lies in a certain interval, specified or understood, such as $[0, 2\pi)$ or $(-\pi, \pi]$, is called the **principal value** of $\arg z$.

Arithmetic, Fundamental Theorem of   See *Fundamental Theorem of Arithmetic*.

arithmetic mean   See *mean*.

arithmetic sequence   An **arithmetic sequence** is a finite or infinite sequence of terms a_1, a_2, a_3, ... with a **common difference** d, so that

$a_2 - a_1 = d$, $a_3 - a_2 = d$, and so on. The first term is usually denoted by a. For example, 2, 5, 8, 11, ... is the arithmetic sequence with $a = 2$, $d = 3$. In such an arithmetic sequence, the n-th term a_n is given by $a_n = a + (n-1)d$.

arithmetic series   An **arithmetic series** is a series $a_1 + a_2 + a_3 + \cdots$ (which may be finite or infinite) in which the terms form an *arithmetic sequence*. Thus the terms have a common difference d, with $a_k - a_{k-1} = d$ for all $k \geq 2$. If the first term equals a, then $a_k = a + (k-1)d$. Let s_n be the sum of the first n terms of an arithmetic series, so that

$$s_n = a + (a+d) + (a+2d) + \cdots + (a + (n-1)d),$$

and let the last term here, $a + (n-1)d$, be denoted by b. Then s_n is given by the formula $s_n = \frac{1}{2}n(a+b)$. The particular case, $a = 1$, $d = 1$, gives the sum of the first n natural numbers:

$$\sum_{r=1}^{n} r = 1 + 2 + \cdots + n = \tfrac{1}{2}n(n+1).$$

arrangement   See *permutation*.

associative   The *binary operation* $\circ$ on a set S is **associative** if, for all a, b and c in S, $(a \circ b) \circ c = a \circ (b \circ c)$.

asymptote   A line l is an **asymptote** to a curve if the distance from a point P to the line l tends to zero as P tends to infinity along some unbounded part of the curve. Consider the following examples:

(i) $y = \dfrac{x+3}{(x+2)(x-1)}$,   (ii) $y = \dfrac{3x^2}{x^2+x+1}$,   (iii) $y = \dfrac{x^3}{x^2+x+1}$.

Example (i) has $x = -2$ and $x = 1$ as vertical asymptotes and has $y = 0$ as a horizontal asymptote. Example (ii) has no vertical asymptotes and has $y = 3$ as a horizontal asymptote. To investigate example (iii), it can be rewritten as

$$y = x - 1 + \frac{1}{x^2 + x + 1}.$$

Then it can be seen that $y = x - 1$ is a **slant asymptote**, that is, an asymptote that is neither vertical nor horizontal.

augmented matrix   For a given set of m linear equations in n unknowns $x_1, x_2, \ldots, x_n$,

$$a_{11}x_1 + a_{12}x_2 + \cdots + a_{1n}x_n = b_1,$$
$$a_{21}x_1 + a_{22}x_2 + \cdots + a_{2n}x_n = b_2,$$
$$\cdots$$
$$a_{m1}x_1 + a_{m2}x_2 + \cdots + a_{mn}x_n = b_m,$$

the **augmented matrix** is the matrix

$$\begin{bmatrix} a_{11} & a_{12} & \cdots & a_{1n} & b_1 \\ a_{21} & a_{22} & \cdots & a_{2n} & b_2 \\ \vdots & \vdots & \ddots & \vdots & \vdots \\ a_{m1} & a_{m2} & \cdots & a_{mn} & b_m \end{bmatrix}$$

obtained by adjoining to the matrix of coefficients an extra column of entries taken from the right-hand sides of the equations. The solutions of a set of linear equations may be investigated by transforming the augmented matrix to echelon or reduced echelon form by elementary row operations. See *Gaussian elimination* and *Gauss-Jordan elimination*.

auxiliary equation   See *linear differential equations with constant coefficients*.

axial plane   An **axial plane** is one of the planes containing two of the coordinate axes in a 3-dimensional Cartesian coordinate system. For example, one of the axial planes is the yz-plane, or (y, z)-plane, containing the y-axis and the z-axis, and it has equation $x = 0$.

axis (plural: axes)   See *coordinates* (in the plane) and *coordinates* (in 3-dimensional space).

axis (of a cone)   See *cone*.

axis (of a cylinder)   See *cylinder*.

axis (of a parabola)   See *parabola*.

B

back substitution   Suppose that a set of linear equations is in *echelon form*. Then the last equation can be solved for the first unknown appearing in it, setting any other unknowns equal to *parameters* taking arbitrary values. This can be substituted into the previous equation, which can then likewise be solved for the first unknown appearing in it. The process that continues in this way is **back substitution**.

base (for representation of numbers)   The integer represented as 4703 in standard decimal notation is written in this way because

$$4703 = (4 \times 10^3) + (7 \times 10^2) + (0 \times 10) + 3.$$

The same integer can be written in terms of powers of 8 as follows:

$$4703 = (1 \times 8^4) + (1 \times 8^3) + (1 \times 8^2) + (3 \times 8) + 7.$$

The expression on the right-hand side is abbreviated to $(11137)_8$ and is the **representation** of this number to **base** 8. In general, if g is an integer greater than 1, any positive integer a can be written uniquely as

$$a = c_n g^n + c_{n-1} g^{n-1} + \cdots + c_1 g + c_0,$$

where each c_i is a non-negative integer less than g. This is the **representation** of a to **base** g and is abbreviated to $(c_n c_{n-1} \ldots c_1 c_0)_g$. Real numbers, not just integers, can also be written to any base, by using figures after a 'decimal' point, just as familiar *decimal* representations of real numbers are obtained to base 10. See also *binary representation*, *decimal* and *hexadecimal*.

base (of exponential function)   See *exponential function to base a*.

base (of logarithms)   See *logarithms*.

base (of natural logarithms)   See *e*.

basis (plural: bases)   A set S of *vectors* is a **spanning set** if any vector can be written as a linear combination of those in S. If, in addition, the vectors in S are *linearly independent*, then S is a **basis**. It follows that any vector can be written *uniquely* as a linear combination of those in a basis. In 3-dimensional space, any set of three non-coplanar vectors $\mathbf{u}$, $\mathbf{v}$ and $\mathbf{w}$ is a basis, since any vector $\mathbf{p}$ can be written uniquely as $\mathbf{p} = x\mathbf{u} + y\mathbf{v} + z\mathbf{w}$. In 2-dimensional space, any set of 2 non-parallel vectors has this property and so is a basis. Any one of the vectors in a set currently being taken as a basis may be called a **basis vector**.

basis vector   See *basis*.

belongs to   If x is an element of a set S, then x **belongs to** S and this is written $x \in S$. Naturally, $x \notin S$ means that x does not belong to S.

Bernoulli family   The Bernoulli family of Basle produced a stream of significant mathematicians, some of them very important indeed. The best known are the brothers, Jacques and Jean, and Jean's son, Daniel. Jacques (1654–1705) did much work on the newly developed calculus but is remembered for his contributions to probability theory: the *Ars Conjectandi* was published, after his death, in 1713. Bernoulli numbers are named after Jacques. The work of Jean (1667–1748) was more definitely within the calculus and he was one of the founders of the Calculus of Variations. In the next generation, Daniel (1700–1782) was the member of the family who worked in hydrodynamics, where he gave his name to Bernoulli's Theorem.

bijection   A **bijection** is a *one-to-one onto mapping*, that is, a mapping that is both *injective* and *surjective*.

bijective mapping   A mapping is **bijective** if it is *injective* (that is, *one-to-one*) and *surjective* (that is, *onto*).

bilateral symmetry   See *symmetrical about a line*.

binary operation   A **binary operation** $\circ$ on a set S is a rule that associates with any elements a and b of S an element denoted by $a \circ b$. If, for all a and b, the element $a \circ b$ also belongs to S, S is said to be **closed under** the operation $\circ$. This is often taken to be implied in saying that $\circ$ is a binary operation on S.

binary relation   A formal definition of a **binary relation** on a set S is as a subset R of the *Cartesian product* $S \times S$. Thus, it can be said that, for a given *ordered pair* (a, b), either $(a, b) \in R$ or $(a, b) \notin R$. However, it is more natural to denote a relation by a symbol such as $\sim$ placed between the elements a and b, where $\sim$ stands for the words 'is related (in some way) to'. Familiar examples are normally written in this way: '$<$' is a binary relation on the set of integers, '$\subseteq$' is a binary relation on the set of subsets of some set E, and 'is perpendicular to' is a binary relation on the set of straight lines in the plane. The letter 'R' may be used in this way, 'aRb' meaning that 'a is related to b'. If this notation is used, the set $\{ (a, b) \mid (a, b) \in S \times S \text{ and } aRb \}$ may be called the *graph* of R. For any relation $\sim$, a corresponding relation $\nsim$ can be defined that holds whenever $\sim$ does not hold.

binary representation   The **binary representation** of a number is its representation to *base* 2. It uses just the two **binary digits** 0 and 1, and this is the reason why it is important in computing. For example, $37 = (100101)_2$, since

$$37 = (1 \times 2^5) + (0 \times 2^4) + (0 \times 2^3) + (1 \times 2^2) + (0 \times 2) + 1.$$

Real numbers, not just integers, can also be written in binary notation, by using binary digits after a 'decimal' point, just as familiar *decimal* representations of real numbers are obtained to base 10. For example, the number $\frac{1}{10}$, which equals 0·1 in decimal notation, has, in binary notation, a recurring representation: $(0·00011001100110011\ldots)_2$.

binary tree   See *tree*.

binomial coefficient   The number, denoted by $\binom{n}{r}$, where n is a positive integer and r is an integer such that $0 \leq r \leq n$, is defined by the formula

$$\binom{n}{r} = \frac{n(n-1)\ldots(n-r+1)}{1.2\ldots r} = \frac{n!}{r!(n-r)!}.$$

Since, by convention, $0! = 1$, we have $\binom{n}{0} = \binom{n}{n} = 1$. These numbers are called **binomial coefficients** because they occur as coefficients in the *Binomial Theorem*. They are sometimes denoted by ^nC_r: this arose as the notation for the number of ways of selecting r objects out of n (see *selection*), but this number can be shown to be equal to the expression given above for the binomial coefficient. The numbers have the following properties:

(i) $\binom{n}{r}$ is an integer (this is not obvious from the definition).

(ii) $\binom{n}{n-r} = \binom{n}{r}$.

(iii) $\binom{n+1}{r} = \binom{n}{r-1} + \binom{n}{r}$.

(iv) $\binom{n}{0} + \binom{n}{1} + \binom{n}{2} + \cdots + \binom{n}{n} = 2^n$.

It is instructive to see the binomial coefficients laid out in the form of *Pascal's triangle*.

binomial series (or **expansion**)   The **binomial series** (or **expansion**) is

$$1 + \frac{\alpha}{1!}x + \frac{\alpha(\alpha-1)}{2!}x^2 + \cdots + \frac{\alpha(\alpha-1)\ldots(\alpha-n+1)}{n!}x^n + \cdots,$$

being the *Maclaurin series* for the function $(1+x)^\alpha$. In general, it is valid for $-1 < x < 1$. If α is a non-negative integer, the expansion is a finite series and so is a polynomial, and then it is equal to $(1+x)^\alpha$ for all x.

Binomial Theorem   The formulae $(x+y)^2 = x^2 + 2xy + y^2$ and $(x+y)^3 = x^3 + 3x^2y + 3xy^2 + y^3$ are used in elementary algebra. The **Binomial Theorem** gives an expansion like this for $(x+y)^n$, where n is any positive integer:

THEOREM: For all positive integers n,

$$(x+y)^n = \sum_{r=0}^{n} \binom{n}{r} x^{n-r} y^r$$

$$= x^n + \binom{n}{1} x^{n-1}y + \binom{n}{2} x^{n-2}y^2 + \cdots + \binom{n}{r} x^{n-r}y^r + \cdots + y^n,$$

where $\binom{n}{r} = \dfrac{n!}{r!(n-r)!}$ (see *binomial coefficient*).

The following is a special case of the Binomial Theorem. It can also be seen as a special case of the *binomial series* when the series is finite:

THEOREM: For all positive integers n,

$$(1+x)^n = \sum_{r=0}^{n} \binom{n}{r} x^r = 1 + \binom{n}{1} x + \binom{n}{2} x^2 + \cdots + \binom{n}{r} x^r + \cdots + x^n.$$

bipartite graph   A **bipartite graph** is a *graph* in which the vertices can be divided into two sets V_1 and V_2, so that no two vertices in V_1 are joined and no two vertices in V_2 are joined. The **complete bipartite graph** $K_{m,n}$ is the bipartite graph with m vertices in V_1 and n vertices in V_2, with every vertex in V_1 joined to every vertex in V_2.

$K_{2,3}$

bisection method   The **bisection method** is a numerical method for finding a root of an equation $f(x) = 0$. If values a and b are found such that $f(a)$ and $f(b)$ have opposite signs and f is *continuous* on the interval $[a, b]$, it is known (by the *Intermediate Value Theorem*) that the equation has a root in (a, b). The method is to bisect the interval and replace it by either one half or the other, thereby closing in on the root.

Let $c = \frac{1}{2}(a + b)$. Calculate $f(c)$. If $f(c)$ has the same sign as $f(a)$, then take c as a new value for a; if not (so that $f(c)$ has the same sign as $f(b)$), take c as a new value for b. (If it should happen that $f(c) = 0$, then c is a root and the aim of finding a root has been achieved.) Repeat this whole process until the length of the interval $[a, b]$ is less than 2ϵ, where ϵ is specified in advance. The midpoint of the interval can then be taken as an approximation to the root and the error will be less than ϵ.

Boole, George (1815–1864)   Boole was an English mathematician and one of the founding fathers of mathematical logic. His major work, published in 1854, is his *Investigation of the Laws of Thought*. The kind of symbolic argument that Boole developed led to the study of Boolean algebras, which are of current significance in computing and algebra. His work, together with that of others in the English School like de Morgan and Peacock, paved the way for the development of modern formal algebra.

bound   Let S be a non-empty subset of **R**. The real number b is said to be an **upper bound** for S if b is greater than or equal to every element of S. If S has an upper bound then S is **bounded above**. Moreover, b is a **supremum** (or **least upper bound**) of S if b is an upper bound for S and no upper bound for S is less than b; this is written $b = \sup S$. For example, if $S = \{0\cdot9, 0\cdot99, 0\cdot999, \dots\}$ then $\sup S = 1$. Similarly, the real number c is a **lower bound** for S if c is less than or equal to every element of S. If S has a lower bound then S is **bounded below**. Moreover, c is an **infimum** (or **greatest lower bound**) of S if c is a lower bound for S and no lower bound for S is greater than c; this is written $c = \inf S$. A set is **bounded** if it is bounded above and below.

It is a non-elementary result about the real numbers that any non-empty set that is bounded above has a supremum, and any non-empty set that is bounded below has an infimum.

bounded function   A *real function* f, defined on a domain S, is **bounded** (on S) if there is a number M such that, for all x in S, $|f(x)| < M$. The fact that if f is *continuous* on a closed interval $[a, b]$ then it is bounded on $[a, b]$ is a property for which a rigorous proof is not elementary (see *continuous function*).

bounded sequence   The sequence $a_1, a_2, a_3, \dots$ is **bounded** if there is a number M such that, for all n, $|a_n| < M$.

bounded set   See *bound*.

Bourbaki, Nicolas   General N. Bourbaki is an obscure French military man with many heads and twice as many legs. Mostly born in this century, much of him is still alive. Since 1939, he has been publishing an encyclopaedic survey of pure mathematics, the *Elements*, the influence of which is variously described as profound or baleful but is undoubtedly extensive. He has been the standard-bearer for what might be called the Structuralist School of modern mathematics.

branch (of a hyperbola)   The two separate parts of a *hyperbola* are called the two **branches**.

bridges of Königsberg   In the early eighteenth century, there were seven bridges in the town of Königsberg (now Kaliningrad). They crossed the different branches of the River Pregel (now Pregolya) as shown in diagrammatic form in the figure. The question was asked whether it was possible, from some starting point, to cross each bridge exactly once and return to the starting point. This prompted Euler to consider the problem in more generality

and to publish what can be thought of as the first research paper in *graph* theory. The original question asked, essentially, whether the graph shown is *Eulerian*. It can be shown that a connected graph is Eulerian if and only if every vertex has even degree and so the answer is no.

C

C   See *complex number*.

cancellation laws   Let ∘ be a *binary operation* on a set S. The **cancellation laws** are said to hold if, for all a, b and c in S,

(i) if $a \circ b = a \circ c$ then $b = c$, (ii) if $b \circ a = c \circ a$ then $b = c$.

It can be shown, for example, that in a *group* the cancellation laws hold.

canonical form   See *quadric*.

Cantor, Georg (1845–1918)   Cantor was born in St Petersburg, but spent most of his life in Halle. The latter part of his life was clouded by repeated mental illness and he spent much time in a sanitorium. His most profound contribution to mathematics was his theory of infinite sets and infinite numbers. Particularly important is his distinction between countable and uncountable sets. He may be thought of as the mathematician who liberated infinity.

cap   The operation ∩ (see *intersection*) is read by some as 'cap', this being derived from the shape of the symbol, and in contrast to *cup* (∪).

cardinality   For a finite set A, the **cardinality** of A, denoted by $n(A)$, is the number of elements in A. The notation $\#(A)$ or $|A|$ is also used. For subsets A, B and C of some universal set E,

(i) $n(A \cup B) = n(A) + n(B) - n(A \cap B)$,
(ii) $n(A \cup B \cup C) = n(A) + n(B) + n(C) - n(A \cap B)$
$$-n(A \cap C) - n(B \cap C) + n(A \cap B \cap C).$$

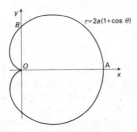

cardioid   The **cardioid** is the curve traced out by a point on the circumference of a circle rolling round another circle of the same radius. Its equation, in which a is the radius of each circle, may be taken in polar coordinates as $r = 2a(1 + \cos\theta)$ $(-\pi < \theta \leq \pi)$. In the figure, $OA = 4a$ and $OB = 2a$.

Cartesian coordinates   See *coordinates* (in the plane) and *coordinates* (in 3-dimensional space).

Cartesian product   The **Cartesian product** $A \times B$, of sets A and B, is the set of all *ordered pairs* (a, b), where $a \in A$ and $b \in B$. In some cases, it may be possible to give a pictorial representation of $A \times B$ by taking two perpendicular axes and displaying the elements of A along one axis and the elements of B along the other axis; the ordered pair (a, b) is represented by the point with, as it were, those coordinates. In particular, if A and B are subsets of $\mathbf{R}$ and are intervals, this gives a pictorial representation as shown. Similarly, the Cartesian product $A \times B \times C$ of sets A, B and C can be defined as the set of all ordered triples (a, b, c), where $a \in A$, $b \in B$ and $c \in C$. More generally, for sets $A_1, A_2, \ldots, A_n$, the Cartesian product $A_1 \times A_2 \times \cdots \times A_n$ can be defined in a similar way.

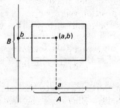

catenary   The **catenary** is the curve in which an ideal flexible heavy rope or chain of uniform density hangs between two points. With suitable axes, the equation of the curve is $y = c \cosh(x/c)$ (see *hyperbolic function*).

Cauchy, Augustin-Louis (1789–1857)   Cauchy was one of the most important mathematicians of the early nineteenth century and a dominating figure in French mathematics. His work ranged over vast areas of mathematics, but he is chiefly remembered as one of the founders of rigorous mathematical analysis. He made deep contributions to the ideas of continuity and convergence and his results in the theory of complex functions are very well known to undergraduates. He was an honourable but pompous and unpopular man, a religious bigot and a royalist.

Cayley-Hamilton Theorem   The *characteristic polynomial* $p(\lambda)$ of an $n \times n$ matrix $\mathbf{A}$ is defined by $p(\lambda) = \det(\mathbf{A} - \lambda \mathbf{I})$. The following result about the characteristic polynomial is called the **Cayley-Hamilton Theorem**:

THEOREM: If the characteristic polynomial $p(\lambda)$ of an $n \times n$ matrix $\mathbf{A}$ is written as

$$p(\lambda) = (-1)^n(\lambda^n + b_{n-1}\lambda^{n-1} + \cdots + b_1\lambda + b_0),$$

then $\mathbf{A}^n + b_{n-1}\mathbf{A}^{n-1} + \cdots + b_1\mathbf{A} + b_0\mathbf{I} = \mathbf{O}$.

central conic   A **central conic** is a *conic* with a *centre of symmetry* and is thus an *ellipse* or a *hyperbola*. The conic with equation $ax^2 + 2hxy + by^2 + 2gx + 2fy + c = 0$ is central if and only if $ab \neq h^2$.

central quadric   A **central quadric** is a non-*degenerate quadric* with a *centre of symmetry* and is thus an *ellipsoid*, a *hyperboloid of one sheet* or a *hyperboloid of two sheets*.

centre   See *circle*, *ellipse* and *hyperbola*.

centre of mass   Suppose that particles $P_1, \ldots, P_k$, with corresponding masses $m_1, \ldots, m_k$, have *position vectors* $\mathbf{r}_1, \ldots, \mathbf{r}_k$, respectively. The **centre of mass** (or **centroid**) is the point with position vector $\mathbf{r}$, where

$$\mathbf{r} = \frac{m_1\mathbf{r}_1 + \cdots + m_k\mathbf{r}_k}{m_1 + \cdots + m_k}.$$

Consider the forces on the particles due to the earth's gravity (assumed to be a uniform gravitational field). How does the centre of mass of the particles move as a result of these forces? It moves in the same way as a single particle, with mass equal to the sum of the masses of the original particles, would move under gravity. Consequently, this point may also be called the **centre of gravity**.

centre of symmetry   See *symmetrical about a point*.

centroid   = *centre of mass*. See also *centroid* (of a triangle).

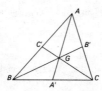

centroid (of a triangle)   The geometrical definition of the **centroid** G of a triangle ABC is as the point at which the *medians* of the triangle are concurrent. It is, in fact, 'two-thirds of the way down each median', so that, for example, if A' is the midpoint of BC, then $AG = 2\,GA'$. This is indeed the point at which a triangular *lamina* of uniform density has its *centre of mass*. It is also the centre of mass of three particles of equal mass situated at the vertices of the triangle. If A, B and C are points in the plane with Cartesian coordinates (x_1, y_1), (x_2, y_2) and (x_3, y_3), then G has coordinates

$$\left(\tfrac{1}{3}(x_1 + x_2 + x_3), \tfrac{1}{3}(y_1 + y_2 + y_3)\right).$$

For points A, B and C in 3-dimensional space with Cartesian coordinates (x_1, y_1, z_1), (x_2, y_2, z_2) and (x_3, y_3, z_3), there is no change in the definition of the centroid G and it has coordinates

$$\left(\tfrac{1}{3}(x_1 + x_2 + x_3), \tfrac{1}{3}(y_1 + y_2 + y_3), \tfrac{1}{3}(z_1 + z_2 + z_3)\right).$$

If A, B and C have *position vectors* $\mathbf{a}$, $\mathbf{b}$ and $\mathbf{c}$, then G has position vector $\tfrac{1}{3}(\mathbf{a} + \mathbf{b} + \mathbf{c})$.

chain rule   The **chain rule** gives the *derivative* of the *composition* of two functions: if $h(x) = (f \circ g)(x) = f(g(x))$ for all x, then $h'(x) = f'(g(x))g'(x)$. For example, if $h(x) = (x^2 + 1)^3$ then $h = f \circ g$, where $f(x) = x^3$ and $g(x) = x^2 + 1$. Then $f'(x) = 3x^2$ and $g'(x) = 2x$. So $h'(x) = 3(x^2 + 1)^2 2x = 6x(x^2 + 1)^2$. Another notation can be used: if $y = f(g(x))$, write $y = f(u)$, where $u = g(x)$. Then the chain rule says that $dy/dx = (dy/du)(du/dx)$. As an example of the use of this notation, suppose that $y = (\sin x)^2$. Then $y = u^2$, where $u = \sin x$. So $dy/du = 2u$ and $du/dx = \cos x$ and hence $dy/dx = 2 \sin x \cos x$.

change of base (of logarithms)   See *logarithm*.

change of coordinates (in the plane)   The simplest changes from one Cartesian coordinate system to another are *translation of axes* and *rotation of axes*. See also *polar coordinates* for the change from Cartesian coordinates to polar coordinates and vice versa.

change of coordinates (in 3-dimensional space)   The simplest change from one Cartesian coordinate system to another is *translation of axes*. See also *cylindrical polar coordinates* and *spherical polar coordinates* for the change from Cartesian coordinates to those coordinate systems and vice versa.

change of variable (in integration)   See *integration*.

characteristic equation   See *characteristic polynomial*.

characteristic polynomial   Let $\mathbf{A}$ be a square matrix. Then $\det(\mathbf{A} - \lambda\mathbf{I})$ is a polynomial in λ and is called the **characteristic polynomial** of $\mathbf{A}$. The equation $\det(\mathbf{A} - \lambda\mathbf{I}) = 0$ is the **characteristic equation** of $\mathbf{A}$ and its roots are the *characteristic values* of $\mathbf{A}$. See also *Cayley-Hamilton Theorem*.

characteristic root   = *characteristic value*.

characteristic value   Let $\mathbf{A}$ be a square matrix. The roots of the *characteristic equation* $\det(\mathbf{A} - \lambda\mathbf{I}) = 0$ are called the **characteristic values**

of **A**. Then λ is a characteristic value of **A** if and only if there is a non-zero vector **x** such that $\mathbf{Ax} = \lambda\mathbf{x}$. Any vector **x** such that $\mathbf{Ax} = \lambda\mathbf{x}$ is called a **characteristic vector** corresponding to the characteristic value λ.

characteristic vector   See *characteristic value*.

chord   Let A and B be two points on a curve. The straight line through A and B, or the *line segment* AB, is called a **chord**, the word being used when a distinction is to be made between the chord AB and the arc AB.

circle   The **circle** with centre C and radius r is the locus of all points in the plane whose distance from C is equal to r. If C has Cartesian coordinates (a, b), this circle has equation $(x - a)^2 + (y - b)^2 = r^2$. An equation of the form $x^2 + y^2 + 2gx + 2fy + c = 0$ represents a circle if $g^2 + f^2 - c > 0$ and is then an equation of the circle with centre $(-g, -f)$ and radius $\sqrt{g^2 + f^2 - c}$.

 The area of a circle of radius r equals πr^2 and the length of the circumference equals $2\pi r$.

circle theorems   The following is a summary of some of the theorems that can be proved concerned with properties of a circle:

 Let A and B be two points on a circle with centre O. If P is any point on the circumference of the circle and on the same side of the chord AB as O, then $\angle AOB = 2\angle APB$. Hence the 'angle at the circumference' $\angle APB$ is independent of the position of P.

 If Q is a point on the circumference and lies on the other side of AB from P, then $\angle AQB = 180° - \angle APB$. Hence opposite angles of a cyclic quadrilateral add up to 180°. When AB is a diameter, the angle at the circumference is the 'angle in a semicircle' and is a right angle. If T is any point on the tangent at A, then $\angle APB = \angle BAT$.

 Suppose now that a circle and a point P are given. Let any line through P meet the circle at points A and B. Then $PA.PB$ is constant, that is, the

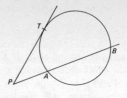

same for all such lines. If P lies outside the circle and a line through P touches the circle at the point T, then $PA \cdot PB = PT^2$.

circular function   The term **circular function** is used to describe one of the *trigonometric functions* sin and cos (and perhaps tan).

circumcentre   The **circumcentre** of a triangle is the centre of the *circumcircle* of the triangle. It is the point O, shown in the figure, at which the perpendicular bisectors of the sides of the triangle are concurrent.

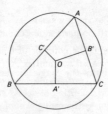

circumcircle   The **circumcircle** of a triangle is the circle that passes through the three vertices. Its centre is at the *circumcentre*.

circumference   The **circumference** of a circle is the boundary of the circle or the length of the boundary, that is, the perimeter. The (length of the) circumference of a circle of radius r is $2\pi r$.

circumscribing cylinder   See *zone*.

cis   The abbreviation **cis** θ is sometimes used for $\cos \theta + i \sin \theta$.

closed disc   See *disc*.

closed half-plane   See *half-plane*.

closed interval   The **closed interval** $[a, b]$ is the set

$$\{ x \mid x \in \mathbf{R} \text{ and } a \leq x \leq b \}.$$

closed (under an operation)   See *operation*.

codomain   See *function* and *mapping*.

coefficient   See *binomial coefficient* and *polynomial*.

cofactor   Let $\mathbf{A}$ be the square matrix $[a_{ij}]$. The **cofactor** of the entry a_{ij} is equal to $(-1)^{i+j}$ times the *determinant* of the matrix obtained by deleting the i-th row and j-th column of $\mathbf{A}$. If $\mathbf{A}$ is the 3×3 matrix shown, the factor $(-1)^{i+j}$ has the effect of introducing a $+$ or $-$ sign according to the pattern alongside:

$$\mathbf{A} = \begin{bmatrix} a_{11} & a_{12} & a_{13} \\ a_{21} & a_{22} & a_{23} \\ a_{31} & a_{32} & a_{33} \end{bmatrix} \qquad \begin{bmatrix} + & - & + \\ - & + & - \\ + & - & + \end{bmatrix}.$$

So, for example,

$$A_{12} = - \begin{vmatrix} a_{21} & a_{23} \\ a_{31} & a_{33} \end{vmatrix}, \qquad A_{31} = + \begin{vmatrix} a_{12} & a_{13} \\ a_{22} & a_{23} \end{vmatrix}.$$

For a 2×2 matrix, the pattern is:

$$\begin{bmatrix} a & b \\ c & d \end{bmatrix} \qquad \begin{bmatrix} + & - \\ - & + \end{bmatrix}.$$

So, the cofactor of a equals d, the cofactor of b equals $-c$, and so on. The following properties hold, for an $n \times n$ matrix $\mathbf{A}$:

   (i) The expression $a_{i1}A_{i1} + a_{i2}A_{i2} + \cdots + a_{in}A_{in}$ has the same value for any i, and is the definition of det $\mathbf{A}$, the determinant of $\mathbf{A}$. This particular expression is the evaluation of det $\mathbf{A}$ by the i-th row.
   (ii) On the other hand, if $i \neq j$, $a_{i1}A_{j1} + a_{i2}A_{j2} + \cdots + a_{in}A_{jn} = 0$.

Results for columns, corresponding to the results (i) and (ii) for rows, also hold.

collinear   Any number of points are said to be **collinear** if there is a straight line passing through all of them.

column operation   See *elementary column operation*.

column matrix   A **column matrix** is a *matrix* with exactly one column, that is, an $m \times 1$ matrix of the form

$$\begin{bmatrix} a_1 \\ a_2 \\ \vdots \\ a_m \end{bmatrix}.$$

Given an $m \times n$ matrix, it may be useful to treat its columns as individual column matrices.

column rank   See *rank*.

column vector   = *column matrix*.

combination   = *selection*.

common difference   See *arithmetic sequence*.

common logarithm   See *logarithm*.

common perpendicular   Let l_1 and l_2 be two straight lines in space that do not intersect and are not parallel. The **common perpendicular** of l_1 and l_2 is the straight line that meets both lines and is perpendicular to both.

common ratio   See *geometric sequence*.

commutative   The *binary operation* ∘ on a set S is **commutative** if, for all a and b in S, $a \circ b = b \circ a$.

commutative ring   See *ring*.

commute   Let ∘ be a *binary operation* on a set S. The elements a and b of S **commute** (under the operation ∘) if $a \circ b = b \circ a$. For example, multiplication on the set of all real 2×2 matrices is not commutative; but if A and B are diagonal matrices then A and B commute.

complement, complementation   Let A be a subset of some *universal set E*. Then the **complement** of A is the *difference set* $E \setminus A$ (or $E - A$). It may be denoted by A' or $\overline{A}$ when the universal set is understood or has previously been specified. **Complementation** (the operation of taking the complement) is a unary operation on the set of subsets of a universal set E. The following properties hold:

    (i) $E' = \emptyset$, $\emptyset' = E$.
    (ii) For all A, $(A')' = A$.
    (iii) For all A, $A \cap A' = \emptyset$, $A \cup A' = E$.

See also *relative complement*.

complementary function   See *linear differential equations with constant coefficients*.

K_3 K_4 K_5

complete graph   A **complete graph** is a *simple graph* in which every vertex is joined to every other. The complete graph with n vertices, denoted by K_n, is *regular* of degree $n - 1$ and has $\frac{1}{2}n(n - 1)$ edges. See also *bipartite graph*.

complete set of residues   A **complete set of residues** modulo n is a set of n integers, one from each of the n *residue classes* modulo n. Thus

$\{0, 1, 2, 3\}$ is a complete set of residues modulo 4; so too are $\{1, 2, 3, 4\}$ and $\{-1, 0, 1, 2\}$.

completing the square   Consider a numerical example: the *quadratic equation* $2x^2 + 5x + 1 = 0$ can be solved by first writing it as

$$x^2 + \frac{5}{2}x = -\frac{1}{2}, \quad \text{and then} \quad \left(x + \frac{5}{4}\right)^2 = -\frac{1}{2} + \frac{25}{16} = \frac{17}{16}.$$

This step is known as **completing the square**: the left-hand side is made into an exact square by adding a suitable constant to both sides. The solution of the quadratic equation can then be accomplished as follows:

$$x + \frac{5}{4} = \pm\frac{\sqrt{17}}{4}, \quad \text{and so} \quad x = \frac{-5 \pm \sqrt{17}}{4}.$$

By proceeding in the same way with $ax^2 + bx + c = 0$, the standard formula for the solution of a quadratic equation can be derived.

complex number   There is no real number x such that $x^2 + 1 = 0$. The introduction of a 'new' number i such that $i^2 = -1$ gives rise to further numbers of the form $a + bi$. A number of the form $a + bi$, where a and b are real, is a **complex number**. Since one may take $b = 0$, this includes all the real numbers. The set of all complex numbers is usually denoted by **C**. (The use of j in place of i is also common.) It is assumed that two such numbers may be added and multiplied using the familiar rules of algebra, with i^2 replaced by -1 whenever it occurs. So,

$$(a + bi) + (c + di) = (a + c) + (b + d)i,$$
$$(a + bi)(c + di) = (ac - bd) + (ad + bc)i.$$

Thus the set **C** of complex numbers is closed under addition and multiplication, and the elements of this enlarged number system satisfy the laws commonly expected of numbers.

The complex number system can be put on a more rigorous basis as follows. Consider the set $\mathbf{R} \times \mathbf{R}$ of all ordered pairs (a, b) of real numbers (see *Cartesian product*). Guided by the discussion above, addition and multiplication are defined on $\mathbf{R} \times \mathbf{R}$ by

$$(a, b) + (c, d) = (a + c, b + d),$$
$$(a, b)(c, d) = (ac - bd, ad + bc).$$

It can be verified that addition and multiplication defined in this way are associative and commutative, that the distributive law holds, that there is a zero element and an identity element, that every element has a negative and every non-zero element has an inverse (see *inverse of a complex number*). This shows that $\mathbf{R} \times \mathbf{R}$ with this addition and multiplication is a *field* whose elements, according to this approach, are called complex numbers. The elements of the form $(a, 0)$ can be seen to behave exactly like the corresponding real numbers a. Moreover, if the element $(0, 1)$ is denoted by i, it is reasonable to write $i^2 = -1$, since $(0, 1)^2 = -(1, 0)$. After providing this rigorous foundation, it is normal to write $a + bi$ instead of (a, b). See also *argument*, *modulus of a complex number* and *polar form of a complex number*.

complex plane   Let points in the plane be given coordinates (x, y) with respect to a Cartesian coordinate system. The plane is called the **complex plane** when the point (x, y) is taken to represent the *complex number* $x + yi$.

component (of a compound statement)   See *compound statement*.

component (of a graph)   A *graph* may be 'in several pieces' and these are called its **components**: two vertices are in the same component if and only if there is a *path* from one to the other. A more precise definition can be given by defining an *equivalence relation* on the set of vertices with u equivalent to v if there is a path from u to v. Then the components are the corresponding *equivalence classes*.

component (of a vector)   In a Cartesian coordinate system in 3-dimensional space, let $\mathbf{i}$, $\mathbf{j}$ and $\mathbf{k}$ be unit vectors along the three coordinate axes. Given a vector $\mathbf{p}$, there are unique real numbers x, y and z such that $\mathbf{p} = x\mathbf{i} + y\mathbf{j} + z\mathbf{k}$. Then x, y and z are the **components** of $\mathbf{p}$ (with respect to the vectors $\mathbf{i}, \mathbf{j}, \mathbf{k}$). These can be determined by using the *scalar product*: $x = \mathbf{p} \cdot \mathbf{i}$, $y = \mathbf{p} \cdot \mathbf{j}$ and $z = \mathbf{p} \cdot \mathbf{k}$. (See also *direction cosines*.)

   More generally, if $\mathbf{u}$, $\mathbf{v}$ and $\mathbf{w}$ are any three non-coplanar vectors, then any vector $\mathbf{p}$ in 3-dimensional space can be expressed uniquely as $\mathbf{p} = x\mathbf{u} + y\mathbf{v} + z\mathbf{w}$, and x, y and z are called the **components** of $\mathbf{p}$ with respect to the basis $\mathbf{u}, \mathbf{v}, \mathbf{w}$. In this case, however, the components cannot be found so simply by using the scalar product.

composite   A positive integer is **composite** if it is neither *prime*, nor equal to 1; that is, if it can be written as a product hk, where the integers h and k are both greater than 1.

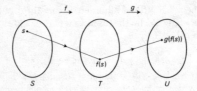

composition   Let $f: S \to T$ and $g: T \to U$ be *mappings*. With each s in S is associated the element $f(s)$ of T and hence the element $g(f(s))$ of U. This rule gives a mapping from S to U, which is denoted by $g \circ f$ (read as 'g circle f') and is the **composition** of f and g. Note that f operates first, then g. Thus $g \circ f: S \to U$ is defined by $(g \circ f)(s) = g(f(s))$ and exists if and only if the domain of g equals the codomain of f. For example, suppose that $f: \mathbf{R} \to \mathbf{R}$ and $g: \mathbf{R} \to \mathbf{R}$ are defined by $f(x) = 1 - x$ and $g(x) = x/(x^2 + 1)$. Then $f \circ g: \mathbf{R} \to \mathbf{R}$ and $g \circ f: \mathbf{R} \to \mathbf{R}$ both exist and

$$(f \circ g)(x) = 1 - \frac{x}{x^2 + 1}, \qquad (g \circ f)(x) = \frac{1 - x}{(1 - x)^2 + 1}.$$

The term 'composition' may be used for the operation $\circ$ as well as for the resulting function. The composition of mappings is associative: if $f: S \to T$, $g: T \to U$ and $h: U \to V$ are mappings, then $h \circ (g \circ f) = (h \circ g) \circ f$. This means that the mappings $h \circ (g \circ f)$ and $(h \circ g) \circ f$ have the same domain S and the same codomain V and, for all s in S, $(h \circ (g \circ f))(s) = ((h \circ g) \circ f)(s)$.

compound interest   Suppose that a sum of money P (measured in £, say) is invested with interest of i per cent a year. After one year, the amount becomes $P + (i/100)P$. This equals $P(1 + i/100)$, so that adding on i per cent is equivalent to multiplying by $1 + i/100$. When interest is compounded annually, the new amount is used to calculate the interest due in the second year and so, after two years, the amount becomes $P(1+i/100)^2$. After n years, the amount becomes

$$P \left(1 + \frac{i}{100}\right)^n.$$

This is the formula for **compound interest**. When points are plotted on graph paper to show how the amount increases, they lie on a curve that illustrates *exponential growth*. This is in contrast to the straight line obtained in the case of *simple interest*.

compound statement   A **compound statement** is formed from simple statements by the use of words such as 'and', 'or', 'not', 'implies' or their corresponding symbols. The simple statements involved are the **components** of the compound statement. For example, $(p \wedge q) \vee (\neg r)$ is a compound statement built up from the components p, q and r.

concave up and **down**   See *concavity*.

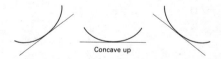
Concave up

concavity   At a point of a graph $y = f(x)$, it may be possible to specify the **concavity** by describing the curve as either concave up or concave down at that point, as follows.

   If the second derivative $f''(x)$ exists and is positive throughout some neighbourhood of a point a, then $f'(x)$ is strictly increasing in that neighbourhood and the curve is said to be **concave up** at a. At that point, the graph $y = f(x)$ and its tangent look like one of the cases shown in the figure above. If $f''(a) > 0$ and f'' is continuous at a, it follows that $y = f(x)$ is concave up at a. Consequently, if $f'(a) = 0$ and $f''(a) > 0$, the function f has a *local minimum* at a. Similarly, if $f''(x)$ exists and is negative throughout some neighbourhood of a, or if $f''(a) < 0$ and f'' is continuous at a, then the graph $y = f(x)$ is **concave down** at a and looks like one of the cases shown in the figure below. If $f'(a) = 0$ and $f''(a) < 0$, the function f has a *local maximum* at a.

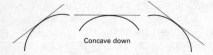

Concave down

concurrent   Any number of lines are said to be **concurrent** if there is a point through which they all pass.

concyclic   A number of points are **concyclic** if there is a circle that passes though all of them.

condition, necessary and **sufficient**   The *implication* $q \Rightarrow p$ can be read as 'if q then p'. When this is true, it may be said that q is a **sufficient condition** for p; that is, the truth of the 'condition' q is sufficient to ensure the truth of p. This means that p is true **if** q is true. On the other hand, when the implication $p \Rightarrow q$ holds, then q is a **necessary condition** for p; that is, the truth of the 'condition' q is a necessary consequence of the truth of p. This means that p is true **only if** q is true. When the implication between p and q holds both ways, p is true **if and only if** q is true, which may be written $p \Leftrightarrow q$. Then q is a **necessary and sufficient condition** for p.

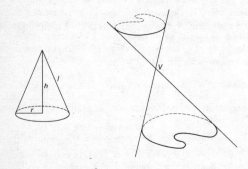

cone   In elementary work, a **cone** usually consists of a circle as base, a vertex lying directly above the centre of the circle, and the curved surface formed by the line segments joining the vertex to the points of the circle. The distance from the vertex to the centre of the base is the **height**, and the length of any of the line segments is the **slant height**. For a cone with base of radius r, height h and slant height l, the volume equals $\frac{1}{3}\pi r^2 h$ and the area of the curved surface equals $\pi r l$.

In more advanced work, a **cone** is the surface consisting of the points of the lines, called **generators**, drawn through a fixed point V, the **vertex**, and the points of a fixed curve, the generators being extended indefinitely in both directions. Then a **right-circular cone** is a cone in which the fixed curve is a circle and the vertex V lies on the line through the centre of the circle and perpendicular to the plane of the circle. The **axis** of a right-circular cone is the line through V and the centre of the circle, and is perpendicular to the plane of the circle. All the generators make the same angle with the axis; this is the **semi-vertical angle** of the cone. The right-circular cone with vertex at the origin, the z-axis as its axis, and semi-vertical angle α, has equation $x^2 + y^2 = z^2 \tan^2 \alpha$. See also *quadric cone*.

conformable   Matrices **A** and **B** are **conformable** (for multiplication) if the number of columns of **A** equals the number of rows of **B**. Then **A** has order $m \times n$ and **B** has order $n \times p$, for some m, n and p, and the product **AB**, of order $m \times p$, is defined. See *multiplication* (of matrices).

congruence (modulo n)   For each positive integer n, the relation of **congruence** between integers is defined as follows: a **is congruent to** b modulo n if $a - b$ is a multiple of n. This is written: $a \equiv b \pmod{n}$. The integer n is the **modulus** of the congruence. Then $a \equiv b \pmod{n}$ if and only if a and b have the same remainder upon division by n. For example, 19 is congruent to 7 modulo 3. The following properties hold, if $a \equiv b \pmod{n}$ and $c \equiv d \pmod{n}$:

   (i) $a + c \equiv b + d \pmod{n}$.
   (ii) $a - c \equiv b - d \pmod{n}$.
   (iii) $ac \equiv bd \pmod{n}$.

It can be shown that congruence modulo n is an *equivalence relation* and so defines a *partition* of the set of integers, where two integers are in the same class if and only if they are congruent modulo n. These classes are the *residue* (or *congruence*) *classes* modulo n.

congruence class $=$ *residue class*.

congruence equation   The following are examples of **congruence equations**:

   (i) $x + 5 \equiv 3 \pmod{7}$; this has the solution $x \equiv 5 \pmod{7}$.
   (ii) $2x \equiv 5 \pmod{4}$; this has no solutions.
   (iii) $x^2 \equiv 1 \pmod{8}$; this has solutions $x \equiv 1, 3, 5$ or $7 \pmod{8}$.
   (iv) $x^2 + 2x + 3 \equiv 0 \pmod{6}$; this has solutions $x \equiv 1$ or $3 \pmod{6}$.

In seeking solutions to a congruence equation, it is only necessary to consider a *complete set of residues* and find solutions in this set. The examples (i) and (ii) above are **linear congruence equations**. The linear congruence equation $ax \equiv b \pmod{n}$ has a solution if and only if (a, n) divides b, where (a, n) is the *greatest common divisor* of a and n.

congruent figures   Two geometrical figures are **congruent** if they are identical in shape and size. This includes the case when one of them is a mirror-image of the other, and so the three triangles shown are all congruent to each other.

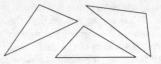

congruent (modulo n)   See *congruence*.

conic   A **conic**, or **conic section**, can be defined as a curve that can be obtained as the plane section of a cone. The figure shows how an ellipse, parabola or hyperbola can be obtained.

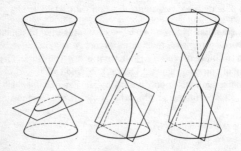

But there are other more convenient characterizations, one of which is by means of the focus and directrix property. Let F be a fixed point (the **focus**) and l a fixed line (the **directrix**), not through F, and let e be a fixed positive number (the **eccentricity**). Then the locus of all points P such that the distance from P to F equals e times the distance from P to l is a curve, and any such curve is a **conic**. The conic is called an *ellipse* if $e < 1$, a *parabola* if $e = 1$ and a *hyperbola* if $e > 1$. Note that a circle is certainly a conic (it is a special case of an ellipse); but it can only be obtained from the focus and directrix property by regarding it as the limiting form of an ellipse as $e \to 0$ and the directrix moves infinitely far away.

In a Cartesian coordinate system, a conic is a curve that has an equation of the second degree, that is, of the form $ax^2 + 2hxy + by^2 + 2gx + 2fy + c = 0$. This equation represents a parabola if $h^2 = ab$, an ellipse if $h^2 < ab$ and a hyperbola if $h^2 > ab$. It represents a circle if $a = b$ and $h = 0$, and a *rectangular hyperbola* if $a + b = 0$. It represents a pair of straight lines (which may coincide) if $\Delta = 0$, where

$$\Delta = \begin{vmatrix} a & h & g \\ h & b & f \\ g & f & c \end{vmatrix}.$$

The *polar equation* of a conic is normally obtained by taking the origin at a focus of the conic and the direction given by $\theta = 0$ perpendicular to the directrix. Then the equation can be written $l/r = 1 + e\cos\theta$ (all θ such that $\cos\theta \neq -1/e$), where e is the eccentricity and l is another constant.

conjugate axis   See *hyperbola*.

conjugate (of a complex number)   For any complex number z, where $z = x + yi$, its **conjugate** $\bar{z}$ (read as 'z bar') is equal to $x - yi$. In the *complex plane*, the points representing a complex number and its conjugate are mirror-images with respect to the real axis. The following properties hold:

(i) $\bar{\bar{z}} = z$; so if $z_1 = \overline{z_2}$ then $z_2 = \overline{z_1}$.

(ii) $z + \bar{z}$ is real; if $z = x + yi$ then $z + \bar{z} = 2x$.

(iii) $z\bar{z} = |z|^2$; if $z = x + yi$ then $z\bar{z} = x^2 + y^2$.

(iv) $\overline{z_1 + z_2} = \overline{z_1} + \overline{z_2}$ and $\overline{z_1 - z_2} = \overline{z_1} - \overline{z_2}$.

(v) $\overline{z_1 z_2} = \overline{z_1}\,\overline{z_2}$ and $\overline{(z_1/z_2)} = \overline{z_1}/\overline{z_2}$.

It is an important fact that if the complex number α is a root of a polynomial equation $z^n + a_1 z^{n-1} + \cdots + a_{n-1}z + a_n = 0$, where $a_1, \ldots, a_n$ are real, then $\bar{\alpha}$ is also a root of this equation.

conjunction   If p and q are statements, then the statement 'p and q', denoted by $p \wedge q$, is the **conjunction** of p and q. For example, if p is 'It is raining' and q is 'It is Monday', then $p \wedge q$ is 'It is raining and it is Monday'. The conjunction of p and q is true only when p and q are both true and so the *truth table* is as follows:

p	q	$p \wedge q$
T	T	T
T	F	F
F	T	F
F	F	F

connected graph   A *graph* is **connected** if there is a *path* from any one vertex to any other. So a graph is connected if it is 'all in one piece', that is, if it has precisely one *component*.

consistent   A set of equations is **consistent** if there is a solution.

constant function   In real analysis, a **constant function** is a *real func-tion* f such that $f(x) = a$ for all x in **R**, where a, the **value** of f, is a fixed real number.

constant of integration   If ϕ is a particular *antiderivative* of a *continuous function* f, then any antiderivative of f differs from ϕ by a constant. It is common practice, therefore, to write

$$\int f(x)\,dx = \phi(x) + c,$$

where c, an arbitrary constant, is the **constant of integration**.

constant term   See *polynomial*.

construction with ruler and compasses   See *duplication of the cube*, *squaring the circle* and *trisection of an angle*.

contained in, contains   It is tempting to say that 'x is contained in S' when $x \in S$, and also to say that 'A is contained in B' if $A \subseteq B$. To distinguish between these two quite different notions, it is better to say that 'x belongs to S' and to say that 'A is included in B' or 'A is a subset of B'. However some authors consistently say 'is contained in' for $\subseteq$. Given the same examples, it is similarly tempting to say that 'S contains x' and also that 'B contains A.' It is again desirable to distinguish between the two by saying that 'B includes A' in the second case, though some authors consistently say 'contains' in this situation. The first case is best avoided or else clarified by saying that 'S contains the element x' or 'S contains x as an element.'

continuous function   The *real function* f of one variable is **continuous** at a if $f(x) \to f(a)$ as $x \to a$ (see *limit* (of $f(x)$)). The rough idea is that, close to a, the function has values close to $f(a)$. It means that the function does not suddenly jump at $x = a$ or take widely differing values arbitrarily close to a.

A function f is **continuous in an open interval** if it is continuous at each point of the interval; and f is **continuous on the closed interval** $[a, b]$, where $a < b$, if it is continuous in the open interval (a, b) and if $\lim_{x \to a+} f(x) = f(a)$ and $\lim_{x \to b-} f(x) = f(b)$. The following properties hold:

 (i) The sum of two continuous functions is continuous.
 (ii) The product of two continuous functions is continuous.
 (iii) The quotient of two continuous functions is continuous at any point or in any interval where the denominator is not zero.
 (iv) Suppose that f is continuous at a, that $f(a) = b$ and that g is continuous at b. Then h, defined by $h(x) = (g \circ f)(x) = g(f(x))$, is continuous at a.
 (v) It can be proved from first principles that the constant functions, and the function f, defined by $f(x) = x$ for all x, are continuous (at any

point or in any interval). By using (i), (ii) and (iii), it follows that any *polynomial function* is continuous and that any *rational function* is continuous at any point or in any interval where the denominator is not zero.

The following properties of continuous functions appear to be obvious if a continuous function is thought of as one whose graph is a continuous curve; but rigorous proofs are not elementary, relying as they do on rather deep properties of the real numbers:

(vi) If f is continuous on a closed interval $[a, b]$ and η is any real number between $f(a)$ and $f(b)$, then, for some c in (a, b), $f(c) = \eta$. This is the *Intermediate Value Theorem* or *Property*.

(vii) If f is continuous on a closed interval $[a, b]$ then f is *bounded* on $[a, b]$. Furthermore, if S is the set of values $f(x)$ for x in $[a, b]$ and $M = \sup S$, then there is a ξ in $[a, b]$ such that $f(\xi) = M$ (and similarly for $m = \inf S$). It is said that 'a continuous function on a closed interval attains its bounds'.

contrapositive   The **contrapositive** of an *implication* $p \Rightarrow q$ is the implication $\neg q \Rightarrow \neg p$. An implication and its contrapositive are *logically equivalent*, so that one is true if and only if the other is. So in giving a proof of a mathematical result, it may on occasion be more convenient to establish the contrapositive rather than the original form of the theorem. For example, the theorem that if n^2 is odd then n is odd could be proved by showing instead that if n is even then n^2 is even.

converse   The **converse** of an *implication* $p \Rightarrow q$ is the implication $q \Rightarrow p$. If an implication is true, then its converse may or may not be true.

convex   A plane or solid figure, such as a polygon or polyhedron, is **convex** if the *line segment* joining any two points inside it lies wholly inside it.

convex up and **down**   Some authors say that a curve is **convex up** when it is *concave down*, and **convex down** when it is *concave up* (see *concavity*).

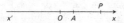

coordinates (on a line)   One way of assigning coordinates to points on a line is as follows. Make the line into a *directed line* by choosing one direction as the positive direction, running say from x' to x. Take a point O on the line as **origin** and a point A on the line such that OA is equal to the *unit length*. If P is any point on the line and $OP = x$, then x is the **coordinate** of P in this coordinate system. (Here OP denotes the *measure*.) The coordinate system on the line is determined by the specified direction of the line, the origin and the given unit of length.

coordinates (in the plane)   One way of assigning coordinates to points in the plane is as follows. Take a *directed line* Ox as x-axis and a directed line Oy

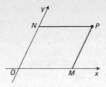

as y-axis, where the point O is the **origin**, and specify the unit of length. For any point P in the plane, let M and N be points on the x-axis and y-axis such that PM is parallel to the y-axis and PN is parallel to the x-axis. If $OM = x$ and $ON = y$, then (x, y) are the **coordinates** of the point P in this coordinate system. The coordinate system is determined by the two directed lines and the given unit of length. When the directed lines intersect at a right angle, the system is a **Cartesian**, or **rectangular**, **coordinate system** and (x, y) are **Cartesian coordinates** of P. Normally, Ox and Oy are chosen so that an anticlockwise rotation of one right angle takes the positive x-direction to the positive y-direction.

There are other methods of assigning coordinates to points in the plane. One such is the method of *polar coordinates*.

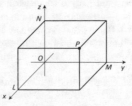

coordinates (in 3-dimensional space)   One way of assigning coordinates to points in space is as follows. Take as **axes**, three mutually perpendicular *directed lines* Ox, Oy and Oz, intersecting at the point O, the **origin**, and forming a *right-handed system*. Let L be the point where the plane through P, parallel to the plane containing the y-axis and the z-axis, meets the x-axis. Alternatively, L is the point on the x-axis such that PL is perpendicular to the x-axis. Let M and N be similarly defined points on the y-axis and the z-axis. The points L, M and N are in fact three of the vertices of the *cuboid* with three of its edges along the coordinate axes and with O and P as opposite vertices. If $OL = x$, $OM = y$ and $ON = z$, then (x, y, z) are the **coordinates** of the point P in this **Cartesian coordinate system**.

There are other methods of assigning coordinates to points in space. One is similar to that described above but using oblique axes. Others are by *spherical polar coordinates* and *cylindrical polar coordinates*.

coplanar points and lines   A number of points and lines are **coplanar** if there is a plane in which they all lie. Three points are always coplanar: indeed, any three points that are not collinear determine a unique plane that passes through them.

coplanar vectors   Let $\overrightarrow{OA}$ and $\overrightarrow{OB}$ be directed line-segments representing non-zero, non-parallel *vectors* **a** and **b**. A vector **p** is **coplanar** with **a** and **b** if **p** can be represented by a directed line-segment $\overrightarrow{OP}$, where P lies in the plane determined by O, A and B. The vector **p** is coplanar with **a** and **b** if and only if there exist scalars λ and μ such that $\mathbf{p} = \lambda\mathbf{a} + \mu\mathbf{b}$.

coprime   = *relatively prime*.

correspondence   See *one-to one correspondence*.

cosecant   See *trigonometric function*.

cosech, cosh   See *hyperbolic function*.

cosine   See *trigonometric function*.

cosine rule   See *triangle*.

cotangent   See *trigonometric function*.

coth   See *hyperbolic function*.

counterexample   Let $p(x)$ be a mathematical sentence involving a symbol x, so that, when x is a particular element of some universal set, $p(x)$ is a statement that is either true or false. What may be of concern is the proving or disproving of the supposed theorem that $p(x)$ is true for all x in the universal set. The supposed theorem can be shown to be false by producing just one particular element of the universal set to serve as x that makes $p(x)$ false. The particular element produced is a **counterexample**. For example, let $p(x)$ say that $\cos x + \sin x = 1$ and consider the supposed theorem that $\cos x + \sin x = 1$ for all real numbers x. This is demonstrably false (though $p(x)$ may be true for some values of x) because $x = \pi/4$ is a counterexample: $\cos(\pi/4) + \sin(\pi/4) \neq 1$.

Cramer's rule   Consider a set of n linear equations in n unknowns x_1, $x_2, \ldots, x_n$, written in matrix form as $\mathbf{Ax} = \mathbf{b}$. When $\mathbf{A}$ is *invertible*, the set of equations has a unique solution $\mathbf{x} = \mathbf{A}^{-1}\mathbf{b}$. Since $\mathbf{A}^{-1} = (1/\det \mathbf{A})\mathrm{adj}\,\mathbf{A}$, this gives the solution

$$\mathbf{x} = \frac{(\mathrm{adj}\,\mathbf{A})\mathbf{b}}{\det \mathbf{A}},$$

which may be written

$$x_j = \frac{b_1 A_{1j} + b_2 A_{2j} + \cdots + b_n A_{nj}}{\det \mathbf{A}} \qquad (j = 1, \ldots, n),$$

using the entries of **b** and the *cofactors* of $\mathbf{A}$. This is **Cramer's rule**. Note that here the numerator is equal to the determinant of the matrix obtained by replacing the j-th column of $\mathbf{A}$ by the column **b**. For example, this gives the solution of

$$ax + by = h,$$
$$cx + dy = k,$$

when $ad - bc \neq 0$, as

$$x = \frac{\begin{vmatrix} h & b \\ k & d \end{vmatrix}}{\begin{vmatrix} a & b \\ c & d \end{vmatrix}} = \frac{hd - bk}{ad - bc}, \qquad y = \frac{\begin{vmatrix} a & h \\ c & k \end{vmatrix}}{\begin{vmatrix} a & b \\ c & d \end{vmatrix}} = \frac{ak - hc}{ad - bc}.$$

critical point   = *stationary point.*

critical value   = *stationary value.*

cross product   = *vector product.*

cube   A **cube** is a solid figure bounded by six square faces. It has eight vertices and twelve edges.

cube root of unity   A **cube root of unity** is a complex number z such that $z^3 = 1$. The three cube roots of unity are 1, ω and ω^2, where

$$\omega = e^{2\pi i/3} = \cos\frac{2\pi}{3} + i\sin\frac{2\pi}{3} = -\frac{1}{2} + \frac{\sqrt{3}}{2}i,$$

$$\omega^2 = e^{4\pi i/3} = \cos\frac{4\pi}{3} + i\sin\frac{4\pi}{3} = -\frac{1}{2} - \frac{\sqrt{3}}{2}i.$$

Properties: (i) $\omega^2 = \overline{\omega}$ (see *conjugate*), (ii) $1 + \omega + \omega^2 = 0$.

cubic equation, cubic polynomial   A **cubic polynomial** is a polynomial of degree three; a **cubic equation** is a polynomial equation of degree three.

cuboid   A **cuboid** is a *parallelepiped* all of whose faces are rectangles.

cup   The operation $\cup$ (see *union*) is read by some as '**cup**', this being derived from the shape of the symbol, and in contrast to *cap* ($\cap$).

curve sketching   When a graph $y = f(x)$ is to be sketched, what is generally required is a sketch showing the general shape of the curve and the behaviour at points of special interest. The different parts of the graph do not have to be to scale. It is normal to investigate the following: *symmetry*, *stationary points*, intervals in which the function is always increasing or always decreasing, *asymptotes* (vertical, horizontal and slant), *concavity*, *points of inflexion*, points of intersection with the axes, and the gradient at points of interest.

cycle (in a graph)   See *Hamiltonian graph* and *tree.*

cyclic group   Let a be an element of a *multiplicative group* G. The elements a^r, where r is an integer (positive, zero or negative), form a *subgroup* of G, called the subgroup generated by a. A group G is **cyclic** if there is an element a in G such that the subgroup generated by a is the whole of G. If G

is a finite cyclic group with identity element e, the set of elements of G may be written $\{e, a, a^2, \ldots, a^{n-1}\}$, where $a^n = e$ and n is the smallest such positive integer. If G is an infinite cyclic group, the set of elements may be written $\{\ldots, a^{-2}, a^{-1}, e, a, a^2, \ldots\}$.

By making appropriate changes, a cyclic *additive group* (or group with any other operation) can be defined. For example, the set $\{0, 1, 2, \ldots, n-1\}$ with addition modulo n is a cyclic group, and the set of all integers with addition is an infinite cyclic group. Any two cyclic groups of the same order are *isomorphic*.

cyclic polygon   A polygon is **cyclic** if there is a circle that passes through all its vertices. From one of the *circle theorems*, it follows that opposite angles of a cyclic quadrilateral add up to 180°.

cycloid   A **cycloid** is the path traced out by a point on the circumference of a circle that rolls without slipping along a straight line. With suitable axes, the cycloid has *parametric equations* $x = a(t - \sin t)$, $y = a(1 - \cos t)$ $(t \in \mathbf{R})$, where a is a constant (equal to the radius of the rolling circle). In the figure, $OA = 2\pi a$.

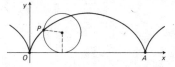

cylinder   In elementary work, a **cylinder**, if taken, say, with its axis vertical, would be reckoned to consist of a circular base, a circular top of the same size, and the curved surface formed by the vertical line segments joining them. For a cylinder with base of radius r and height h, the volume equals $\pi r^2 h$ and the area of the curved surface equals $2\pi r h$.

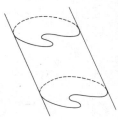

In more advanced work, a **cylinder** is a surface, consisting of the points of the lines, called **generators**, drawn through the points of a fixed curve and parallel to a fixed line, the generators being extended indefinitely in both directions. Then a **right-circular cylinder** is one in which the fixed curve is a circle and the fixed line is perpendicular to the plane of the circle. The

axis of a right-circular cylinder is the line through the centre of the circle and perpendicular to the plane of the circle, that is, parallel to the generators.

cylindrical polar coordinates   Suppose that three mutually perpendicular directed lines Ox, Oy and Oz, intersecting at the point O and forming a right-handed system, are taken as coordinate axes. For any point P, let M and N be the projections of P onto the xy-plane and the z-axis respectively. Then $ON = PM = z$, the z-coordinate of P. Let $\rho = |PN|$, the distance of P from the z-axis, and let ϕ be the angle $\angle xOM$ in radians ($0 \leq \phi < 2\pi$). Then (ρ, ϕ, z) are the **cylindrical polar coordinates** of P. (It should be noted that the points of the z-axis give no value for ϕ.) The two coordinates (ρ, ϕ) can be seen as polar coordinates of the point M and, as with polar coordinates, $\phi + 2k\pi$, where k is an integer, may be allowed in place of ϕ.

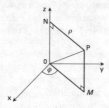

The Cartesian coordinates (x, y, z) of P can be found from (ρ, ϕ, z) by: $x = \rho \cos \phi$, $y = \rho \sin \phi$, and $z = z$. Conversely, the cylindrical polar coordinates can be found from (x, y, z) by: $\rho = \sqrt{x^2 + y^2}$, ϕ is such that $\cos \phi = x/\sqrt{x^2 + y^2}$ and $\sin \phi = y/\sqrt{x^2 + y^2}$, and $z = z$. Cylindrical polar coordinates can be useful in treating problems involving right-circular cylinders. Such a cylinder with its axis along the z-axis then has equation $\rho = $ constant.

D

decimal Any real number a between 0 and 1 has a **decimal representation**, written $\cdot d_1 d_2 d_3 \ldots$, where each d_i is one of the digits 0, 1, 2, ..., 9; this means that

$$a = d_1 \times 10^{-1} + d_2 \times 10^{-2} + d_3 \times 10^{-3} + \cdots.$$

This notation can be extended to enable any positive real number to be written as

$$c_n c_{n-1} \ldots c_1 c_0 \cdot d_1 d_2 d_3 \ldots$$

using, for the integer part, the normal representation $c_n c_{n-1} \ldots c_1 c_0$ to base 10 (see *base*). If, from some stage on, the representation consists of the repetition of a string of one or more digits, it is called a **recurring** or **repeating decimal**. For example, the recurring decimal $\cdot 12748748748 \ldots$ can be written $\cdot 12\dot{7}4\dot{8}$, where the dots above indicate the beginning and end of the repeating string. The repeating string may consist of just one digit, and then, for example, $\cdot 16666 \ldots$ is written as $\cdot 1\dot{6}$. If the repeating string consists of a single zero, this is generally omitted and the representation may be called a **terminating decimal**.

The decimal representation of any real number is unique except that, if a number can be expressed as a terminating decimal, it can also be expressed as a decimal with a recurring 9. Thus $\cdot 25$ and $\cdot 24\dot{9}$ are representations of the same number. The numbers that can be expressed as recurring (including terminating) decimals are precisely the *rational numbers*.

decimal places In *rounding* or *truncation* of a number to n **decimal places**, the original is replaced by a number with just n digits after the decimal point. When the rounding or truncation takes place to the left of the decimal point, a phrase such as 'to the nearest 10' or 'to the nearest 1000' has to be used. To say that $a = 1\cdot 9$ to 1 decimal place means that the exact value of a becomes $1\cdot 9$ after rounding to 1 decimal place, and so $1\cdot 85 \leq a \leq 1\cdot 95$.

decreasing function A *real function* f is **decreasing** in or on an interval I if $f(x_1) \geq f(x_2)$ whenever x_1 and x_2 are in I with $x_1 < x_2$. Also f is **strictly decreasing** if $f(x_1) > f(x_2)$ whenever $x_1 < x_2$.

decreasing sequence A sequence $a_1, a_2, a_3, \ldots$ is said to be **decreasing** if $a_i \geq a_{i+1}$ for all i, and **strictly decreasing** if $a_i > a_{i+1}$ for all i.

Dedekind, Richard (1831–1916) Dedekind was a German mathematician who spent some years at the University at Göttingen and much of the rest of his life teaching in a technical college. He is famous for the Dedekind cut. This refers to his formal construction of the real number system from the rational numbers. This was an important step towards the formalization of mathematics that we have seen in this century, albeit one that was anticipated by Eudoxus, 2000 years earlier. The reader is directed to Dedekind's very readable account of his work in the essay *Continuity and Irrational Numbers*.

definite integral   See *integral*.

degenerate conic   A *conic* is **degenerate** if it consists of a pair of (possibly coincident) straight lines. The equation $ax^2 + 2hxy + by^2 + 2gx + 2fy + c = 0$ represents a degenerate conic if $\Delta = 0$, where

$$\Delta = \begin{vmatrix} a & h & g \\ h & b & f \\ g & f & c \end{vmatrix}.$$

degenerate quadric   The *quadric* with equation $ax^2 + by^2 + cz^2 + 2fyz + 2gzx + 2hxy + 2ux + 2vy + 2wz + d = 0$ is **degenerate** if $\Delta = 0$, where

$$\Delta = \begin{vmatrix} a & h & g & u \\ h & b & f & v \\ g & f & c & w \\ u & v & w & d \end{vmatrix}.$$

The non-degenerate quadrics are the *ellipsoid*, the *hyperboloid of one sheet*, the *hyperboloid of two sheets*, the *elliptic paraboloid* and the *hyperbolic paraboloid*.

degree (angular measure)   The method of measuring angles in **degrees** dates back to Babylonian mathematics around 2000 BC. A complete revolution is divided into 360 degrees (°); a right angle measures 90°. Each degree is divided into 60 minutes (′) and each minute into 60 seconds (″). In more advanced work, angles should be measured in *radians*.

degree (of a polynomial)   See *polynomial*.

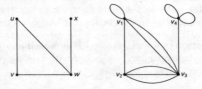

degree (of a vertex of a graph)   The **degree** of a vertex v of a *graph* is the number of edges ending at v. (If *loops* are allowed, each loop joining v to itself contributes two to the degree of v.)

In the graph on the left, the vertices u, v, w and x have degrees 2, 2, 3 and 1. The graph on the right has vertices v_1, v_2, v_3 and v_4 with degrees 5, 4, 6 and 5.

de Moivre's Theorem   From the definition of *multiplication* (of a complex number), $(\cos\theta_1 + i\sin\theta_1)(\cos\theta_2 + i\sin\theta_2) = \cos(\theta_1 + \theta_2) + i\sin(\theta_1 + \theta_2)$. This leads to the following result known as **de Moivre's Theorem**, which is crucial to any consideration of the powers z^n of a complex number z:

THEOREM: For all positive integers n, $(\cos\theta + i\sin\theta)^n = \cos n\theta + i\sin n\theta$.

The result is also true for negative (and zero) integer values of n, and this may be considered as either included in or forming an extension of de Moivre's Theorem.

de Morgan's laws   For all sets A and B (subsets of a *universal set*), $(A \cup B)' = A' \cap B'$ and $(A \cap B)' = A' \cup B'$. These are **de Morgan's laws**.

derivative   For the *real function* f, if $(f(a+h) - f(a))/h$ has a *limit* as $h \to 0$, this limit is the **derivative** of f at a and is denoted by $f'(a)$. (The term 'derivative' may also be used loosely for the *derived function*.)

Consider the graph $y = f(x)$. If (x, y) are the coordinates of a general point P on the graph and $(x+\Delta x, y+\Delta y)$ are those of a nearby point Q on the graph, it can be said that a change Δx in x produces a change Δy in y. The quotient $\Delta y/\Delta x$ is the gradient of the chord PQ. Also $\Delta y = f(x+\Delta x) - f(x)$. So the derivative of f at x is the limit of the quotient $\Delta y/\Delta x$ as $\Delta x \to 0$. This limit can be denoted by dy/dx, which is thus an alternative notation for $f'(x)$. The notation y' is also used.

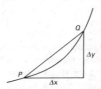

The derivative $f'(x)$ may be denoted by $(d/dx)(\quad)$, where the brackets contain a formula for $f(x)$. Some authors use the notation df/dx. The derivative $f'(a)$ gives the gradient of the curve $y = f(x)$, and hence the gradient of the tangent to the curve, at the point given by $x = a$. Suppose now, with a different notation, that x is a function of t, where t is some measurement of time. Then the derivative dx/dt, which is the *rate of change* of x with respect to t, may be denoted by $\dot{x}$. The derivatives of certain common functions are given in the Table of Derivatives (Appendix 2). See also *differentiation*, *left and right derivative*, *higher derivative* and *partial derivative*.

derived function   The function f', where $f'(x)$ is the *derivative* of f at x, is the **derived function** of f. See also *differentiation*.

Descartes, René (1596–1650)   To most people, the Frenchman Descartes is best known as a philosopher. Within the physical sciences, he is remembered for his theory of vortices as an explanation of planetary motion, a theory that was crushed by Newton. In mathematics, he is known mainly for his development of Cartesian geometry, using *coordinates* to change geometry into algebra. This seems very simple and obvious nowadays, but one should realize that very little of modern mathematics could have developed without it, including the whole notion of functional dependence. When living in Sweden, Descartes is reputed to have kept warm by working inside a stove.

determinant   For the square matrix $\mathbf{A}$, the **determinant** of $\mathbf{A}$, denoted by $\det \mathbf{A}$ or $|\mathbf{A}|$, can be defined as follows. Consider, in turn, 1×1, 2×2, 3×3, and $n \times n$ matrices.

The determinant of the 1×1 matrix $[a]$ is simply equal to a. If $\mathbf{A}$ is the 2×2 matrix below, then $\det \mathbf{A} = ad - bc$, and the determinant can also be written as shown:

$$\mathbf{A} = \begin{bmatrix} a & b \\ c & d \end{bmatrix}, \qquad \det \mathbf{A} = \begin{vmatrix} a & b \\ c & d \end{vmatrix}.$$

If $\mathbf{A}$ is a 3×3 matrix $[a_{ij}]$, then $\det \mathbf{A}$, which may be denoted by

$$\begin{vmatrix} a_{11} & a_{12} & a_{13} \\ a_{21} & a_{22} & a_{23} \\ a_{31} & a_{32} & a_{33} \end{vmatrix},$$

is given by

$$\det \mathbf{A} = a_{11} \begin{vmatrix} a_{22} & a_{23} \\ a_{32} & a_{33} \end{vmatrix} - a_{12} \begin{vmatrix} a_{21} & a_{23} \\ a_{31} & a_{33} \end{vmatrix} + a_{13} \begin{vmatrix} a_{21} & a_{22} \\ a_{31} & a_{32} \end{vmatrix}.$$

Notice how each 2×2 determinant occurring here is obtained by deleting the row and column containing the entry by which the 2×2 determinant is multiplied. This expression for the determinant of a 3×3 matrix can be written $a_{11}A_{11} + a_{12}A_{12} + a_{13}A_{13}$, where A_{ij} is the *cofactor* of a_{ij}. This is the evaluation of $\det \mathbf{A}$, 'by the first row'. In fact, $\det \mathbf{A}$ may be found by using evaluation by any row or column: for example, $a_{31}A_{31} + a_{32}A_{32} + a_{33}A_{33}$ is the evaluation by the third row and $a_{12}A_{12} + a_{22}A_{22} + a_{32}A_{32}$ is the evaluation by the second column. The determinant of an $n \times n$ matrix $\mathbf{A}$ may be defined similarly, as $a_{11}A_{11} + a_{12}A_{12} + \cdots + a_{1n}A_{1n}$, and the same value is obtained using a similar evaluation by any row or column. The following properties hold:

(i) If two rows (or two columns) of a square matrix $\mathbf{A}$ are identical, $\det \mathbf{A} = 0$.

(ii) If two rows (or two columns) of a square matrix $\mathbf{A}$ are interchanged, then only the sign of $\det \mathbf{A}$ is changed.

(iii) The value of $\det \mathbf{A}$ is unchanged if a multiple of one row is added to another row, or if a multiple of one column is added to another column.

(iv) If **A** and **B** are square matrices of the same order, $\det(\mathbf{AB}) = (\det \mathbf{A})(\det \mathbf{B})$.

(v) If **A** is *invertible*, $\det(\mathbf{A}^{-1}) = (\det \mathbf{A})^{-1}$.

(vi) If **A** is an $n \times n$ matrix, $\det k\mathbf{A} = k^n \det \mathbf{A}$.

In particular cases, the determinant of a given matrix may be evaluated by using operations of the kind described in (iii) to produce a matrix whose determinant is easier to evaluate.

diagonal entry   For a square matrix $[a_{ij}]$, the **diagonal entries** are the entries $a_{11}, a_{22}, \ldots, a_{nn}$ and they are said to form the **main diagonal**.

diagonal matrix   A square matrix is **diagonal** if all the entries not in the main diagonal are zero.

difference equation   Let $u_0, u_1, u_2, \ldots, u_n, \ldots$ be a sequence (where it is convenient to start with a term u_0). If the terms satisfy the **first-order difference equation** $u_{n+1} + au_n = 0$, it is easy to see that $u_n = A(-a)^n$, where $A \ (= u_0)$ is arbitrary.

Suppose that the terms satisfy the **second-order difference equation** $u_{n+2} + au_{n+1} + bu_n = 0$. Let α and β be the roots of the quadratic equation $x^2 + ax + b = 0$. It can be shown that (i) if $\alpha \neq \beta$, $u_n = A\alpha^n + B\beta^n$, (ii) if $\alpha = \beta$, $u_n = (A + Bn)\alpha^n$, where A and B are arbitrary constants. The *Fibonacci sequence* is given by the difference equation $u_{n+2} = u_{n+1} + u_n$, with $u_0 = 1$, $u_1 = 1$, and the above method gives

$$u_n = \frac{1}{2}\left(\frac{1+\sqrt{5}}{2}\right)^n + \frac{1}{2}\left(\frac{1-\sqrt{5}}{2}\right)^n.$$

Difference equations, also called **recurrence relations**, do not necessarily have constant coefficients like those considered above; they have similarities with differential equations.

difference quotient $=$ *Newton quotient.*

difference set   The **difference** $A \backslash B$ of sets A and B (subsets of a *universal set*) is the set consisting of all elements of A that are not elements of B. The notation $A - B$ is also used. The set is represented by the shaded region of the *Venn diagram* shown.

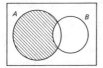

difference of two squares   Since $a^2 - b^2 = (a - b)(a + b)$, any expression with the form of the left-hand side, known as the **difference of two squares**, can be factorized into the form of the right-hand side.

differentiable function   The *real function* f of one variable is **differentiable** at a if $(f(a + h) - f(a))/h$ has a limit as $h \to 0$; that is, if the *derivative* of f at a exists. The rough idea is that a function is differentiable if it is possible to define the gradient of the graph $y = f(x)$ and hence define a tangent at the point. The function f is differentiable in an open interval if it is differentiable at every point in the interval; and f is differentiable on the closed interval $[a, b]$, where $a < b$, if it is differentiable in (a, b) and if the *right derivative* of f at a and the *left derivative* of f at b exist.

differential calculus   The term **differential calculus** is used to describe that part of mathematics that develops from the definition of the *derivative* of a function or the gradient of a graph. The derivative is obtained as the limit of the Newton quotient, and this is equivalent to the notion of the gradient of a graph as the limit of the gradient of a chord of the graph. From another point of view, the subject is concerned essentially with the *rate of change* of one quantity with respect to another.

differential coefficient   = *derivative*.

differential equation   Suppose that y is a function of x and that y', y'', ..., $y^{(n)}$ denote the *derivatives* dy/dx, d^2y/dx^2, ..., d^ny/dx^n. An **ordinary differential equation** is an equation involving x, y, y', y'', ... (The term 'ordinary' is used here to make the distinction from **partial differential equations**, which involve *partial derivatives* and which will not be discussed here.) The **order** of the differential equation is the order n of the highest derivative $y^{(n)}$ that appears.

The problem of solving a differential equation is to find functions y whose derivatives satisfy the equation. In certain circumstances, it can be shown that a differential equation of order n has a **general solution**, that is, a function y, involving n arbitrary constants, that gives all the solutions. A solution given by some set of values of the arbitrary constants is a **particular solution**. Here are some examples of differential equations and their general solutions, where A, B and C are arbitrary constants:

(i) $y' - y = 3$ has general solution $y = Ae^x - 3$.

(ii) $y' = (2x + 3y + 2)/(4x + 6y - 3)$ has general solution $\ln|2x + 3y| = 2y - x + C$.

(iii) $y'' + y = 0$ has general solution $y = A\cos x + B\sin x$.

(iv) $y'' - 2y' - 3y = e^{-x}$ has general solution $y = Ae^{-x} + Be^{3x} - \frac{1}{4}xe^{-x}$.

Example (ii) shows that it is not necessarily possible to express y explicitly as a function of x.

A differential equation of the first order (that is, of order one) can be expressed in the form $dy/dx = f(x, y)$. Whether or not it can be solved depends upon the function f. Among those that may be solvable are *separable*, *homogeneous* and *linear first-order differential equations*. Among higher-order differential equations that may be solvable reasonably easily are *linear differential equations with constant coefficients*.

differentiation   **Differentiation** is the process of obtaining the *derived function* f' from the function f, where $f'(x)$ is the *derivative* of f at x. The derivatives of certain common functions are given in the Table of Derivatives (Appendix 2), and from these many other functions can be differentiated using the following rules of differentiation:

(i) If $h(x) = k f(x)$ for all x, where k is a constant, then $h'(x) = k f'(x)$.

(ii) If $h(x) = f(x) + g(x)$ for all x, then $h'(x) = f'(x) + g'(x)$.

(iii) The **product rule**: If $h(x) = f(x)g(x)$ for all x, then

$$h'(x) = f(x)g'(x) + f'(x)g(x).$$

(iv) The **reciprocal rule**: If $h(x) = 1/f(x)$ and $f(x) \neq 0$ for all x, then

$$h'(x) = -\frac{f'(x)}{(f(x))^2}.$$

(v) The **quotient rule**: If $h(x) = f(x)/g(x)$ and $g(x) \neq 0$ for all x, then

$$h'(x) = \frac{g(x)f'(x) - f(x)g'(x)}{(g(x))^2}.$$

(vi) The *chain rule*: If $h(x) = (f \circ g)(x) = f(g(x))$ for all x, then

$$h'(x) = f'(g(x))g'(x).$$

digraph   A **digraph** (or **directed graph**) consists of a number of **vertices**, some of which are joined by **arcs**, where an **arc**, or **directed edge**, joins one vertex to another and has an arrow on it to indicate its direction. The arc from the vertex u to the vertex v may be denoted by the ordered pair (u, v). The digraph with vertices u, v, w, x and arcs (u, v), (u, w), (v, u), (w, v), (w, x) is shown on the left below.

As for *graphs*, and with a similar terminology, there may be multiple arcs and loops. A digraph with multiple arcs and loops is shown on the right.

dilatation   A **dilatation** of the plane from O with scale factor c $(\neq 0)$ is the *transformation* of the plane in which the origin O is mapped to itself and a point P is mapped to the point P', where O, P and P' are collinear and $OP' = c\,OP$. This is given in terms of Cartesian coordinates by $x' = cx$, $y' = cy$.

direct proof   For a theorem that has the form $p \Rightarrow q$, a **direct proof** is one that supposes p and shows that q follows. Compare this with an *indirect proof*.

directed graph   = *digraph*.

directed line   A **directed line** is a straight line with a specified direction along the line. The specified direction may be called the **positive direction** and the opposite the **negative direction**. It may be convenient to distinguish the ends of the line by labelling them x' and x, where the positive direction runs from x' to x. Alternatively, a directed line may be denoted by Ox, where O is a point on the line and the positive direction runs towards the end x.

directed line-segment   If A and B are two points on a straight line, the part of the line between and including A and B, together with a specified direction along the line, is a **directed line-segment**. Thus $\overrightarrow{AB}$ is the directed line-segment from A to B, and $\overrightarrow{BA}$ is the directed line-segment from B to A. See also *vector*.

direction cosines   In a Cartesian coordinate system in 3-dimensional space, a certain direction can be specified as follows. Take a point P such that $\overrightarrow{OP}$ has the given direction and $|OP| = 1$. Let α, β and γ be the three angles $\angle xOP$, $\angle yOP$ and $\angle zOP$, measured in radians ($0 \leq \alpha \leq \pi$, $0 \leq \beta \leq \pi$, $0 \leq \gamma \leq \pi$). Then $\cos \alpha$, $\cos \beta$, $\cos \gamma$ are the **direction cosines** of the given direction or of $\overrightarrow{OP}$. They are not independent, however, since $\cos^2 \alpha + \cos^2 \beta + \cos^2 \gamma = 1$. The point P has coordinates $(\cos \alpha, \cos \beta, \cos \gamma)$ and, using the standard unit vectors $\mathbf{i}$, $\mathbf{j}$ and $\mathbf{k}$ along the coordinate axes, the position vector $\mathbf{p}$ of P is given by $\mathbf{p} = (\cos \alpha)\mathbf{i} + (\cos \beta)\mathbf{j} + (\cos \gamma)\mathbf{k}$. So the direction cosines are the components of $\mathbf{p}$. The direction cosines of the x-axis are $1, 0, 0$; of the y-axis, $0, 1, 0$; and of the z-axis, $0, 0, 1$.

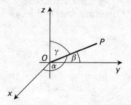

direction ratios   Suppose that a direction has *direction cosines* $\cos \alpha$, $\cos \beta$, $\cos \gamma$. Any triple of numbers l, m, n, not all zero, such that $l = k \cos \alpha$, $m = k \cos \beta$, $n = k \cos \gamma$, are called **direction ratios** of the given direction. Since $\cos^2 \alpha + \cos^2 \beta + \cos^2 \gamma = 1$, it follows that

$$\cos \alpha = \frac{\pm l}{\sqrt{l^2 + m^2 + n^2}}, \quad \cos \beta = \frac{\pm m}{\sqrt{l^2 + m^2 + n^2}}, \quad \cos \gamma = \frac{\pm n}{\sqrt{l^2 + m^2 + n^2}},$$

where either the $+$ sign or the $-$ sign is taken throughout. So any triple of numbers, not all zero, determine two possible sets of direction cosines, corresponding to opposite directions. The triple l, m, n are said to be direction ratios of a straight line when they are direction ratios of either direction of the line.

directrix (plural: directrices)   See *conic*, *ellipse*, *hyperbola* and *parabola*.

disc   The circle, centre C, with coordinates (a, b), and radius r, has equation $(x-a)^2 + (y-b)^2 = r^2$. The set of points (x, y) such that $(x-a)^2 + (y-b)^2 < r^2$ forms the interior of the circle and may be called the **open disc**, centre C, radius r. The **closed disc**, centre C, radius r, is the set of points (x, y) such that $(x - a)^2 + (y - b)^2 \leq r^2$.

discriminant   For the *quadratic equation* $ax^2 + bx + c = 0$, the quantity $b^2 - 4ac$ is the **discriminant**. The equation has two distinct real roots, equal roots (that is, one root) or no real roots according as the discriminant is positive, zero or negative.

disjoint   Sets A and B are **disjoint** if they have no elements in common; that is, if $A \cap B = \emptyset$.

disjunction   If p and q are statements, then the statement 'p or q', denoted by $p \vee q$, is the **disjunction** of p and q. For example, if p is 'It is raining' and q is 'It is Monday' then $p \vee q$ is 'It is raining or it is Monday'. To be quite clear, notice that $p \vee q$ means 'p or q *or both*': the disjunction of p and q is true when *at least* one of the statements p and q is true. The *truth table* is therefore as follows:

p	q	$p \vee q$
T	T	T
T	F	T
F	T	T
F	F	F

displacement   Suppose that a particle is moving in a straight line, with a point O on the line taken as origin and one direction along the line taken as positive. Let $|OP|$ be the distance between O and P, where P is the position of the particle at time t. Then the **displacement** x is equal to $|OP|$ if $\overrightarrow{OP}$ is in the positive direction and equal to $-|OP|$ if $\overrightarrow{OP}$ is in the negative direction. Indeed, the displacement is equal to the *measure* OP.

dissection (of an interval) $=$ *partition* (of an interval).

distance (in the complex plane)   If P_1 and P_2 represent the complex numbers z_1 and z_2, the **distance** $|P_1 P_2|$ is equal to $|z_1 - z_2|$, the *modulus* of $z_1 - z_2$.

distance between two points (in the plane)   Let A and B have coordinates (x_1, y_1) and (x_2, y_2). It follows from Pythagoras' Theorem that the **distance** $|AB|$ is equal to $\sqrt{(x_2 - x_1)^2 + (y_2 - y_1)^2}$.

distance between two points (in 3-dimensional space)   Let A and B have coordinates (x_1, y_1, z_1) and (x_2, y_2, z_2). Then the **distance** $|AB|$ is equal to $\sqrt{(x_2 - x_1)^2 + (y_2 - y_1)^2 + (z_2 - z_1)^2}$.

distance between two lines (in 3-dimensional space)   Let l_1 and l_2 be lines in space that do not intersect. There are two cases. If l_1 and l_2 are parallel, the **distance between the two lines** is the length of any line segment $N_1 N_2$, with N_1 on l_1 and N_2 on l_2, perpendicular to both lines. If l_1 and l_2 are not parallel, there are unique points N_1 on l_1 and N_2 on l_2 such that the length of the line segment $N_1 N_2$ is the shortest possible. The length $|N_1 N_2|$ is the **distance between the two lines**. In fact, the line $N_1 N_2$ is the *common perpendicular* of l_1 and l_2.

distance from a point to a line (in the plane)   The **distance** from the point P to the line l is the shortest distance between P and a point on l. It is equal to $|PN|$, where N is the point on l such that the line PN is perpendicular to l. If P has coordinates (x_1, y_1) and l has equation $ax + by + c = 0$, the distance from P to l is equal to

$$\frac{|ax_1 + by_1 + c|}{\sqrt{a^2 + b^2}},$$

where $|ax_1 + by_1 + c|$ is the *absolute value* of $ax_1 + by_1 + c$.

distance from a point to a plane (in 3-dimensional space)   The **distance** from the point P to the plane p is the shortest distance between P and a point in p, and is equal to $|PN|$, where N is the point in p such that the line PN is normal to p. If P has coordinates (x_1, y_1, z_1) and p has equation $ax + by + cz + d = 0$, the distance from P to p is equal to

$$\frac{|ax_1 + by_1 + cz_1 + d|}{\sqrt{a^2 + b^2 + c^2}},$$

where $|ax_1 + by_1 + cz_1 + d|$ is the *absolute value* of $ax_1 + by_1 + cz_1 + d$.

distributive   Suppose that $\circ$ and $*$ are *binary operations* on a set S. Then $\circ$ is **distributive** over $*$ if, for all a, b and c in S,

$$a \circ (b * c) = (a \circ b) * (a \circ c) \quad \text{and} \quad (a * b) \circ c = (a \circ c) * (b \circ c).$$

If the two operations are multiplication and addition, 'the distributive laws' normally means those that say that multiplication is distributive over addition.

divides   Let a and b be integers. Then a **divides** b (which may be written as $a \mid b$) if there is an integer c such that $ac = b$. It is said that a is a **divisor** or **factor** of b, that b is **divisible** by a, and that b is a **multiple** of a.

divisible   See *divides*.

Division Algorithm   The so-called **Division Algorithm** is the following theorem of elementary number theory:

THEOREM: For integers a and b, with $b > 0$, there exist unique integers q and r such that $a = bq + r$, where $0 \leq r < b$.

In the division of a by b, the number q is the **quotient** and r is the **remainder**.

divisor   See *divides*.

divisor of zero   If in a *ring* there are non-zero elements a and b such that $ab = 0$, then a and b are **divisors of zero**. For example, in the ring of 2×2 real matrices,

$$\begin{bmatrix} 0 & 1 \\ 0 & 0 \end{bmatrix} \begin{bmatrix} 1 & 0 \\ 0 & 0 \end{bmatrix} = \begin{bmatrix} 0 & 0 \\ 0 & 0 \end{bmatrix},$$

and so each of the matrices on the left-hand side is a divisor of zero. In the ring $\mathbf{Z}_6$, consisting of the set $\{0, 1, 2, 3, 4, 5\}$ with addition and multiplication modulo 6, the element 4 is a divisor of zero since $4.3 = 0$.

dodecahedron (plural: dodecahedra)   See *polyhedron*.

domain   See *function* and *mapping*.

dot product $=$ *scalar product*.

double root   See *root*.

dummy variable   A variable appearing in an expression is a **dummy variable** if the letter being used could equally well be replaced by another letter. For example, the two expressions

$$\int_0^1 x^2 \, dx, \qquad \int_0^1 t^2 \, dt,$$

represent the same definite integral, and so x and t are dummy variables. Similarly, the summation

$$\sum_{r=1}^5 r^2$$

denotes the sum $1^2 + 2^2 + 3^2 + 4^2 + 5^2$, and would still do so if the letter r were replaced by the letter s, say; so r here is a dummy variable.

duplication of the cube   One of the problems that Greek geometers attempted (like *squaring the circle* and *trisection of an angle*) was to find a construction, with ruler and pair of compasses, to obtain the side of a cube whose volume was twice the volume of a given cube. This is equivalent to finding a geometrical construction to obtain a length of $\sqrt[3]{2}$ from a given unit length. Now constructions of the kind envisaged can only give lengths belonging to a class of numbers obtained, essentially, by addition, subtraction, multiplication, division and the taking of square roots. Since $\sqrt[3]{2}$ does not belong to this class of numbers, the duplication of the cube is impossible.

E

e   The number *e* is the base of natural logarithms. There are several ways of defining it. Probably the most satisfactory is this. First define ln as in approach **2** to the *logarithmic function*. Then define exp as the inverse function of ln (see approach **2** to the *exponential function*). Then define *e* as equal to exp 1. This amounts to saying that *e* is the number that makes

$$\int_1^e \frac{1}{t}\,dt = 1.$$

It is necessary to go on to show that e^x and exp x are equal and so are identical as functions, and also that ln and $\log_e$ are identical functions.

The number *e* has important properties derived from some of the properties of ln and exp. For example,

$$e = \lim_{h\to 0}(1 + h)^{1/h} = \lim_{n\to\infty}\left(1 + \frac{1}{n}\right)^n.$$

Also, *e* is the sum of the series

$$1 + \frac{1}{1!} + \frac{1}{2!} + \cdots + \frac{1}{n!} + \cdots.$$

Another approach, but not a recommended one, is to make one of these properties the definition of *e*. Then exp x would be defined as e^x, ln x would be defined as its inverse function, and the properties of these functions would have to be proved.

The value of *e* is 2·71828183 (to 8 decimal places). The proof that *e* is *irrational* is comparatively easy. In 1873, Hermite proved that *e* is *transcendental* and his proof was subsequently simplified by Hilbert.

eccentricity   See *conic*, *ellipse* and *hyperbola*.

echelon form   Suppose that a row of a matrix is called zero if all its entries are zero. Then a matrix is in **echelon form** if (i) all the zero rows come below the non-zero rows and (ii) the first non-zero entry in each non-zero row is 1 and occurs in a column to the right of the leading 1 in the row above. For example, these two matrices are in echelon form:

$$\begin{bmatrix} 1 & 6 & -1 & 4 & 2 \\ 0 & 0 & 1 & 2 & -3 \\ 0 & 0 & 0 & 1 & 5 \end{bmatrix}, \qquad \begin{bmatrix} 1 & 6 & -1 & 4 & 2 \\ 0 & 1 & 2 & -3 & 5 \\ 0 & 0 & 0 & 0 & 0 \end{bmatrix}.$$

Any matrix can be transformed to a matrix in echelon form using *elementary row operations*, by a method known as *Gaussian elimination*. The solutions of a set of linear equations may be investigated by transforming the *augmented matrix* to echelon form. Further elementary row operations may be used to transform a matrix to *reduced echelon form*. A set of linear equations is said to be in echelon form if its augmented matrix is.

edge (of a graph), **edge-set**   See *graph*.

eigenvalue, eigenvector   = *characteristic value, characteristic vector*.

Einstein, Albert (1879–1955)   Einstein's work was the single most important influence on the development of physics since Newton. He was responsible for the Special (1905) and General (1916) Theories of Relativity. He made a fundamental contribution to the birth of quantum theory and had an important influence on thermodynamics. He is perhaps most widely known for his equation $E = mc^2$, quantifying the equivalence of matter and energy. He regarded himself as a physicist rather than as a mathematician, but his work has triggered off many developments in modern mathematics. Contrary to the popular image of a white-haired professor scribbling incomprehensible symbols on a blackboard, Einstein's great strength was his ability to ask simple questions and give simple answers. In that way he changed our view of the universe and our concepts of space and time. Nothing could be more fundamental. He once remarked that what really interested him was whether God had any choice in the creation of the world.

element   An object in a set is an **element** of that set.

elementary column operation   The following operations on the columns of a matrix are the **elementary column operations**:

  (i) interchange two columns,
  (ii) multiply a column by a non-zero scalar,
  (iii) add a multiple of one column to another column.

An elementary column operation can be produced by post-multiplication by the appropriate *elementary matrix*.

elementary function   The **elementary functions** consist of the following real functions: the *rational functions*, the *trigonometric functions*, the *logarithmic* and *exponential functions*, the functions f defined by $f(x) = x^{m/n}$ (where m and n are non-zero integers), and all those functions that can be obtained from these by using addition, subtraction, multiplication, division, *composition* and the taking of *inverse functions*.

elementary matrix   An **elementary matrix** is a square matrix obtained from the identity matrix **I** by an *elementary row operation*. Thus there are three types of elementary matrix. Here is an example of each type:

$$
\text{(i)} \begin{bmatrix} 1 & 0 & 0 & 0 & 0 & 0 & 0 \\ 0 & 0 & 0 & 0 & 1 & 0 & 0 \\ 0 & 0 & 1 & 0 & 0 & 0 & 0 \\ 0 & 0 & 0 & 1 & 0 & 0 & 0 \\ 0 & 1 & 0 & 0 & 0 & 0 & 0 \\ 0 & 0 & 0 & 0 & 0 & 1 & 0 \\ 0 & 0 & 0 & 0 & 0 & 0 & 1 \end{bmatrix}, \quad \text{(ii)} \begin{bmatrix} 1 & 0 & 0 & 0 & 0 & 0 & 0 \\ 0 & 1 & 0 & 0 & 0 & 0 & 0 \\ 0 & 0 & -3 & 0 & 0 & 0 & 0 \\ 0 & 0 & 0 & 1 & 0 & 0 & 0 \\ 0 & 0 & 0 & 0 & 1 & 0 & 0 \\ 0 & 0 & 0 & 0 & 0 & 1 & 0 \\ 0 & 0 & 0 & 0 & 0 & 0 & 1 \end{bmatrix},
$$

$$
\text{(iii)} \begin{bmatrix} 1 & 0 & 0 & 0 & 0 & 0 & 0 \\ 0 & 1 & 0 & 0 & 4 & 0 & 0 \\ 0 & 0 & 1 & 0 & 0 & 0 & 0 \\ 0 & 0 & 0 & 1 & 0 & 0 & 0 \\ 0 & 0 & 0 & 0 & 1 & 0 & 0 \\ 0 & 0 & 0 & 0 & 0 & 1 & 0 \\ 0 & 0 & 0 & 0 & 0 & 0 & 1 \end{bmatrix}.
$$

The matrix (i) is obtained from $\mathbf{I}$ by interchanging the second and fifth rows, matrix (ii) by multiplying the third row by -3, and matrix (iii) by adding 4 times the fifth row to the second row. Pre-multiplication of an $m \times n$ matrix $\mathbf{A}$ by an $m \times m$ elementary matrix produces the result of the corresponding row operation on $\mathbf{A}$.

Alternatively, an elementary matrix can be seen as one obtained from the identity matrix by an *elementary column operation*; and post-multiplication of an $m \times n$ matrix $\mathbf{A}$ by an $n \times n$ elementary matrix produces the result of the corresponding column operation on $\mathbf{A}$.

elementary row operation   The following operations on the rows of a matrix are the **elementary row operations**:

(i) interchange two rows,
(ii) multiply a row by a non-zero scalar,
(iii) add a multiple of one row to another row.

An elementary row operation can be produced by pre-multiplication by the appropriate *elementary matrix*. Elementary row operations are applied to the *augmented matrix* of a set of linear equations to transform it into *echelon* or *reduced echelon form*. Each elementary row operation corresponds to an operation on the set of linear equations that does not alter the solution set of the equations.

ellipse   An **ellipse** is a particular 'oval' shape, obtained, it could be said, by stretching or squashing a circle. If it has length $2a$ and width $2b$, its area equals πab.

In more advanced work, a more precise definition of an ellipse is required. One approach is to define it as a *conic* with eccentricity less than 1. Thus it is the locus of all points P such that the distance from P to a fixed point F_1 (the **focus**) equals e (< 1) times the distance from P to a fixed line l_1 (the **directrix**). It turns out that there is another point F_2 and another line l_2

such that the same locus would be obtained with these as focus and directrix. An ellipse is also the conic section that results when a plane cuts a cone in such a way that a finite section is obtained (see *conic*).

The line through F_1 and F_2 is the **major axis**, and the points V_1 and V_2 where it cuts the ellipse are the **vertices**. The length $|V_1V_2|$ is the **length of the major axis** and is usually taken to be $2a$. The midpoint of V_1V_2 is the **centre** of the ellipse. The line through the centre perpendicular to the major axis is the **minor axis** and the distance, usually taken to be $2b$, between the points where it cuts the ellipse is the **length of the minor axis**. The three constants a, b and e are related by $b^2 = a^2(1 - e^2)$ or, in another form, $e^2 = 1 - b^2/a^2$. The eccentricity e determines the shape of the ellipse. The value $e = 0$ is permitted and gives rise to a circle, though this requires the directrices to be infinitely far away and invalidates the focus and directrix approach.

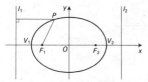

By taking a coordinate system with origin at the centre of the ellipse and x-axis along the major axis, the foci have coordinates $(ae, 0)$ and $(-ae, 0)$, the directrices have equations $x = a/e$ and $x = -a/e$, and the ellipse has equation

$$\frac{x^2}{a^2} + \frac{y^2}{b^2} = 1,$$

where $a > b > 0$. When investigating the properties of an ellipse, it is a common practice to choose this convenient coordinate system. It may be useful to take $x = a \cos\theta$, $y = b \sin\theta$ $(0 \le \theta < 2\pi)$ as *parametric equations*.

(An ellipse with its centre at the origin and its major axis, of length $2a$, along the y-axis instead has equation $y^2/a^2 + x^2/b^2 = 1$, where $a > b > 0$, and its foci are at $(0, ae)$ and $(0, -ae)$.)

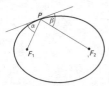

The ellipse has two important properties:

(i) If P is any point of the ellipse with foci F_1 and F_2 and length of major axis $2a$, then $|PF_1| + |PF_2| = 2a$. The fact that an ellipse can be seen as the locus of all such points is the basis of a practical method of drawing an ellipse using a string between two points.

(ii) For any point P on the ellipse, let α be the angle between the tangent at P and the line PF_1 and β the angle between the tangent at P and the line PF_2, as shown in the figure; then $\alpha = \beta$. This property is analogous to that of the parabolic reflector (see *parabola*).

ellipsoid   An **ellipsoid** is a *quadric* whose equation in a suitable coordinate system is

$$\frac{x^2}{a^2} + \frac{y^2}{b^2} + \frac{z^2}{c^2} = 1.$$

The three axial planes are planes of symmetry. All non-empty plane sections are ellipses.

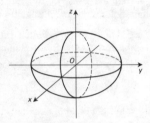

elliptic cylinder   An **elliptic cylinder** is a *cylinder* in which the fixed curve is an *ellipse* and the fixed line to which the generators are parallel is perpendicular to the plane of the ellipse. It is a *quadric* and in a suitable coordinate system has equation

$$\frac{x^2}{a^2} + \frac{y^2}{b^2} = 1.$$

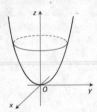

elliptic paraboloid   An **elliptic paraboloid** (shown above) is a *quadric* whose equation in a suitable coordinate system is

$$\frac{x^2}{a^2} + \frac{y^2}{b^2} = \frac{2z}{c}.$$

Here the yz-plane and the zx-plane are planes of symmetry. Sections by planes $z = k$, where $k \geq 0$, are ellipses (circles if $a = b$); planes $z = k$, where $k < 0$, have no points of intersection with the paraboloid. Sections by planes parallel to the yz-plane and to the zx-plane are parabolas. Planes through the z-axis cut the paraboloid in parabolas with vertex at the origin.

empty set   The **empty set**, denoted by $\emptyset$, is the set with no elements in it. Consequently, its *cardinality*, $n(\emptyset)$, is zero.

entry   See *matrix*.

equality (of complex numbers)   See *equating real and imaginary parts*.

equality (of matrices)   Matrices $\mathbf{A}$ and $\mathbf{B}$, where $\mathbf{A} = [a_{ij}]$ and $\mathbf{B} = [b_{ij}]$, are **equal** if and only if they have the same order and $a_{ij} = b_{ij}$ for all i and j.

equality (of sets)   Sets A and B are **equal** if they consist of the same elements. In order to establish that $A = B$, a technique that can be useful is to show, instead, that both $A \subseteq B$ and $B \subseteq A$.

equality (of vectors)   See *vector*.

equating coefficients   Let $f(x)$ and $g(x)$ be polynomials, and let

$$f(x) = a_n x^n + a_{n-1} x^{n-1} + \cdots + a_1 x + a_0,$$
$$g(x) = b_n x^n + b_{n-1} x^{n-1} + \cdots + b_1 x + b_0,$$

where it is not necessarily assumed that $a_n \neq 0$ and $b_n \neq 0$. If $f(x) = g(x)$ for all values of x, then $a_n = b_n$, $a_{n-1} = b_{n-1}$, ..., $a_1 = b_1$, $a_0 = b_0$. Using this fact is known as **equating coefficients**. The result is obtained by applying the *Fundamental Theorem of Algebra* to the polynomial $h(x)$, where $h(x) = f(x) - g(x)$. If $h(x) = 0$ for all values of x (or, indeed, for more than n values of x), the only possibility is that $h(x)$ is the zero polynomial with all its coefficients zero. The method can be used, for example, to find numbers A, B, C and D such that

$$x^3 = A(x-1)(x-2)(x-3) + B(x-1)(x-2) + C(x-1) + D$$

for all values of x. It is often used to find the unknowns in *partial fractions*.

equating real and imaginary parts   Complex numbers $a + bi$ and $c + di$ are **equal** if and only if $a = c$ and $b = d$. Using this fact is called **equating real and imaginary parts**. For example, if $(a + bi)^2 = 5 + 12i$, then $a^2 - b^2 = 5$ and $2ab = 12$.

equiangular spiral   An **equiangular spiral** is a curve whose equation in polar coordinates is $r = ae^{k\theta}$, where a (> 0) and k are constants. Let O be the origin and P be any point on the curve. The curve derives its name from the property that the angle α between OP and the tangent at P is constant.

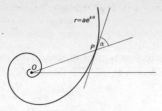

In fact, $k = \cot \alpha$. The equation can be written $\ln r = k\theta + b$ and the curve is also called the **logarithmic spiral**.

equivalence class   For an *equivalence relation* $\sim$ on a set S, an **equivalence class** $[a]$ is the set of elements of S equivalent to a; that is to say, $[a] = \{\, x \mid x \in S \text{ and } a \sim x \,\}$. It can be shown that if two equivalence classes have an element in common then the two classes are, as sets, equal. The collection of distinct equivalence classes, having the property that every element of S belongs to exactly one of them, is a *partition* of S.

equivalence relation   A *binary relation* $\sim$ on a set S is an **equivalence relation** if it is *reflexive*, *symmetric* and *transitive*. For an equivalence relation $\sim$, a is said to be **equivalent** to b when $a \sim b$. It is an important fact that, from an equivalence relation on S, *equivalence classes* can be defined to obtain a *partition* of S.

equivalent   See *equivalence relation*.

Eratosthenes   See *sieve of Eratosthenes*.

error   Let x be an approximation to a value X. According to some authors, the **error** is $X - x$; for example, when 1·9 is used as an approximation for 1·875, the error equals $-0\cdot025$. Others define the error to be $x - X$. Whichever of these definitions is used, the error can be positive or negative. Yet other authors define the error to be $|X - x|$, the difference between the true value and the approximation, in which case the error is always greater than or equal to zero. When contrasted with *relative error*, the error may be called the **absolute error**.

Euclid (about 300 BC)   Euclid was a Hellenic mathematician who worked in Alexandria. He was the author of what may well be the second most influential book in Western Culture: the *Elements*. We know little of the man and it is not clear to what extent the book describes original work and to what extent it is a textbook. The *Elements* develops a large section of geometry, specifically up to the construction of the five *Platonic solids*, by rigorous logic starting from 'undeniable' axioms. It has served for two millenia as a model of what pure mathematics is about. It is not to be confused with old school textbooks of the same name, which, in the interests of simplicity, usually destroyed the whole delicate structure of Euclid's work.

Euclidean Algorithm   The **Euclidean Algorithm** is a process, based on the *Division Algorithm*, for finding the *greatest common divisor* (a, b) of two positive integers a and b. Assuming that $a > b$, write $a = bq_1 + r_1$, where $0 \leq r_1 < b$. If $r_1 = 0$, the g.c.d. (a, b) is equal to b; if $r_1 \neq 0$ then $(a, b) = (b, r_1)$, so the step is repeated with b and r_1 in place of a and b. After further repetitions, the last non-zero remainder obtained is the required g.c.d. For example, for $a = 1274$ and $b = 871$, write

$$1274 = 1 \times 871 + 403,$$
$$871 = 2 \times 403 + 65,$$
$$403 = 6 \times 65 + 13,$$
$$65 = 5 \times 13,$$

and then $(1274, 871) = (871, 403) = (403, 65) = (65, 13) = 13$.

The algorithm also enables s and t to be found so that the g.c.d. can be expressed as $sa + tb$: use the equations in turn to express each remainder in this form. Thus,

$$403 = 1274 - 1 \times 871 = a - b,$$
$$65 = 871 - 2 \times 403 = b - 2(a - b) = 3b - 2a,$$
$$13 = 403 - 6 \times 65 = (a - b) - 6(3b - 2a) = 13a - 19b.$$

Eudoxus (about 380 BC)   Eudoxus was undoubtedly one of the greatest mathematicians of antiquity. Unfortunately, all his works have been lost, but we do know that he was responsible for the work in Book 5 of Euclid's *Elements*. That alone would serve to make him great, for it is, in the language of the day, a precise and rigorous development of the real number system. The ideas in this are so sophisticated that its significance was soon forgotten and was not really appreciated until similar problems beset the mathematicians of the nineteenth century.

Euler, Leonhard (1707–1783)   Beyond comparison, the most prolific of famous mathematicians, Euler's collected works stretch to over 90 large volumes (admittedly in large print). It was said that he calculated as easily as he breathed. Even more remarkable is the fact that a significant proportion of this work was done after he went blind. He was born in Switzerland but is most closely associated with the Berlin of Frederick the Great and the St Petersburg of Catherine the Great. It is difficult to pin down Euler's contribution to mathematics in a single paragraph. He worked in that fantastically productive period when the newly developed calculus was being extended in all directions at once and he made contributions to most areas of mathematics. Ironically, or perhaps not, he is best remembered by the notations that he introduced or popularized. Among his contributions to the language are the basic symbols π, e, i, the summation notation Σ and our standard function notation $f(x)$. His *Introductio In Analysin Infinitorum* was the most important mathematics text of the late eighteenth century. From the vast bulk of his work, let us just present one famous result of which Euler was justifiably proud:

$$1 + \frac{1}{2^2} + \frac{1}{3^2} + \cdots + \frac{1}{n^2} + \cdots = \frac{\pi^2}{6}.$$

Eulerian graph   One area of graph theory is concerned with the possibility of travelling around a *graph*, going along edges in such a way as to use every edge exactly once. A *connected* graph is called **Eulerian** if there is a sequence $v_0, e_1, v_1, \ldots, e_k, v_k$ of alternately vertices and edges (where e_i is an edge joining v_{i-1} and v_i), with $v_0 = v_k$ and with every edge of the graph occurring exactly once. Simply put, it means that 'you can draw the graph without taking your pencil off the paper or retracing any lines, ending at your starting-point'. The name arises from Euler's consideration of the problem of whether the *bridges of Königsberg* could be crossed in this way. It can be shown that a connected graph is Eulerian if and only if every vertex has even degree.

Euler's constant   Let $a_n = 1 + \frac{1}{2} + \frac{1}{3} + \cdots + (1/n) - \ln n$. This sequence has a limit whose value is known as **Euler's constant** γ; that is, $a_n \to \gamma$. The value equals $0 \cdot 57721566$, to 8 decimal places. It is not known whether γ is *rational* or *irrational*.

Euler line   In a triangle, the *circumcentre* O, the *centroid* G and the *orthocentre* H lie on a straight line called the **Euler line**. On this line, $OG : GH = 1 : 2$.

Euler's formula   The equation $\cos \theta + i \sin \theta = e^{i\theta}$, a special case of which gives $e^{i\pi} + 1 = 0$, is sometimes called **Euler's formula**.

Euler's function   For a positive integer n, let $\phi(n)$ be the number of positive integers less than n that are *relatively prime* to n. For example, $\phi(12) = 4$, since four numbers, 1, 5, 7 and 11, are relatively prime to 12. This function ϕ, defined on the set of positive integers, is **Euler's function**. It can be shown that, if the prime decomposition of n is $n = p_1^{\alpha_1} p_2^{\alpha_2} \cdots p_r^{\alpha_r}$, then

$$\phi(n) = p_1^{\alpha_1 - 1} p_2^{\alpha_2 - 1} \cdots p_r^{\alpha_r - 1} (p_1 - 1)(p_2 - 1) \cdots (p_r - 1),$$
$$= n \left(1 - \frac{1}{p_1}\right) \left(1 - \frac{1}{p_2}\right) \cdots \left(1 - \frac{1}{p_r}\right).$$

Euler proved the following extension of *Fermat's Little Theorem*: If n is a positive integer and a is any integer such that $(a, n) = 1$, then $a^{\phi(n)} \equiv 1 \pmod{n}$.

Euler's Theorem   If a *planar graph* G is drawn in the plane, so that no two edges cross, the plane is divided into a number of regions which may be called 'faces'. **Euler's Theorem** (for planar graphs) is the following:

THEOREM: Let G be a connected planar graph drawn in the plane. If there are v vertices, e edges and f faces, then $v - e + f = 2$.

An application of this gives **Euler's Theorem** (for polyhedra):

THEOREM: If a convex polyhedron has v vertices, e edges and f faces, then $v - e + f = 2$.

For particular polyhedra, it is easy to confirm the result stated in the theorem. For example, a cube has $v = 8$, $e = 12$, $f = 6$ and a tetrahedron has $v = 4$, $e = 6$, $f = 4$.

even function   The *real function* f is an **even function** if $f(-x) = f(x)$ for all x (in the domain of f). Thus the graph $y = f(x)$ of an even function has the y-axis as a line of symmetry. For example, f is an even function when $f(x)$ is defined as any of the following: 5, x^2, $x^6 - 4x^4 + 1$, $1/(x^2 - 3)$, $\cos x$.

existential quantifier   See *quantifier*.

exponent   = *index*. See also *floating-point*.

exponential decay   Suppose that $y = Ae^{kt}$, where A (> 0) and k are constants, and t represents some measurement of time. (See *exponential growth*.) When $k < 0$, y can be said to be exhibiting **exponential decay**. In such circumstances, the length of time it takes for y to be reduced to half its value is the same, whatever the value. This length of time, called the **half-life**, is a useful measure of the rate of decay. It is applicable, for example, to the decay of radioactive isotopes.

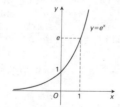

exponential function   The **exponential function** is the function f such that $f(x) = e^x$, or $\exp x$, for all x in **R**. The two notations arise from different approaches described below but are used interchangeably. Among the important properties that the exponential function has are the following:

(i) $\exp(x + y) = (\exp x)(\exp y)$, $\exp(-x) = 1/\exp x$, $(\exp x)^r = \exp rx$.
    (These hold by the usual rules for indices once the equivalence of $\exp x$ and e^x has been established.)

(ii) The exponential function is the *inverse function* of the *logarithmic function*: $y = \exp x$ if and only if $x = \ln y$.

(iii) $\dfrac{d}{dx}(\exp x) = \exp x$.

(iv) $\exp x$ is the sum of the series $1 + \dfrac{x}{1!} + \dfrac{x^2}{2!} + \cdots + \dfrac{x^n}{n!} + \cdots$.

(v) As $n \to \infty$, $\left(1 + \dfrac{x}{n}\right)^n \to \exp x$.

Three approaches can be used:

1. Suppose that the value of e has already been obtained independently. Then it is possible to define e^x, the exponential function to base e, by using approach **1** to the *exponential function to base a*. Then $\exp x$ can be taken to mean just e^x. The problem with this approach is its reliance on a prior definition of e and the difficulty of subsequently proving some of the other properties of exp.

2. Define ln as in approach **2** to the *logarithmic function* and take exp as its inverse function. It is then possible to define the value of e as $\exp 1$, establish the equivalence of $\exp x$ and e^x, and prove the other properties. This is widely held to be the most satisfactory approach mathematically, but it has to be admitted that it is artificial and does not match up with any of the ways in which exp is usually first encountered.

3. Some other property of exp may be used as a definition. It may be defined as the unique function that satisfies the differential equation $dy/dx = y$ (that is, as a function that is equal to its own derivative), with $y = 1$ when $x = 0$. Alternatively, property (iv) or (v) above could be taken as the definition of $\exp x$. In each case, it has to be shown that the other properties follow.

exponential function to base a   Let a be a positive number not equal to 1. The **exponential function to base a** is the function f such that $f(x) = a^x$ for all x in **R**. This must be clearly distinguished from what is commonly called 'the' *exponential function*. The graphs $y = 2^x$ and $y = (\frac{1}{2})^x$ illustrate the essential difference between the cases when $a > 1$ and $a < 1$. See also *exponential growth* and *exponential decay*.

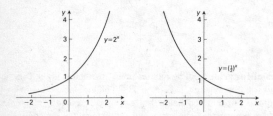

Clarifying just what is meant by a^x can be done in two ways:

1. The familiar rules for indices (see *index*) give a meaning to a^x for rational values of x. For x not rational, take a sequence of rationals that more and more closely approximate to x. For example, when $x = \sqrt{2}$, such a sequence could be 1·4, 1·41, 1·414, ... Now each of the values $a^{1·4}$, $a^{1·41}$, $a^{1·414}$, ... has a meaning, since in each case the index is rational. It can be proved that this sequence of values has a limit and this limit is then taken as the definition of $a^{\sqrt{2}}$. The method is applicable for any real value of x.

2. Alternatively, suppose that exp has been defined (say by approach **2** to the *exponential function*) and that ln is its *inverse function*. Then the following can be taken as a definition: $a^x = \exp(x \ln a)$. This approach is less elementary but really more satisfactory than **1**. It follows that $\ln(a^x) = x \ln a$, as would be expected, and the following can be proved:

(i) $a^{x+y} = a^x a^y$, $a^{-x} = 1/a^x$, $(a^x)^y = a^{xy}$.

(ii) When n is a positive integer, a^n, defined in this way, is indeed equal to the product $a \times a \times \cdots \times a$ with n occurrences of a, and $a^{1/n}$ is equal to $\sqrt[n]{a}$,

(iii) $\dfrac{d}{dx}(a^x) = a^x \ln a$.

exponential growth   When $y = Ae^{kt}$, where A (> 0) and k are constants, and t represents some measurement of time, y can be said to be exhibiting **exponential growth**. This occurs when $dy/dt = ky$; that is, when the *rate of change* of the quantity y at any time is proportional to the value of y at that time. When $k > 0$, then y is growing larger with x and moreover the rate at which y is increasing increases with x. In fact, any quantity with exponential growth (with $k > 0$) ultimately outgrows any quantity growing linearly or in proportion to a fixed power of t. When $k < 0$, the term *exponential decay* may be used.

exterior angle   See *polygon*.

extrapolation   Suppose that certain values $f(x_0)$, $f(x_1)$, ..., $f(x_n)$ of a function f are known, where $x_0 < x_1 < \cdots < x_n$. A method of finding, from these, an approximation for $f(x)$, for a given value of x that lies outside the interval $[x_0, x_n]$, is called **extrapolation**. Such methods are normally far less reliable than *interpolation*, in which x lies between x_0 and x_n.

F

factor   See *divides*.

factorial   For a positive integer n, the notation $n!$ (read as 'n **factorial**') is used for the product $n(n-1)(n-2)\cdots\times 2\times 1$. For example, $4! = 4\times 3\times 2\times 1 = 24$ and $10! = 10\times 9\times 8\times 7\times 6\times 5\times 4\times 3\times 2\times 1 = 3{,}628{,}800$. Also, by definition, $0! = 1$.

Factor Theorem   The following result, known as the **Factor Theorem**, is an immediate consequence of the *Remainder Theorem*:

THEOREM: Let $f(x)$ be a polynomial. Then $x - h$ is a factor of $f(x)$ if and only if $f(h) = 0$.

The theorem is valuable for finding factors of polynomials. For example, to factorize $2x^3 + 3x^2 - 12x - 20$, look first for possible factors $x - h$, where h is an integer. Here h must divide 20. Try possible values for h and calculate $f(h)$. Eventually it is found that $f(-2) = -16 + 12 + 24 - 20 = 0$ and so $x + 2$ is a factor. Now divide the polynomial by this factor to obtain a quadratic which it may be possible to factorize further.

feasible region   See *linear programming*.

Fermat, Pierre de (1601–1665)   Professionally, Fermat was a judge in Toulouse. In his spare time, he was one of the founders of the modern era of mathematics. His work on tangents was an acknowledged inspiration to Newton in his development of the calculus. Fermat's minimization principle in optics had profound consequences throughout later physics. Above all, he is remembered for his work in the theory of numbers, including *Fermat's Little Theorem* and the still unproven conjecture known as *Fermat's Last Theorem*.

Fermat prime   A **Fermat prime** is a *prime* of the form $2^{2^r} + 1$. At present, the only known primes of this form are those given by $r = 0, 1, 2, 3$ and 4.

Fermat's Last 'Theorem'   No proof has yet been given of **Fermat's Last 'Theorem'** so its status is in fact that of a conjecture. It states that, for all integers $n > 2$, the equation $x^n + y^n = z^n$ has no solutions in positive integers. Fermat wrote in the margin of a book that he had a proof of this, but he died without providing it.

Fermat's Little Theorem   The name **Fermat's Little Theorem** is sometimes given to this result:

THEOREM: Let p be a prime and let a be an integer not divisible by p. Then $a^{p-1} \equiv 1 \pmod{p}$.

Sometimes the name is given instead to the following, which is a corollary of the preceding result:

THEOREM: If p is a prime and a is any integer, then $a^p \equiv a \pmod{p}$.

Fibonacci (about 1170–1250)   Leonardo of Pisa, known as Fibonacci (son of Bonaccio), was one of the first European mathematicians to emerge after the Dark Ages. He did significant work on Euclidean geometry but is best remembered for his sequence of *Fibonacci numbers*. This has turned out to be surprisingly important in modern mathematics and computing.

Fibonacci number   A **Fibonacci number** is one of the numbers in the Fibonacci sequence 1, 1, 2, 3, 5, 8, 13, ..., where each number after the second is the sum of the two preceding numbers in the sequence. This sequence has many interesting properties. For instance, the sequence consisting of the ratios of one Fibonacci number to the previous one, $\frac{1}{1}, \frac{2}{1}, \frac{3}{2}, \frac{5}{3}, \frac{8}{5}, \frac{13}{8}, \ldots$, has the limit τ, the *golden ratio*. See also *difference equation*.

field   A **field** is a commutative ring with identity (see *ring*) with the following additional property:

   10. For each a ($\neq 0$), there is an element a^{-1} such that $a^{-1}a = 1$.

(The axiom numbering here follows on from that used for ring and *integral domain*.) From the defining properties of a field, Axioms **1** to **8** and Axiom **10**, it can be shown that $ab = 0$ only if $a = 0$ or $b = 0$. Thus Axiom **9** holds, and so any field is an integral domain. Familiar examples of fields are the set **Q** of rational numbers, the set **R** of real numbers, and the set **C** of complex numbers, each with the usual addition and multiplication. Another example is $\mathbf{Z}_p$, consisting of the set $\{0, 1, 2, \ldots, p-1\}$ with addition and multiplication modulo p, where p is a prime.

finite sequence   See *sequence*.

finite series   See *series*.

first derivative   The *derivative* may be called the **first derivative** when it is being contrasted with *higher derivatives*.

fixed point   See *transformation* (of the plane).

fixed-point iteration   To find a root of an equation $f(x) = 0$ by the method of **fixed-point iteration**, the equation is first rewritten in the form $x = g(x)$. Starting with an initial approximation x_0 to the root, the values x_1, x_2, x_3, ... are calculated using $x_{n+1} = g(x_n)$. The method is said to converge if these values tend to a limit α. If they do, then $\alpha = g(\alpha)$ and so α is a root of the original equation.

   A root of $x = g(x)$ occurs where the graph $y = g(x)$ meets the line $y = x$. It can be shown that, if $|g'(x)| < 1$ in an interval containing both the root and the value x_0, the method will converge, but not if $|g'(x)| > 1$. This can be illustrated in diagrams such as those below; these show cases in which $g'(x)$ is positive. For example, the equation $x^3 - x - 1 = 0$ has a root between 1 and 2, so take $x_0 = 1.5$. The equation can be written in the form $x = g(x)$ in several ways, such as (i) $x = x^3 - 1$, (ii) $x = (x+1)^{1/3}$. In case (i), $g'(x) = 3x^2$, which does not satisfy $|g'(x)| < 1$ near x_0. In case (ii), $g'(x) = \frac{1}{3}(x+1)^{-2/3}$ and $g'(1.5) \approx 0.2$, so it is likely that with this formulation the method converges.

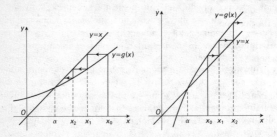

floating-point   One method of writing real numbers, used in computing, is **floating-point** notation: a number is written as $a \times 10^n$, where $0.1 \le a < 1$ and n is an integer. The number a is called the **mantissa** and n the **exponent**. Thus 634·8 and 0·00234 are written as 0.6348×10^3 and 0.234×10^{-2}. (There is also a base 2 version similar to the base 10 version just described.)

This is in contrast to **fixed-point** notation, in which all numbers are given by means of a fixed number of digits with a fixed number of digits after the decimal point. For example, if numbers are given by means of 8 digits with four of them after the decimal point, the two numbers above would be written (with an approximation) as 0634·8000 and 0000·0023. Integers are likely to be written in fixed-point notation; consequently, in the context of computers, some authors use 'fixed-point' to mean 'integer'.

focus (plural: foci)   See *conic*, *ellipse*, *hyperbola* and *parabola*.

foot of the perpendicular   See *projection* (of a point on a line) and *projection* (of a point on a plane).

Four Colour Theorem   It has been observed by map makers through the centuries that any geographical map, that is, a division of the plane into regions, can be coloured with just four colours in such a way that no two neighbouring regions have the same colour. A proof of this, the **Four Colour Theorem**, was sought by mathematicians from about the 1850s. In 1890, Heawood proved that five colours would suffice but it was not until 1976 that Appel and Haken proved the Four Colour Theorem itself. Initially, some mathematicians were sceptical of the proof because it relied, in an essential way, on a massive amount of checking of configurations by computer that could not easily be verified independently. However, the proof is now generally accepted and considered a magnificent achievement.

Fourier, Joseph (1768–1830)   Fourier was an engineer-mathematician and one of Napoleon's most able administrators. He made fundamental contributions to the theory of heat conduction and is best known for his theory of trigonometric series, now called Fourier series. These are of immense importance throughout mathematics, physics and engineering. Indeed, much of modern applied mathematics would be inconceivable without them.

fourth root of unity   A **fourth root of unity** is a complex number z such that $z^4 = 1$. There are 4 fourth roots of unity and they are $1, i, -1, -i$. (See *n-th root of unity*.)

fractional part   For any real number x, its **fractional part** is equal to $x - [x]$, where $[x]$ is the *integer part* of x. It may be denoted by $\{x\}$. The fractional part r of any real number always satisfies $0 \le r < 1$.

frustum (plural: frusta)   A **frustum** of a *right-circular cone* is the part between two parallel planes perpendicular to the axis. Suppose that the planes are at a distance h apart and that the circles that form the top and bottom of the frustum have radii a and b. Then the volume of the frustum equals $\frac{1}{3}\pi h(a^2 + ab + b^2)$. Let l be the **slant height** of the frustum, that is, the length of the part of a generator between the top and bottom of the frustum. Then the area of the curved surface of the frustum equals $\pi(a+b)l$.

function   A **function** f from S to T, where S and T are non-empty sets, is a rule that associates with each element of S (the **domain**) a unique element of T (the **codomain**). Thus it is the same thing as a *mapping*. The word 'function' tends to be used when the domain S is the set **R** of real numbers, or some subset of **R**, and the codomain T is **R** (see *real function*). The notation $f: S \to T$, read as 'f from S to T', is used. If $x \in S$, then $f(x)$ is the **image** of x under f. The subset of T consisting of those elements that are images of elements of S under f, that is, the set $\{ y \mid y = f(x),$ for some x in $S \}$, is the **range** of f. If $f(x) = y$, it is said that f-**maps** x to y, written $f: x \mapsto y$. If the graph of f is then taken to be $y = f(x)$, it may be said that y is a function of x. When $x = a$, $f(a)$ is the corresponding **value** of the function.

Fundamental Theorem of Algebra   A most important theorem in mathematics, concerned with the roots of polynomial equations, is called the **Fundamental Theorem of Algebra**:

THEOREM: Every polynomial equation

$$a_n z^n + a_{n-1} z^{n-1} + \cdots + a_1 z + a_0 = 0,$$

where the a_i are real or complex numbers and $a_n \ne 0$, has a root in the set of complex numbers.

It follows that, if $f(z) = a_n z^n + a_{n-1} z^{n-1} + \cdots + a_1 z + a_0$, there exist complex numbers $\alpha_1, \alpha_2, \ldots, \alpha_n$ (not necessarily distinct) such that

$$f(z) = a_n(z - \alpha_1)(z - \alpha_2) \ldots (z - \alpha_n).$$

Hence the equation $f(z) = 0$ cannot have more than n distinct roots.

Fundamental Theorem of Arithmetic   = the *Unique Factorization Theorem* (for integers).

Fundamental Theorem of Calculus   A sound approach to integration defines the *integral*

$$\int_a^b f(x)\, dx$$

as the limit, in a certain sense, of a sum. That this can be evaluated, when f is continuous, by finding an *antiderivative* of f, is the result embodied in the so-called **Fundamental Theorem of Calculus**. It establishes that integration is the reverse process to differentiation.

THEOREM: If f is continuous on $[a, b]$ and ϕ is a function such that $\phi'(x) = f(x)$ for all x in $[a, b]$, then

$$\int_a^b f(x)\, dx = \phi(b) - \phi(a).$$

G

Galois, Evariste (1811–1832)   Galois is one of the great tragedies of mathematical history. By the age of 19, he had made major contributions to the theory of equations in an area now known as Galois Theory. At the age of 21 he died, shot in a duel.

Gauss, Carl Friedrich (1777–1855)   Gauss has some claim to be regarded as the greatest of all pure mathematicians. He also made enormous contributions to many other parts of mathematics and physics. He had the advantage of an early start, correcting his father's financial accounts at the age of three. At the age of 18, he invented the method of least squares. By the age of 24, he was ready to publish his *Disquisitiones Arithmeticae*, a book which was to have a profound influence on the theory of numbers. He had proved both the *Fundamental Theorem of Arithmetic* and the *Fundamental Theorem of Algebra*. Gauss's *theorema egregium* gave substance to the theory of curved surfaces and led, in time, to Einstein's cosmology. Gauss himself considered the possibility of the curvature of the universe. His work on complex functions was fundamental but was not published in his lifetime, which is why we refer to Cauchy's Theorem. Statisticians now use what is known as the Gaussian distribution, and in magnetism there is a unit called the gauss. His development of statistical technique and his great powers of mental calculation allowed him to calculate the orbits of comets and asteroids from limited observational data. He is particularly associated with the orbit of Ceres. The list goes on and on.

Gaussian elimination   **Gaussian elimination** is the name given to a particular systematic procedure for solving a set of linear equations in several unknowns. This is normally carried out by applying *elementary row operations* to the augmented matrix

$$\begin{bmatrix} a_{11} & a_{12} & \dots & a_{1n} & b_1 \\ a_{21} & a_{22} & \dots & a_{2n} & b_2 \\ \vdots & \vdots & \ddots & \vdots & \vdots \\ a_{m1} & a_{m2} & \dots & a_{mn} & b_m \end{bmatrix}$$

to transform it to *echelon form*. The method is to divide the first row by a_{11} and then subtract suitable multiples of the first row from the subsequent rows, to obtain a matrix of the form

$$\begin{bmatrix} 1 & a'_{12} & \cdots & a'_{1n} & b'_1 \\ 0 & a'_{22} & \cdots & a'_{2n} & b'_2 \\ \vdots & \vdots & \ddots & \vdots & \vdots \\ 0 & a'_{m2} & \cdots & a'_{mn} & b'_m \end{bmatrix}.$$

(If $a_{11} = 0$, it is necessary to interchange two rows first.) The first row now remains untouched and the process is repeated with the remaining rows, dividing the second row by a'_{22} to produce a 1, and subtracting suitable multiples of the new second row from the subsequent rows to produce zeros below that 1. The method continues in the same way. The essential point is that the corresponding set of equations at any stage has the same solution set as the original. (See also *simultaneous linear equations*.)

Gauss-Jordan elimination   **Gauss-Jordan elimination** is an extension of the method of *Gaussian elimination*. At the stage when the i-th row has been divided by a suitable value to obtain a 1, suitable multiples of this row are subtracted not only from subsequent rows but also from preceding rows to produce zeros both below and above the 1. The result of this systematic method is that the augmented matrix is transformed into *reduced echelon form*. As a method for solving *simultaneous linear equations*, Gauss-Jordan elimination in fact requires more work than Gaussian elimination followed by *back substitution* and so is not in general recommended.

g.c.d.   = *greatest common divisor*.

general solution   See *differential equation*.

generator   See *cone* and *cylinder*.

geometrical representation (of a vector)   = *representation* (of a vector).

geometric mean   See *mean*.

geometric sequence   A **geometric sequence** is a finite or infinite sequence $a_1, a_2, a_3, \ldots$ with a **common ratio** r, so that $a_2/a_1 = r$, $a_3/a_2 = r$, and so on. The first term is usually denoted by a. For example, 3, 6, 12, 24, 48, $\ldots$ is the geometric sequence with $a = 3$, $r = 2$. In such a geometric sequence, the n-th term a_n is given by $a_n = ar^{n-1}$.

geometric series   A **geometric series** is a series $a_1 + a_2 + a_3 + \cdots$ (which may be finite or infinite) in which the terms form a *geometric sequence*. Thus the terms have a **common ratio** r with $a_k/a_{k-1} = r$ for all k. If the first term a_1 equals a, then $a_k = ar^{k-1}$. Let s_n be the sum of the first n terms, so that $s_n = a + ar + ar^2 + \cdots + ar^{n-1}$. Then s_n is given (when $r \neq 1$) by the formulae

$$s_n = \frac{a(1 - r^n)}{1 - r} = \frac{a(r^n - 1)}{r - 1}.$$

If the common ratio r satisfies $-1 < r < 1$, then $r^n \to 0$ and it can be seen that $s_n \to a/(1-r)$. The value $a/(1-r)$ is called the **sum to infinity** of the series $a + ar + ar^2 + \cdots$. In particular, for $-1 < x < 1$, the geometric series $1 + x + x^2 + \cdots$ has sum to infinity equal to $1/(1-x)$. For example, putting $x = \frac{1}{2}$, the series $1 + \frac{1}{2} + \frac{1}{4} + \frac{1}{8} + \cdots$ has sum 2. If $x \leq -1$ or $x \geq 1$, then s_n does not tend to a limit and the series has no sum to infinity.

Gödel, Kurt (1906–1978)   In 1931, Gödel published a result which undermined many of the hopes of modern mathematical logic. Mathematicians had been trying to put the theory of elementary arithmetic on to a sound formal footing. A necessary requirement for any such formal system is that it be self-consistent and complete. Gödel showed that the consistency of elementary arithmetic could not be proved from within the theory itself. He gave us the notion of unprovability, a concept that has become significant in modern computer science.

Goldbach's conjecture   In 1742, Christian Goldbach conjectured that every even integer greater than 2 is the sum of two *primes*. Neither proved nor disproved, **Goldbach's conjecture** remains one of the most famous unsolved problems in number theory.

golden ratio, golden rectangle   See *golden section*.

golden section   A line segment is divided in **golden section** if the ratio of the whole length to the larger part is equal to the ratio of the larger part to the smaller part. This definition implies that, if the smaller part has unit length and the larger part has length τ, then $(\tau + 1)/\tau = \tau/1$. Hence $\tau^2 - \tau - 1 = 0$, which gives $\tau = \frac{1}{2}(1 + \sqrt{5}) = 1\cdot 6180$, to 4 decimal places. This number τ is the **golden ratio**. A **golden rectangle**, whose sides are in this ratio, has throughout history been considered to have a particularly pleasing shape. It has the property that the removal of a square from one end of it leaves a rectangle that has the same shape.

gradient (of a straight line)   In coordinate geometry, suppose that A and B are two points on a given straight line and let M be the point where the line through A parallel to the x-axis meets the line through B parallel to the y-axis. Then the **gradient** of the straight line is equal to MB/AM. (Notice that here MB is the *measure* of $\overrightarrow{MB}$, where the line through M and B has positive direction upwards. In other words, MB equals the length $|MB|$ if B is above M, and equals $-|MB|$ if B is below M. Similarly, $AM = |AM|$ if

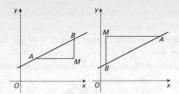

M is to the right of A, and $AM = -|AM|$ if M is to the left of A. Two cases are illustrated in the figure.)

The gradient of the line through A and B may be denoted by m_{AB}, and, if A and B have coordinates (x_1, y_1) and (x_2, y_2), with $x_1 \neq x_2$,

$$m_{AB} = \frac{y_2 - y_1}{x_2 - x_1}.$$

Though defined in terms of two points A and B on the line, the gradient of the line is independent of the choice of A and B. The line in the figure has gradient $\frac{1}{2}$.

Alternatively, the gradient may be defined as equal to $\tan \theta$, where either direction of the line makes an angle θ with the positive x-axis. (The different possible values for θ give the same value for $\tan \theta$.) If the line through A and B is vertical, that is, parallel to the y-axis, it is customary to say that the gradient is infinite. The following properties hold:

(i) Points A, B and C are collinear if and only if $m_{AB} = m_{AC}$. (This includes the case when m_{AB} and m_{AC} are both infinite.)

(ii) The lines with gradients m_1 and m_2 are parallel (to each other) if and only if $m_1 = m_2$. (This includes m_1 and m_2 both infinite.)

(iii) The lines with gradients m_1 and m_2 are perpendicular (to each other) if and only if $m_1 m_2 = -1$. (This must be reckoned to include the cases when $m_1 = 0$ and m_2 is infinite and vice versa.)

graph   A **graph** consists of a number of **vertices** (or **points** or **nodes**), some of which are joined by **edges**. The edge joining the vertex u and the vertex v may be denoted by (u, v) or (v, u). The **vertex-set**, that is, the set of vertices, of a graph G may be denoted by $V(G)$ and the **edge-set** by $E(G)$. For example, the graph shown on the left above has $V(G) = \{\, u, v, w, x \,\}$ and $E(G) = \{\, (u, v), (u, w), (v, w), (w, x) \,\}$.

In general, a graph may have more than one edge joining a pair of vertices; when this occurs, these edges are called **multiple edges**. Also, a graph may have loops — a **loop** is an edge that joins a vertex to itself. In the other graph shown, there are 2 edges joining v_1 and v_3 and 3 edges joining v_2 and v_3; the graph also has three loops.

Normally, $V(G)$ and $E(G)$ are finite, but if this is not so, the result may also be called a graph, though some prefer to call this an **infinite graph**.

graph (of a function or mapping)   For a *real function* f, the **graph** of f is the set of all pairs (x, y) in $\mathbf{R} \times \mathbf{R}$ such that $y = f(x)$, and x is in the domain of the function. For many real functions of interest, this gives a set of points that form a curve of some sort, possibly in a number of parts, that can be drawn in the plane. Such a curve defined by $y = f(x)$ is also called the graph of f. See also *mapping*.

graph (of a relation)   Let R be a *binary relation* on a set S, so that, when a is related to b, this is written as aRb. The **graph** of R is the corresponding subset of the *Cartesian product* $S \times S$, namely, the set of all pairs (a, b) such that aRb.

great circle   A **great circle** (in contrast to a *small circle*) is a circle on the surface of a sphere with its centre at the centre of the sphere.

greatest common divisor   For two non-zero integers a and b, any integer that is a divisor of both is a **common divisor**. Of all the common divisors, the greatest is the **greatest common divisor** (or **g.c.d.**), denoted by (a, b). The g.c.d. of a and b has the property of being divisible by every other common divisor of a and b. It is an important theorem that there are integers s and t such that the g.c.d. can be expressed as $sa + tb$. If the prime decomposition of a and b are known, the g.c.d. is easily found: for example, if $a = 168 = 2^3 \times 3 \times 7$ and $b = 180 = 2^2 \times 3^2 \times 5$ then the g.c.d. is $2^2 \times 3 = 12$. Otherwise, the g.c.d. can be found by the *Euclidean Algorithm*, which can be used also to find s and t to express the g.c.d. as $sa + tb$. Similarly, any finite set of non-zero integers $a_1, a_2, \ldots, a_n$ has a g.c.d., denoted by $(a_1, a_2, \ldots, a_n)$, and there are integers $s_1, s_2, \ldots, s_n$ such that this can be expressed as $s_1 a_1 + s_2 a_2 + \cdots + s_n a_n$.

greatest lower bound   = *infimum*.

greatest value   Let f be a *real function* and D a subset of its domain. If there is a point c in D such that $f(c) \geq f(x)$ for all x in D, then $f(c)$ is the **greatest value** of f in D. There may be no such point: consider, for example, either the function f defined by $f(x) = 1/x$ or the function f defined by $f(x) = x$, with the open interval $(0, 1)$ as D; or the function f defined by $f(x) = x - [x]$, with the closed interval $[0, 1]$ as D. If the greatest value does exist, it may be attained at more than one point of D.

That a *continuous function* on a closed interval has a greatest value is ensured by the non-elementary theorem that such a function 'attains its bounds'.

An important theorem states that a function, continuous on $[a, b]$ and *differentiable* in (a, b), attains its greatest value either at a *local maximum* (which is a *stationary point*) or at an end-point of the interval.

group   An operation on a set is only worth considering if it has properties likely to lead to interesting and useful results. Certain basic properties recur in different parts of mathematics and, if these are recognized, use can be made of the similarities that exist in the different situations. One such set of basic properties is specified in the definition of a group. The following, then, are all examples of groups: the set of real numbers with addition, the set of non-zero real numbers with multiplication, the set of 2×2 real matrices with matrix addition, the set of vectors in 3-dimensional space with vector addition, the set of all bijective mappings from a set S onto itself with composition of mappings, the four complex numbers 1, i, -1, $-i$ with multiplication. The definition is as follows: a **group** is a set G closed under an operation $\circ$ such that

1. for all a, b and c in G, $a \circ (b \circ c) = (a \circ b) \circ c$,
2. there is an identity element e in G such that $a \circ e = e \circ a = a$ for all a in G,
3. for each a in G, there is an inverse element a' in G such that $a \circ a' = a' \circ a = e$.

The group may be denoted by $\langle G, \circ \rangle$, or $(G, \circ)$, when it is necessary to specify the operation, but may be called simply the group G when the intended operation is clear.

H

half-life   See *exponential decay*.

half-plane   In coordinate geometry, if a line l has equation $ax + by + c = 0$, the set of points (x, y) such that $ax + by + c > 0$ forms the **open half-plane** on one side of l and the set of points (x, y) such that $ax + by + c < 0$ forms the open half-plane on the other side of l. When the line $ax + by + c = 0$ has been drawn, there is a useful method, if $c \neq 0$, of determining which half-plane is which: find out which of the two inequalities is satisfied by the origin. Thus the half-plane containing the origin is the one given by $ax + by + c > 0$ if $c > 0$, and is the one given by $ax + by + c < 0$ if $c < 0$.

A **closed half-plane** is a set of points (x, y) such that $ax + by + c \geq 0$ or such that $ax + by + c \leq 0$. The use of open and closed half-planes is the basis of elementary *linear programming*.

half-turn symmetry   See *symmetrical about a point*.

Hamilton, William Rowan (1805–1865)   Hamilton is Ireland's greatest mathematician. He was a child prodigy. It is claimed that at the age of 13 he could speak 13 languages. He became professor at Dublin at the age of 22. Hamilton's main achievement was in the subject of geometrical optics, for which he laid a theoretical foundation that came close to anticipating quantum theory. His work is also of great significance for general mechanics. He is perhaps best known among pure mathematicians for his algebraic theory of complex numbers, the invention of quaternions and his exploitation of non-commutative algebra, in which $ab \neq ba$.

Hamiltonian graph   In graph theory, one area of study has been concerned with the possibility of travelling around a *graph*, going along edges in such a way as to visit every vertex exactly once. The precise definitions can be given as follows. A **cycle** in a graph is a sequence v_0, e_1, v_1, ..., e_k, v_k ($k \geq 1$) of alternately vertices and edges (where e_i is an edge joining v_{i-1} and v_i), with all the edges different and all the vertices different, except that $v_0 = v_k$. Then a **Hamiltonian cycle** is a cycle that contains every vertex, and a graph is called **Hamiltonian** if it has a Hamiltonian cycle. The term arises from *Hamilton*'s interest in the existence of such cycles in the graph of the dodecahedron — the graph with vertices and edges corresponding to the vertices and edges of a dodecahedron.

handshaking lemma   In any *graph*, the sum of the degrees of all the vertices is even, a simple result called the **handshaking lemma**. (The name arises from its application to the total number of hands shaken when some members of a group of people shake hands.) It follows from the simple observation that the sum of the degrees of all the vertices of a graph is equal to twice the number of edges. A result that follows from it is that, in any graph, the number of vertices of odd degree is even.

harmonic mean   See *mean*.

harmonic series   The **harmonic series** is the series $1 + \frac{1}{2} + \frac{1}{3} + \frac{1}{4} + \cdots$, where the n-th term a_n equals $1/n$. For this series, $a_n \to 0$. However, the series does not have a sum to infinity for, if s_n is the sum of the first n terms, then $s_n \to \infty$. For large values of n, $s_n \approx \ln n + \gamma$, where γ is *Euler's constant*.

h.c.f.   = *highest common factor*.

helix   A **helix** is a curve on the surface of a (right-circular) cylinder that cuts the generators of the cylinder at a constant angle. Thus it is 'like a spiral staircase'.

heptagon   A **heptagon** is a seven-sided polygon.

Hero's formula   See *triangle*.

hexadecimal   Numbers are written in **hexadecimal** notation when they are written to *base* 16. In this system, 16 digits are required and it is normal to take 0, 1, 2, 3, 4, 5, 6, 7, 8, 9, A, B, C, D, E, F, where A to F represent the numbers that, in decimal notation, are denoted by 10, 11, 12, 13, 14 and 15. Then the hexadecimal representation of the decimal number 712, for example, is found by writing

$$712 = 2 \times 16^2 + 12 \times 16 + 8 = (2C8)_{16}.$$

It is particularly simple to change the representation of a number to base 2 (binary) to its representation to base 16 (hexadecimal) and vice versa: each block of 4 digits in base 2 (form blocks of 4, starting from the right-hand end) can be made to correspond to its hexadecimal equivalent. Thus

$$(101101001001101)_2 = (101|1010|0100|1101)_2 = (5A4D)_{16}.$$

Real numbers, not just integers, can also be written in hexadecimal notation, by using hexadecimal digits after a 'decimal' point, just as familiar *decimal* representations of real numbers are obtained to base 10. Hexadecimal notation is important in computing. It translates easily into binary notation but is more concise and easier to read.

hexagon   A **hexagon** is a six-sided polygon.

higher derivative   If the function f is *differentiable* on an interval, its *derived function* f' is defined. If f' is also differentiable, then the derived function of this, denoted by f'', is the **second derived function** of f; its value at x, denoted by $f''(x)$, or d^2f/dx^2, is the **second derivative** of f at x. (The term 'second derivative' may be used loosely also for the second derived function f''.)

Similarly, if f'' is differentiable, $f'''(x)$ or d^3f/dx^3, the third derivative of f at x, can be formed, and so on. The **n-th derivative** of f at x is denoted by $f^{(n)}(x)$ or $d^n f/dx^n$. The n-th derivatives, for $n \geq 2$, are the **higher derivatives** of f. When $y = f(x)$, the higher derivatives may be denoted by $d^2y/dx^2, \ldots, d^n y/dx^n$ or $y'', y''', \ldots, y^{(n)}$. If, with a different notation, x is a function of t and the derivative dx/dt is denoted by $\dot{x}$, the second derivative d^2x/dt^2 is denoted by $\ddot{x}$.

higher-order partial derivative   Given a function f of n variables x_1, $x_2, \ldots, x_n$, the *partial derivative* $\partial f/\partial x_i$, where $1 \leq i \leq n$, may also be reckoned to be a function of $x_1, x_2, \ldots, x_n$. So the partial derivatives of $\partial f/\partial x_i$ can be considered. Thus

$$\frac{\partial}{\partial x_i}\left(\frac{\partial f}{\partial x_i}\right) \quad \text{and} \quad \frac{\partial}{\partial x_j}\left(\frac{\partial f}{\partial x_i}\right) \quad (\text{for } j \neq i)$$

can be formed and these are denoted, respectively, by

$$\frac{\partial^2 f}{\partial x_i^2} \quad \text{and} \quad \frac{\partial^2 f}{\partial x_j \partial x_i}.$$

These are the **second-order partial derivatives**. When $j \neq i$,

$$\frac{\partial^2 f}{\partial x_i \partial x_j} \quad \text{and} \quad \frac{\partial^2 f}{\partial x_j \partial x_i}$$

are different by definition, but the two are equal for most 'straightforward' functions f that are likely to be met. (It is not possible to describe here just what conditions are needed for equality.) Similarly, third-order partial derivatives such as

$$\frac{\partial^3 f}{\partial x_1^3}, \quad \frac{\partial^3 f}{\partial x_1 \partial x_2^2}, \quad \frac{\partial^3 f}{\partial x_1 \partial x_2 \partial x_3}, \quad \frac{\partial^3 f}{\partial x_3 \partial x_3 \partial x_1},$$

can be defined as can fourth-order partial derivatives, and so on. Then the n-th-order partial derivatives, where $n \geq 2$, are the **higher-order partial derivatives**.

When f is a function of two variables x and y and the partial derivatives are denoted by f_x and f_y, then $f_{xx}, f_{xy}, f_{yx}, f_{yy}$ are used to denote

$$\frac{\partial^2 f}{\partial x^2}, \quad \frac{\partial^2 f}{\partial y \partial x}, \quad \frac{\partial^2 f}{\partial x \partial y}, \quad \frac{\partial^2 f}{\partial y^2}$$

respectively, noting particularly that f_{xy} means $(f_x)_y$ and f_{yx} means $(f_y)_x$. This notation can be extended to third-order (and higher) partial derivatives and to functions of more variables. With the value of f at (x, y) denoted by $f(x, y)$ and the partial derivatives denoted by f_1 and f_2, the second-order partial derivatives can be denoted by f_{11}, f_{12}, f_{21} and f_{22}, and this notation can also be extended to third-order (and higher) partial derivatives and to functions of more variables.

highest common factor   = *greatest common divisor.*

Hilbert, David (1862–1943)   Born in Germany and eventually almost identified with the University of Göttingen, Hilbert was one of the founding fathers of twentieth-century mathematics and in many ways the originator of the Formalist school of mathematics that has been so dominant in the pure mathematics of this century. One of his fundamental contributions to formalism was his *Foundations of Geometry*, which served to put geometry on a proper axiomatic basis, unlike the rather more intuitive 'axiomatization' of Euclid. He also made a major contribution to mathematical analysis. At the International Congress of Mathematics in 1900, Hilbert opened the new century by posing his famous list of 23 problems — problems that have kept mathematicians busy ever since and have generated a significant amount of the important work of the last eighty years. Hilbert is, for these reasons, often thought of as a thorough-going pure mathematician, but he was also the chairman of the famous atomic physics seminar at Göttingen that had a great influence on the development of quantum theory.

homogeneous first-order differential equation   The first-order differential equation $dy/dx = f(x, y)$ is **homogeneous** if the function f, of two variables, has the property that $f(kx, ky) = f(x, y)$ for all k. Examples of such functions are

$$\frac{x^2 + 3y^2}{2x^2 - 5xy}, \qquad 1 + e^{x/y}, \qquad \frac{x}{\sqrt{x^2 + y^2}}.$$

Any such function f can be written as a function of one variable v, where $v = y/x$. The method of solving homogeneous first-order differential equations is therefore to let $y = vx$ so that $dy/dx = x\,dv/dx + v$. The differential equation for v as a function of x that is obtained is always *separable*.

homogeneous linear differential equation   See *linear differential equation with constant coefficients.*

homogeneous set of linear equations   A **homogeneous set** of m **linear equations** in n unknowns $x_1, x_2, \ldots, x_n$ has the form

$$a_{11}x_1 + a_{12}x_2 + \cdots + a_{1n}x_n = 0,$$
$$a_{21}x_1 + a_{22}x_2 + \cdots + a_{2n}x_n = 0,$$
$$\cdots$$
$$a_{m1}x_1 + a_{m2}x_2 + \cdots + a_{mn}x_n = 0.$$

Here, unlike the non-homogeneous case, the numbers on the right-hand sides of the equations are all zero. In matrix notation, this set of equations can be written $\mathbf{Ax} = \mathbf{0}$, where the unknowns form a column matrix $\mathbf{x}$. Thus $\mathbf{A}$ is the $m \times n$ matrix $[a_{ij}]$ and

$$\mathbf{x} = \begin{bmatrix} x_1 \\ \vdots \\ x_n \end{bmatrix}.$$

If $\mathbf{x}$ is a solution of a homogeneous set of linear equations, then so is any scalar multiple $k\mathbf{x}$ of it. There is always the trivial solution $\mathbf{x} = \mathbf{0}$. What is generally of concern is whether it has other solutions besides this one. For a homogeneous set consisting of the same number of equations as unknowns, the matrix of coefficients $\mathbf{A}$ is a square matrix and the set of equations has non-trivial solutions if and only if $\det \mathbf{A} = 0$.

hyperbola   A **hyperbola** is a *conic* with eccentricity greater than 1. Thus it is the locus of all points P such that the distance from P to a fixed point F_1 (the **focus**) is equal to e (> 1) times the distance from P to a fixed line l_1 (the **directrix**). It turns out that there is another point F_2 and another line l_2 such that the same set of points would be obtained with these as focus and directrix. The hyperbola is also the conic section that results when a plane cuts a (double) cone in such a way that a section in two separate parts is obtained (see *conic*).

The line through F_1 and F_2 is the **transverse axis** and the points V_1 and V_2 where it cuts the hyperbola are the **vertices**. The length $|V_1 V_2|$ is the **length of the transverse axis** and is usually taken to be $2a$. The midpoint of $V_1 V_2$ is the **centre** of the hyperbola. The line through the centre perpendicular to the transverse axis is the **conjugate axis**. It is usual to introduce b (> 0) defined by $b^2 = a^2(e^2 - 1)$, so that $e^2 = 1 + b^2/a^2$. It may be convenient to consider the points $(0, -b)$ and $(0, b)$ on the conjugate axis, despite the fact that the hyperbola does not cut the conjugate axis at all. The two separate parts of the hyperbola are the two *branches*.

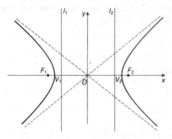

By taking a coordinate system with origin at the centre of the hyperbola, and x-axis along the transverse axis, the foci have coordinates $(ae, 0)$ and $(-ae, 0)$, the directrices have equations $x = a/e$ and $x = -a/e$, and the hyperbola has equation

$$\frac{x^2}{a^2} - \frac{y^2}{b^2} = 1.$$

Unlike the comparable equation for an ellipse, it is not necessarily the case here that $a > b$. When investigating the properties of a hyperbola, it is normal to choose this convenient coordinate system. It may be useful to take $x = a \sec \theta$, $y = b \tan \theta$ ($0 \leq \theta < 2\pi$, $\theta \neq \pi/2, 3\pi/2$) as *parametric equations*. The alternative parametric equations $x = a \cosh t$, $y = b \sinh t$ ($t \in \mathbf{R}$) (see *hyperbolic function*) may also be used, but give only one branch of the hyperbola.

(A hyperbola with its centre at the origin and its transverse axis, of length $2a$, along the y-axis instead has equation $y^2/a^2 - x^2/b^2 = 1$ and has foci at $(0, ae)$ and $(0, -ae)$.)

The hyperbola

$$\frac{x^2}{a^2} - \frac{y^2}{b^2} = 1$$

has two *asymptotes*, $y = (b/a)x$ and $y = (-b/a)x$. The shape of the hyperbola is determined by the eccentricity or, what is equivalent, by the ratio of b to a. The particular value $e = \sqrt{2}$ is important for this gives $b = a$. Then the asymptotes are perpendicular and the curve, which is of special interest, is a *rectangular hyperbola*.

hyperbolic cylinder   A **hyperbolic cylinder** is a *cylinder* in which the fixed curve is a *hyperbola* and the fixed line to which the generators are parallel is perpendicular to the plane of the hyperbola. It is a *quadric* and in a suitable coordinate system has equation

$$\frac{x^2}{a^2} - \frac{y^2}{b^2} = 1.$$

hyperbolic function   The **hyperbolic functions** are cosh, sinh, tanh, sech, cosech and coth, defined as follows:

$$\cosh x = \tfrac{1}{2}(e^x + e^{-x}), \qquad \sinh x = \tfrac{1}{2}(e^x - e^{-x}),$$

$$\tanh x = \frac{\sinh x}{\cosh x}, \qquad \coth x = \frac{\cosh x}{\sinh x} \quad (x \neq 0),$$

$$\operatorname{sech} x = \frac{1}{\cosh x}, \qquad \operatorname{cosech} x = \frac{1}{\sinh x} \quad (x \neq 0).$$

The functions derive their name from the possibility of using $x = a \cosh t$, $y = b \sinh t$ ($t \in \mathbf{R}$) as *parametric equations* for (one branch of) a *hyperbola*. (The pronunciation of these functions causes difficulty. For instance, tanh may be pronounced as 'tansh' or 'than' (with the 'th' as in 'thing'); and sinh may be pronounced as 'shine' or 'sinch'. Some prefer to say 'hyperbolic tan' and 'hyperbolic sine'.) Many of the formulae satisfied by the hyperbolic functions are similar to corresponding formulae for the trigonometric functions, but

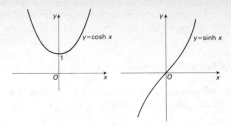

some changes of sign must be noted. For example:

$$\cosh^2 x = 1 + \sinh^2 x,$$
$$\text{sech}^2 x = 1 - \tanh^2 x,$$
$$\sinh(x + y) = \sinh x \cosh y + \cosh x \sinh y,$$
$$\cosh(x + y) = \cosh x \cosh y + \sinh x \sinh y,$$
$$\sinh 2x = 2 \sinh x \cosh x,$$
$$\cosh 2x = \cosh^2 x + \sinh^2 x.$$

Since $\cosh(-x) = \cosh x$ and $\sinh(-x) = -\sinh x$, cosh is an *even function* and sinh is an *odd function*. The graphs of $\cosh x$ and $\sinh x$ are shown above. It is instructive to sketch both of them, together with the graphs of e^x and e^{-x}, on the same diagram.

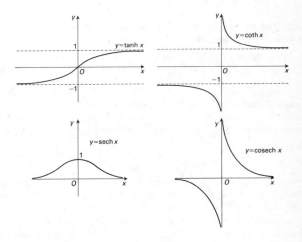

The following derivatives are easily established:

$$\frac{d}{dx}(\cosh x) = \sinh x, \qquad \frac{d}{dx}(\sinh x) = \cosh x, \qquad \frac{d}{dx}(\tanh x) = \operatorname{sech}^2 x.$$

See also *inverse hyperbolic function*.

hyperbolic paraboloid   A **hyperbolic paraboloid** is a *quadric* whose equation in a suitable coordinate system is

$$\frac{x^2}{a^2} - \frac{y^2}{b^2} = \frac{2z}{c}.$$

The yz-plane and the zx-plane are planes of symmetry. Sections by planes parallel to the xy-plane are hyperbolas, the section by the xy-plane itself being a pair of straight lines. Sections by planes parallel to the other axial planes are parabolas. Planes through the z-axis cut the paraboloid in parabolas with vertex at the origin. The origin is a *saddle-point*.

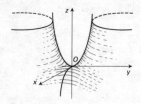

hyperboloid of one sheet   A **hyperboloid of one sheet** is a *quadric* whose equation in a suitable coordinate system is

$$\frac{x^2}{a^2} + \frac{y^2}{b^2} - \frac{z^2}{c^2} = 1.$$

The axial planes are planes of symmetry. The section by a plane $z = k$, parallel to the xy-plane, is an ellipse (circle if $a = b$). The hyperboloid is all in one piece or **sheet**. Sections by planes parallel to the other two axial planes are hyperbolas.

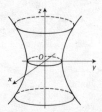

hyperboloid of two sheets   A **hyperboloid of two sheets** is a *quadric* whose equation in a suitable coordinate system is

$$\frac{x^2}{a^2} + \frac{y^2}{b^2} - \frac{z^2}{c^2} = -1.$$

The axial planes are planes of symmetry. The section by a plane $z = k$, parallel to the xy-plane, is, when non-empty, an ellipse (circle if $a = b$). When k lies between $-c$ and c, the plane $z = k$ has no points of intersection with the hyperboloid and the hyperboloid is thus in two pieces or **sheets**. Sections by planes parallel to the other two axial planes are hyperbolas. Planes through the z-axis cut the hyperboloid in hyperbolas with vertices at $(0, 0, c)$ and $(0, 0, -c)$.

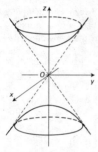

hypotenuse   The **hypotenuse** of a right-angled triangle is the side opposite the right angle.

I

i   See *complex number*.

icosahedron (plural: icosahedra)   See *polyhedron*.

identity element   See *neutral element*.

identity mapping   The **identity mapping** on a set S is the *mapping* $i_S: S \rightarrow S$ defined by $i_S(s) = s$ for all s in S. Identity mappings have the property that if $f: S \rightarrow T$ is a mapping then $f \circ i_S = f$ and $i_T \circ f = f$.

identity matrix   The $n \times n$ **identity matrix I**, or $\mathbf{I}_n$, is the $n \times n$ matrix,

$$\begin{bmatrix} 1 & 0 & 0 & \ldots & 0 \\ 0 & 1 & 0 & \ldots & 0 \\ 0 & 0 & 1 & \ldots & 0 \\ \vdots & \vdots & \vdots & \ddots & \vdots \\ 0 & 0 & 0 & \ldots & 1 \end{bmatrix},$$

with each diagonal entry equal to 1 and all other entries equal to 0. It is the identity element for the set of $n \times n$ matrices with multiplication.

if and only if   See *condition, necessary and sufficient*.

image   See *function* and *mapping*.

imaginary axis   In the *complex plane*, the y-axis is called the **imaginary axis**. Its points represent *pure imaginary* numbers.

imaginary part   A *complex number* z can be written $x + yi$, where x and y are real, and then y is the **imaginary part**. It is denoted by $\operatorname{Im} z$ or $\Im z$.

implication   If p and q are statements, the statement 'p implies q' or 'if p then q' is an **implication** and is denoted by $p \Rightarrow q$. It is reckoned to be false only in the case when p is true and q is false. So its *truth table* is as follows:

p	q	$p \Rightarrow q$
T	T	T
T	F	F
F	T	T
F	F	T

The statement that 'p implies q and q implies p' may be denoted by $p \Leftrightarrow q$, to be read as 'p if and only if q'.

implicit differentiation   When x and y satisfy a single equation, it may be possible to regard this as defining y as a function of x with a suitable domain, even though there is no explicit formula for y. In such a case, it may be possible to obtain the *derivative* of y by a method, called **implicit differentiation**, that consists of differentiating the equation as it stands and making use of the *chain rule*. For example, if $xy^2 + x^2y^3 - 1 = 0$, then

$$x2y\frac{dy}{dx} + y^2 + x^2 3y^2\frac{dy}{dx} + 2xy^3 = 0$$

and so, if $2xy + 3x^2y^2 \neq 0$,

$$\frac{dy}{dx} = -\frac{y^2 + 2xy^3}{2xy + 3x^2y^2}.$$

improper integrals   There are two kinds of **improper integral**. The first kind is one in which the interval of integration is infinite as, for example, in

$$\int_a^\infty f(x)\,dx.$$

It is said that this integral exists, and that its value is l, if the value of the integral from a to X tends to a limit l as $X \to \infty$. For example,

$$\int_1^X \frac{1}{x^2}\,dx = 1 - \frac{1}{X}$$

and, as $X \to \infty$, the right-hand side tends to 1. So

$$\int_1^\infty \frac{1}{x^2}\,dx = 1.$$

A similar definition can be given for the improper integral from $-\infty$ to a. If both the integrals

$$\int_{-\infty}^a f(x)\,dx, \qquad \int_a^\infty f(x)\,dx,$$

exist and have values l_1 and l_2, then it is said that the integral from $-\infty$ to ∞ exists and that its value is $l_1 + l_2$.

The second kind of improper integral is one in which the function becomes infinite at some point. Suppose first that the function becomes infinite at one of the limits of integration as, for example, in

$$\int_0^1 \frac{1}{\sqrt{x}}\,dx.$$

The function $1/\sqrt{x}$ is not bounded on the closed interval $[0, 1]$, so, in the normal way, this integral is not defined. However, the function is bounded on the interval $[\delta, 1]$, where $0 < \delta < 1$, and

$$\int_\delta^1 \frac{1}{\sqrt{x}} \, dx = 2 - 2\sqrt{\delta}.$$

As $\delta \to 0$, the right-hand side tends to the limit 2. So the integral above, from 0 to 1, is taken, by definition, to be equal to 2; in the same way, any such integral can be given a value equal to the appropriate limit, if it exists. A similar definition can be made for an integral in which the function becomes infinite at the upper limit.

Finally, an integral in which the function becomes infinite at a point between the limits is dealt with as follows. It is written as the sum of two integrals, where the function becomes infinite at the upper limit of the first and at the lower limit of the second. If both these integrals exist, the original integral is said to exist and, in this way, its value can be obtained.

incentre   The **incentre** of a triangle is the centre of the *incircle* of the triangle. It is the point at which the three internal bisectors of the angles of the triangle are concurrent.

incircle   The **incircle** of a triangle is the circle that lies inside the triangle and touches the three sides.

include   See *subset*.

inconsistent   A set of equations is **inconsistent** if its solution set is empty.

increasing function   A *real function* f is **increasing** in or on an interval I if $f(x_1) \le f(x_2)$ whenever x_1 and x_2 are in I with $x_1 < x_2$. Also, f is **strictly increasing** if $f(x_1) < f(x_2)$ whenever $x_1 < x_2$.

increasing sequence   A sequence $a_1, a_2, a_3, \ldots$ is **increasing** if $a_i \le a_{i+1}$ for all i, and **strictly increasing** if $a_i < a_{i+1}$ for all i.

indefinite integral   See *integral*.

index (plural: indices)   Suppose that a is a real number. When the product $a \times a \times a \times a \times a$ is written as a^5, the number 5 is called the **index**. When the index is a positive integer p, then a^p means $a \times a \times \cdots \times a$, where there are p occurrences of a. It can then be shown that

  (i) $a^p \times a^q = a^{p+q}$,
  (ii) $a^p/a^q = a^{p-q}$ $(a \ne 0)$,
  (iii) $(a^p)^q = a^{pq}$,
  (iv) $(ab)^p = a^p b^p$,

where, in (ii), for the moment, it is required that $p > q$. The meaning of a^p can however be extended so that p is not restricted to being a positive integer. This is achieved by giving a meaning for a^0, for a^{-p} and for $a^{m/n}$, where m

is an integer and n is a positive integer. To ensure that (i) to (iv) hold when p and q are any rational numbers, it is necessary to take the following as definitions:

(v) $a^0 = 1$,
(vi) $a^{-p} = 1/a^p \quad (a \neq 0)$,
(vii) $a^{m/n} = \sqrt[n]{a^m} \quad$ (m an integer, n a positive integer).

Together, (i) to (vii) form the basic rules for indices.

The same notation is used in other contexts; for example, to define z^p, where z is a complex number, to define $\mathbf{A}^p$, where $\mathbf{A}$ is a square matrix, or to define g^p, where g is an element of a multiplicative group. In such cases, some of the above rules may hold and others may not.

indirect proof   A theorem of the form $p \Rightarrow q$ can be proved by establishing instead its *contrapositive*, by supposing $\neg q$ and showing that $\neg p$ follows. Such a method is called an **indirect proof**. Another example of an indirect proof is the method of *proof by contradiction*.

induction   See *mathematical induction*.

infimum (plural: infima)   See *bound*.

infinite product   From an infinite sequence a_1, a_2, a_3, ..., an **infinite product** $a_1 a_2 a_3 \ldots$ can be formed and denoted by

$$\prod_{r=1}^{\infty} a_r.$$

Let P_n be the n-th *partial product*, so that

$$P_n = \prod_{r=1}^{n} a_r.$$

If P_n tends to a limit P as $n \to \infty$, then P is the **value** of the infinite product. For example,

$$\prod_{r=2}^{\infty} \left(1 - \frac{1}{r^2}\right)$$

has the value $\frac{1}{2}$, since it can be shown that $P_n = (n+1)/2n$ and $P_n \to \frac{1}{2}$.

infinite sequence   See *sequence*.

infinite series   See *series*.

inflection   = *inflexion*.

inflexion   See *point of inflexion*.

injection   = *one-to-one mapping*.

injective mapping   A *mapping* is **injective** if it is *one-to-one*.

integer   An **integer** is one of the 'whole' numbers: $\ldots$, -3, -2, -1, 0, 1, 2, 3, $\ldots$. The set of all integers is often denoted by $\mathbf{Z}$. With the normal addition and multiplication, $\mathbf{Z}$ forms an *integral domain*.

integer part   For any real number x, there is a unique integer n such that $n \le x < n + 1$. This integer n is the **integer part** of x and is denoted by $[x]$. For example, $\left[\frac{9}{4}\right] = 2$ and $[\pi] = 3$, but notice that $\left[-\frac{9}{4}\right] = -3$. In a computer language, the function INT(X) may well convert the real number X into an integer by truncating. If so, INT(9/4)=2 and INT(PI)=3, but INT(-9/4)=-2. So INT(X) agrees with $[x]$ for $x \ge 0$ but not for $x < 0$.

integral   Let f be a function defined on the closed interval $[a, b]$. Take points x_0, x_1, x_2, $\ldots$, x_n such that $a = x_0 < x_1 < x_2 < \cdots < x_{n-1} < x_n = b$, and in each subinterval $[x_i, x_{i+1}]$ take a point c_i. Form the sum

$$\sum_{i=0}^{n-1} f(c_i)(x_{i+1} - x_i),$$

that is, $f(c_0)(x_1 - x_0) + f(c_1)(x_2 - x_1) + \cdots + f(c_{n-1})(x_n - x_{n-1})$. Such a sum is called a **Riemann sum** for f over $[a, b]$. Geometrically, it gives the sum of the areas of n rectangles and is an approximation to the area under the curve $y = f(x)$ between $x = a$ and $x = b$.

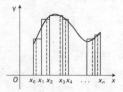

The (**Riemann**) **integral** of f over $[a, b]$ is defined to be the limit I (in a sense that needs more clarification than can be given here) of such a Riemann sum as n, the number of points, increases and the size of the subintervals gets smaller. The value of I is denoted by

$$\int_a^b f(x)\, dx, \quad \text{or} \quad \int_a^b f(t)\, dt,$$

where it is immaterial what letter, such as x or t, is used in the integral. The intention is that the value of the integral is equal to what is intuitively understood to be the area under the curve $y = f(x)$. Such a limit does not always exist, but it can be proved that it does if, for example, f is *continuous* on $[a, b]$.

If f is continuous on $[a, b]$ and F is defined by

$$F(x) = \int_a^x f(t)\, dt,$$

then $F'(x) = f(x)$ for all x in $[a, b]$, so that F is an *antiderivative* of f. Moreover, if an antiderivative ϕ of f is known, the integral

$$\int_a^b f(t)\, dt$$

can be easily evaluated: the *Fundamental Theorem of Calculus* gives its value as $\phi(b) - \phi(a)$. Of the two integrals

$$\int_a^b f(x)\, dx, \quad \int f(x)\, dx,$$

the first, with limits, is called a **definite integral** and the second, which denotes an antiderivative of f, is an **indefinite integral**.

integral calculus   The subject of **integral calculus** arose from the problem of trying to find the area of a region with a curved boundary. In general, this is calculated by a limiting process that obtains gradually better approximations to the value. The *integral* is defined by a limiting process based on an intuitive idea of the area under a curve and the fundamental discovery was the link that exists between this and the *differential calculus*.

integral domain   An **integral domain** is a commutative ring R with identity (see *ring*) with the additional property that

9. For all a and b in R, $ab = 0$ only if $a = 0$ or $b = 0$.

(The axiom numbering follows on from that used for ring.) Thus an integral domain is a commutative ring with identity with no *divisors of zero*. The natural example is the set $\mathbf{Z}$ of all integers with the usual addition and multiplication. Any *field* is an integral domain. Further examples of integral domains (these are not fields) are: the set $\mathbf{Z}[\sqrt{2}]$ of all real numbers of the form $a + b\sqrt{2}$, where a and b are integers, and the set $\mathbf{R}[x]$ of all polynomials in an indeterminate x, with real coefficients, each with the normal addition and multiplication.

integral part   = *integer part*.

integrand   In either of the integrals

$$\int_a^b f(x)\, dx, \quad \int f(x)\, dx,$$

the expression $f(x)$ is the **integrand**.

integrating factor   See *linear first-order differential equations*.

integration   The process of finding an *antiderivative* of a given function f is called **integration**: 'Integrate f' means 'Find an antiderivative of f'. Such an antiderivative may be called an indefinite integral of f and be denoted by

$$\int f(x)\, dx.$$

The term 'integration' is also used for any method of evaluating a definite integral. The definite integral

$$\int_a^b f(x)\,dx$$

can be evaluated if an antiderivative ϕ of f can be found, because then its value is $\phi(b)-\phi(a)$. (This is provided that a and b both belong to an interval in which f is continuous.) However, for many functions f, there is no antiderivative expressible in terms of elementary functions, and other methods for evaluating the definite integral have to be sought, one such being so-called *numerical integration*.

What ways are there then of finding an antiderivative? If the given function can be recognized as the derivative of a familiar function, an antiderivative is immediately known. Some standard integrals are also given in the Table of Integrals (Appendix 3); more extensive tables of integrals are available. Certain **techniques of integration** may also be tried, among which are the following:

CHANGE OF VARIABLE. If it is possible to find a suitable function g such that the *integrand* can be written as $f(g(x))g'(x)$, it may be possible to find an indefinite integral using the **change of variable** $u = g(x)$; this is because

$$\int f(g(x))g'(x)\,dx = \int f(u)\,du,$$

a rule derived from the *chain rule* for differentiation. For example, in the integral

$$\int 2x(x^2 + 1)^8\,dx,$$

let $u = g(x) = x^2 + 1$. Then $g'(x) = 2x$ (this can be written: '$du = 2x\,dx$'), and, using the rule above with $f(u) = u^8$, the integral equals

$$\int (x^2 + 1)^8\,2x\,dx = \int u^8\,du = \tfrac{1}{9}u^9 = \tfrac{1}{9}(x^2 + 1)^9.$$

SUBSTITUTION. The rule above, derived from the chain rule for differentiation, can be written as

$$\int f(x)\,dx = \int f(g(u))g'(u)\,du.$$

It is used in this form to make a **substitution** $x = g(u)$. For example, in the integral

$$\int \frac{1}{(1 + x^2)^{3/2}}dx,$$

let $x = g(u) = \tan u$. Then $g'(u) = \sec^2 u$ (this can be written: '$dx = \sec^2 u\,du$'), and the integral equals

$$\int \frac{\sec^2 u}{(1 + \tan^2 u)^{3/2}}du = \int \frac{1}{\sec u}du = \int \cos u\,du = \sin u = \frac{x}{\sqrt{1 + x^2}}.$$

INTEGRATION BY PARTS. The rule for **integration by parts**,

$$\int f(x)g'(x)\,dx = f(x)g(x) - \int g(x)f'(x)\,dx,$$

is derived from the rule for differentiating a product $f(x)g(x)$, and is useful when the integral on the right-hand side is easier to find than the integral on the left. For example, in the integral

$$\int x\cos x\,dx,$$

let $f(x) = x$ and $g'(x) = \cos x$. Then $g(x)$ can be taken as $\sin x$ and $f'(x) = 1$, so the method gives

$$\int x\cos x\,dx = x\sin x - \int \sin x\,1\,dx = x\sin x + \cos x.$$

See also *reduction formula* and *partial fractions*.

integration by parts   See *integration*.

intercept   See *straight line* (in the plane).

interior point   When the *real line* is being considered, the real number x is an **interior point** of the set S of real numbers if there is an open interval $(x - \delta, x + \delta)$, where $\delta > 0$, included in S.

Intermediate Value Theorem   An important property of *continuous functions* is stated in the **Intermediate Value Theorem**:

THEOREM: If the real function f is continuous on the closed interval $[a, b]$ and η is a real number between $f(a)$ and $f(b)$, then, for some c in (a, b), $f(c) = \eta$.

The theorem is useful for locating roots of equations. For example, suppose that $f(x) = x - \cos x$. Then f is continuous on $[0, 1]$ and $f(0) < 0$ and $f(1) > 0$, and so it follows from the Intermediate Value Theorem that the equation $f(x) = 0$ has a root in the interval $(0, 1)$.

interpolation   Suppose that the values $f(x_0)$, $f(x_1)$, ..., $f(x_n)$ of a certain function f are known for the particular values x_0, x_1, ..., x_n. A method of finding an approximation for $f(x)$, for a given value of x, somewhere between these particular values, is called **interpolation**. If $x_0 < x < x_1$, the method known as **linear interpolation** gives

$$f(x) \approx f(x_0) + \frac{x - x_0}{x_1 - x_0}\left(f(x_1) - f(x_0)\right).$$

This is obtained by supposing, as an approximation, that between x_0 and x_1 the graph of the function is a straight line joining the points $(x_0, f(x_0))$

and $(x_1, f(x_1))$. More complicated methods of interpolation use the values of the function at more than two values.

intersection   The **intersection** of sets A and B (subsets of a *universal set*) is the set consisting of all objects that belong to A and belong to B, and it is denoted by $A \cap B$ (read as 'A **intersection** B'). Thus the term 'intersection' is used for both the resulting set and the operation, a *binary operation* on the set of all subsets of a universal set. The following properties hold:

(i) For all A, $A \cap A = A$, $A \cap \varnothing = \varnothing$.
(ii) For all A and B, $A \cap B = B \cap A$; that is, $\cap$ is commutative.
(iii) For all A, B and C, $(A \cap B) \cap C = A \cap (B \cap C)$; that is, $\cap$ is associative.

In view of (iii), the intersection $A_1 \cap A_2 \cap \cdots \cap A_n$ of more than two sets can be written without brackets, and it may also be denoted by

$$\bigcap_{i=1}^{n} A_i.$$

interval   A **finite interval** on the real line is a subset of $\mathbf{R}$ defined in terms of end-points a and b. Since each end-point may or may not belong to the subset, there are four types of finite interval:

(i) the closed interval $\{\, x \mid x \in \mathbf{R} \text{ and } a \le x \le b \,\}$, denoted by $[a, b]$,
(ii) the open interval $\{\, x \mid x \in \mathbf{R} \text{ and } a < x < b \,\}$, denoted by (a, b),
(iii) the interval $\{\, x \mid x \in \mathbf{R} \text{ and } a \le x < b \,\}$, denoted by $[a, b)$,
(iv) the interval $\{\, x \mid x \in \mathbf{R} \text{ and } a < x \le b \,\}$, denoted by $(a, b]$.

There are also four types of **infinite interval**:

(v) $\{\, x \mid x \in \mathbf{R} \text{ and } a \le x \,\}$, denoted by $[a, \infty)$,
(vi) $\{\, x \mid x \in \mathbf{R} \text{ and } a < x \,\}$, denoted by (a, ∞),
(vii) $\{\, x \mid x \in \mathbf{R} \text{ and } x \le a \,\}$, denoted by $(-\infty, a]$,
(viii) $\{\, x \mid x \in \mathbf{R} \text{ and } x < a \,\}$, denoted by $(-\infty, a)$.

Here ∞ (read as 'infinity') and $-\infty$ (read as 'minus infinity') are not, of course, real numbers but the use of these symbols provides a convenient notation.

If I is any of the intervals (i) to (iv), the **open interval determined by** I is (a, b); if I is (v) or (vi), it is (a, ∞) and, if I is (vii) or (viii), it is $(-\infty, a)$.

inverse element   Suppose that, for the *binary operation* $\circ$ on the set S, there is a *neutral element* e. An element a' is an **inverse** (or **inverse element**) of the element a if $a \circ a' = a' \circ a = e$. If the operation is called multiplication, the neutral element is normally called the *identity* element and may be denoted by 1. Then the inverse a' may be called a **multiplicative inverse** of a and be denoted by a^{-1}, so that $aa^{-1} = a^{-1}a = 1$ (or e). If the operation is addition, the neutral element is denoted by 0, and the inverse a' may be called an **additive inverse** (or a **negative**) of a and be denoted by $-a$, so that $a + (-a) = (-a) + a = 0$. See also *group*.

inverse function   For a *real function* f, its inverse function f^{-1} is to be a function such that if $y = f(x)$ then $x = f^{-1}(y)$. The conditions under which such a function exists need careful consideration. Suppose that f has domain S and range T, so that $f: S \to T$ is onto. The **inverse function** f^{-1}, with domain T and range S, can be defined, provided that f is *one-to-one*, as follows. For y in T, $f^{-1}(y)$ is the unique element x of S such that $f(x) = y$.

If the domain S is an interval I and f is *strictly increasing* on I or *strictly decreasing* on I, then f is certainly one-to-one. When f is *differentiable*, a sufficient condition can be given in terms of the sign of $f'(x)$. Thus, if f is continuous on an interval I and differentiable in the open interval (a, b) determined by I (see *interval*), and $f'(x) > 0$ in (a, b) (or $f'(x) < 0$ in (a, b)), then, for f (with domain I), an inverse function exists.

When an inverse function is required for a given function f, it may be necessary to restrict the domain and obtain instead the inverse function of this *restriction* of f. For example, suppose that $f: \mathbf{R} \to \mathbf{R}$ is defined by $f(x) = x^2 - 4x + 5$. This function is not one-to-one. However, since $f'(x) = 2x - 4$, it can be seen that $f'(x) > 0$ for $x > 2$. Use f now to denote the function defined by $f(x) = x^2 - 4x + 5$ with domain $[2, \infty)$. The range is $[1, \infty)$ and the function $f: [2, \infty) \to [1, \infty)$ has an inverse function $f^{-1}: [1, \infty) \to [2, \infty)$. A formula for f^{-1} can be found by setting $y = x^2 - 4x + 5$ and, remembering that $x \in [2, \infty)$, obtaining $x = 2 + \sqrt{y - 1}$. So, with a change of notation, $f^{-1}(x) = 2 + \sqrt{x - 1}$ for $x \geq 1$.

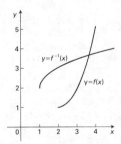

When the inverse function exists, the graphs $y = f(x)$ and $y = f^{-1}(x)$ are reflections of each other in the line $y = x$. The derivative of the inverse function can be found as follows. Suppose that f is differentiable and has inverse denoted now by g, so that if $y = f(x)$ then $x = g(y)$. Then, if $f'(x) \neq 0$, g is differentiable at y and

$$g'(y) = \frac{1}{f'(x)} = \frac{1}{f'(g(y))}.$$

When $f'(x)$ is denoted by dy/dx, then $g'(y)$ may be denoted by dx/dy and the preceding result says that, if $dy/dx \neq 0$,

$$\frac{dx}{dy} = \frac{1}{dy/dx}.$$

This can only safely be used if it known that the function in question has an inverse. For examples, see *inverse hyperbolic function* and *inverse trigonometric function*.

inverse hyperbolic function   Each of the *hyperbolic functions* sinh and tanh is strictly increasing throughout the whole of its domain **R**, so in each case an inverse function exists. In the case of cosh, the function has to be restricted to a suitable domain (see *inverse function*), taken to be $[0, \infty)$. The domain of the inverse function is, in each case, the range of the original function (after the restriction of the domain, in the case of cosh). The following inverse functions are obtained: $\cosh^{-1}: [1, \infty) \to [0, \infty)$; $\sinh^{-1}: \mathbf{R} \to \mathbf{R}$; $\tanh^{-1}: (-1, 1) \to \mathbf{R}$. These functions are given by the formulae:

$$\cosh^{-1} x = \ln\left(x + \sqrt{x^2 - 1}\right), \quad \text{for } x \geq 1,$$

$$\sinh^{-1} x = \ln\left(x + \sqrt{x^2 + 1}\right), \quad \text{for all } x,$$

$$\tanh^{-1} x = \ln\sqrt{\frac{1+x}{1-x}}, \quad \text{for } -1 < x < 1.$$

It is not so surprising that the inverse functions can be expressed in terms of the logarithmic function, since the original functions were defined in terms of the exponential function. The following derivatives can be obtained:

$$\frac{d}{dx}(\cosh^{-1} x) = \frac{1}{\sqrt{x^2 - 1}} \quad (x \neq 1), \qquad \frac{d}{dx}(\sinh^{-1} x) = \frac{1}{\sqrt{x^2 + 1}},$$

$$\frac{d}{dx}(\tanh^{-1} x) = \frac{1}{1 - x^2}.$$

inverse mapping   Let $f: S \to T$ be a bijection, that is, a mapping that is *one-to-one* and *onto*. Then a mapping, denoted by f^{-1}, from T to S, may be defined as follows: for t in T, $f^{-1}(t)$ is the unique element s of S such that $f(s) = t$. The mapping $f^{-1}: T \to S$, which is also a bijection, is the **inverse mapping** of f. It has the property that $f \circ f^{-1} = i_T$ and $f^{-1} \circ f = i_S$, where i_S and i_T are the identity mappings on S and T, and $\circ$ denotes composition.

inverse matrix   An **inverse** of a square matrix $\mathbf{A}$ is a matrix $\mathbf{X}$ such that $\mathbf{AX} = \mathbf{I}$ and $\mathbf{XA} = \mathbf{I}$. (A matrix that is not square cannot have an inverse.) A square matrix $\mathbf{A}$ may or may not have an inverse, but if it has then that inverse is unique and $\mathbf{A}$ is said to be **invertible**. A matrix is invertible if and only if it is *non-singular*. Consequently, the term 'non-singular' is sometimes used for 'invertible'.

When $\det \mathbf{A} \neq 0$, the matrix $(1/\det \mathbf{A})\,\mathrm{adj}\,\mathbf{A}$ is the inverse of $\mathbf{A}$, where $\mathrm{adj}\,\mathbf{A}$ is the *adjoint* of $\mathbf{A}$. For example, the 2×2 matrix $\mathbf{A}$ below is invertible if $ad - bc \neq 0$, and its inverse $\mathbf{A}^{-1}$ is as shown:

$$\mathbf{A} = \begin{bmatrix} a & b \\ c & d \end{bmatrix}, \qquad \mathbf{A}^{-1} = \frac{1}{ad - bc}\begin{bmatrix} d & -b \\ -c & a \end{bmatrix}.$$

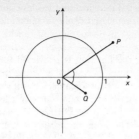

inverse of a complex number   If z is a non-zero complex number and $z = x + yi$, the (**multiplicative**) **inverse** of z, denoted by z^{-1} or $1/z$, is

$$\frac{x}{x^2 + y^2} - \frac{y}{x^2 + y^2}i.$$

When z is written in *polar form*, so that $z = re^{i\theta} = r(\cos\theta + i\sin\theta)$, where $r \neq 0$, the inverse of z is $(1/r)e^{-i\theta} = (1/r)(\cos\theta - i\sin\theta)$. If z is represented by P in the *complex plane*, then z^{-1} is represented by Q, where $\angle xOQ = -\angle xOP$ and $|OP| . |OQ| = 1$.

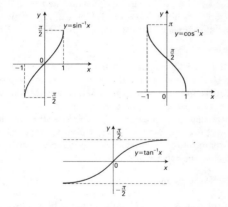

inverse trigonometric function   The inverse sine function $\sin^{-1}$ is, to put it briefly, the inverse function of sine, so that $y = \sin^{-1}x$ if $x = \sin y$. Thus $\sin^{-1}\frac{1}{2} = \pi/6$ because $\sin(\pi/6) = \frac{1}{2}$. However, $\sin(5\pi/6) = \frac{1}{2}$ also, so it might be thought that $\sin^{-1}\frac{1}{2} = \pi/6$ or $5\pi/6$. It is necessary to avoid such ambiguity so it is normally agreed that the value to be taken is the one lying in the interval $[-\pi/2, \pi/2]$. Similarly, $y = \tan^{-1}x$ if $x = \tan y$ and the value y is taken to lie in the interval $(-\pi/2, \pi/2)$. Also, $y = \cos^{-1}x$ if $x = \cos y$ and the value y is taken in the interval $[0, \pi]$.

A more advanced approach provides more explanation. The inverse function of a trigonometric function exists only if the original function is restricted to a suitable domain. This can be an interval I in which the function is strictly increasing or strictly decreasing (see *inverse function*). So, to obtain an inverse function for $\sin x$, the function is restricted to a domain consisting of the interval $[-\pi/2, \pi/2]$; $\tan x$ is restricted to the interval $(-\pi/2, \pi/2)$; and $\cos x$ is restricted to $[0, \pi]$. The domain of the inverse function is, in each case, the range of the restricted function. Hence the following inverse functions are obtained: $\sin^{-1}: [-1, 1] \rightarrow [-\pi/2, \pi/2]$; $\tan^{-1}: \mathbf{R} \rightarrow (-\pi/2, \pi/2)$; $\cos^{-1}: [-1, 1] \rightarrow [0, \pi]$. The notation arcsin, arctan and arccos, for $\sin^{-1}$, $\tan^{-1}$ and $\cos^{-1}$, is also used. The following derivatives can be obtained:

$$\frac{d}{dx}(\sin^{-1} x) = \frac{1}{\sqrt{1-x^2}} \quad (x \neq \pm 1), \quad \frac{d}{dx}(\cos^{-1} x) = -\frac{1}{\sqrt{1-x^2}} \quad (x \neq \pm 1),$$

$$\frac{d}{dx}(\tan^{-1} x) = \frac{1}{1+x^2}.$$

invertible matrix   See *inverse matrix*.

irrational number   A real number that is not *rational* is **irrational**. A famous proof, sometimes attributed to Pythagoras, shows that $\sqrt{2}$ is irrational. The same method shows that numbers such as $\sqrt{3}$ and $\sqrt{7}$ are also irrational. It follows that numbers like $1 + \sqrt{2}$ and $1/(1 + \sqrt{2})$ are irrational. The proof that e is irrational is reasonably easy, and in 1761 Lambert showed that π is irrational.

isometry   If P and Q are points in the plane, $|PQ|$ denotes the distance between P and Q. An **isometry** is a *transformation* of the plane that preserves the distance between points: it is a transformation with the property that, if P and Q are mapped to P' and Q', then $|P'Q'| = |PQ|$. Examples of isometries are *translations*, *rotations* and *reflections*. It can be shown that all the isometries of the plane can be obtained from translations, rotations and reflections, by composition. Two figures are *congruent* if there is an isometry that maps one onto the other.

isomorphic   See *isomorphism*.

isomorphism (of groups)   Let $\langle G, \circ \rangle$ and $\langle G', \star \rangle$ be *groups*, so that $\circ$ is the operation on G and $\star$ is the operation on G'. An **isomorphism** between $\langle G, \circ \rangle$ and $\langle G', \star \rangle$ is a *one-to-one onto mapping* f from the set G to the set G' such that, for all a and b in G, $f(a \circ b) = f(a) \star f(b)$. This means that, if f maps a to a' and b to b', then f maps $a \circ b$ to $a' \star b'$. If there is an isomorphism between two groups, the two groups are **isomorphic** to each other. Two groups that are isomorphic to one another have essentially the same structure: the actual elements of one group may be quite different objects from the elements of the other, but the way in which they behave with respect to the operation is the same. For example, the group of complex numbers 1, i, -1, $-i$ with multiplication is isomorphic to the group of elements 0, 1, 2, 3 with addition modulo 4.

isomorphism (of rings)   Suppose that $\langle R, +, \times \rangle$ and $\langle R', \oplus, \otimes \rangle$ are *rings*. An **isomorphism** between them is a *one-to-one onto mapping* f from the set R to the set R' such that, for all a and b in R, $f(a + b) = f(a) \oplus f(b)$ and $f(a \times b) = f(a) \otimes f(b)$. If there is an isomorphism between two rings, the rings are **isomorphic** to each other and, as with isomorphic groups, the two have essentially the same structure.

iteration   A method uses **iteration** if it obtains successive approximations to a required value by repeating a certain procedure. Examples are *fixed-point iteration* and *Newton's method* for finding a root of an equation $f(x) = 0$.

J

j   In the notation for *complex numbers*, some authors, especially engineers, use *j* instead of *i*.

K

al-Khwârizmi (about AD 800)   From the name of this mathematician of the Arabic school, we derive the word 'algorithm'. The title of his work *Al-jabr wa'l muqabalah* gives us the word 'algebra'.

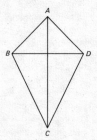

kite   A **kite** is a quadrilateral that has two adjacent sides of equal length and the other two sides of equal length. If the kite $ABCD$ has $AB = AD$ and $CB = CD$, the diagonals AC and BD are perpendicular and AC bisects BD.

L

Lagrange, Joseph-Louis (1736–1813)   With Euler, Lagrange was possibly the greatest of eighteenth-century mathematicians. Although he was born in Turin, and spent the early part of his life there, he eventually settled in Paris and is normally deemed to be French. Italians may think this unfair. Much of his important work was done in Berlin, where he was Euler's successor at the Academy. His work, in common with that of most important mathematicians of the time, covers the whole range of mathematics. He is probably best remembered as a leading figure in the development of *theoretical* mechanics. In particular, he was mainly responsible for the methods of the Calculus of Variations and the consequent Lagrangian method in mechanics. In ordinary maximum-minimum theory, you have to find the value of x that minimizes, say, the value of $F(x)$. In the basic form of the Calculus of Variations, you have to solve the much more difficult problem of finding the *function* f that minimizes the value of an integral like $\int_a^b F(x, f(x), f'(x))\, dx$. A famous problem in this subject is that of finding the curve joining two given points in a vertical plane along which a particle sliding under gravity will take the least time to get from the upper point to the lower.

lamina   A **lamina** is a thin plate or sheet, normally considered to have uniform density but idealized as having no thickness.

Laplace, Pierre-Simon, Marquis de (1749–1827)   Luckily for him, the Frenchman Laplace was not born an aristocrat but was politically adept. He became the Minister of the Interior under Napoleon (not a success) but seems to have got on just as well with the restored monarchy. He is best known for his work on planetary motion, enshrined in his *Mécanique Céleste*, and for his fundamental contributions to the theory of probability. It was Laplace who pushed Newton's gravitational theory forward to the study of the whole solar system. He developed the strongly deterministic view that, once you knew the *starting conditions* of a closed dynamical system, such as the universe, its future development was then totally determined. Napoleon asked him where God fitted into all this. 'I have no need of that hypothesis,' replied Laplace.

latus rectum   The **latus rectum** of a *parabola* is the chord through the focus and perpendicular to the axis. For the parabola $y^2 = 4ax$, the latus rectum has length $4a$.

l.c.m.   = *least common multiple*.

leading diagonal   = *main diagonal*.

least common multiple   For two non-zero integers a and b, an integer that is a multiple of both is a **common multiple**. Of all the positive common multiples, the least is the **least common multiple (l.c.m.)** and is denoted by $[a, b]$. The l.c.m. of a and b has the property of dividing any other common multiple of a and b. If the prime decompositions of a and b are known, the l.c.m. is easily obtained: for example, if $a = 168 = 2^3 \times 3 \times 7$ and $b = 180 = 2^2 \times 3^2 \times 5$, then the l.c.m. is $2^3 \times 3^2 \times 5 \times 7 = 2520$. For positive integers a and b, the l.c.m. is equal to $ab/(a, b)$, where (a, b) is the *greatest common divisor*.

Similarly, any finite set of non-zero integers, a_1, a_2, ..., a_n has an l.c.m. denoted by $[a_1, \ldots, a_n]$. However, when $n > 2$, it is not true, in general, that $[a_1, \ldots, a_n]$ is equal to $a_1 a_2 \ldots a_n/(a_1, \ldots, a_n)$, where $(a_1, \ldots, a_n)$ is the g.c.d.

least upper bound   = *supremum*.

least value   Let f be a *real function* and D a subset of its domain. If there is a point c in D such that $f(c) \leq f(x)$ for all x in D, then $f(c)$ is the **least value** of f in D. There may be no such point: consider, for example, either the function f defined by $f(x) = -1/x$ or the function f defined by $f(x) = x$, with the open interval $(0, 1)$ as D; or the function f defined by $f(x) = [x] - x$, with the closed interval $[0, 1]$ as D. If the least value does exist, it may be attained at more than one point of D.

That a *continuous function* on a closed interval has a least value is ensured by the non-elementary theorem that such a function 'attains its bounds'. An important theorem states that a function, continuous on $[a, b]$ and *differentiable* in (a, b), attains its least value either at a *local minimum* (which is a *stationary point*) or at an end-point of the interval.

left and **right derivative**   For the *real function* f, if

$$\lim_{h \to 0-} \frac{f(a + h) - f(a)}{h}$$

exists, this limit is the **left derivative** of f at a. Similarly, if

$$\lim_{h \to 0+} \frac{f(a + h) - f(a)}{h}$$

exists, this limit is the **right derivative** of f at a. (See *limit from the left, and right*.) The *derivative* $f'(a)$ exists if and only if the left derivative and the right derivative of f at a exist and are equal. An example where the left and right derivatives both exist but are not equal is provided by the function f, where $f(x) = |x|$ for all x. At 0, the left derivative equals -1 and the right derivative equals $+1$.

left-handed system   See *right-handed system*.

Legendre, Adrien-Marie (1752–1833)   The famous trio of French mathematicians associated with the period of the French Revolution are also associated by the fact that their names all start with L: Lagrange, Laplace, Legendre.

Legendre was well known in the nineteenth century for his textbook of geometry — Euclid 'done proper', by the standards of the time. His real work was much more concerned with the calculus. He was responsible for the classification of elliptic integrals into their standard forms. Students of more advanced mathematics soon come across the Legendre polynomials which are among the most important of special functions. In an entirely different area, Legendre did significant work on number theory. Along with Euler, he conjectured and partially proved the Law of Quadratic Reciprocity. The full proof had to wait for Gauss.

Leibniz, Gottfried (1646–1716)   Leibniz was a famous German philosopher and polymath. In mathematics he was, with Newton, the founder of the calculus. He also made significant contributions to the development of symbolic logic, a lead which was not followed up until the end of the nineteenth century. A major international row blew up, in about 1712, over the rival claims of Newton and Leibniz to be the inventor of the calculus. Leibniz's behaviour in this feud was honourable — unlike Newton's, and unlike his own with regard to Spinoza.

Leibniz's Theorem   The following result about the n-th derivative of a product is sometimes known as **Leibniz's Theorem**:

THEOREM: If $h(x) = f(x)g(x)$ for all x, the n-th derivative of h is given by

$$h^{(n)}(x) = \sum_{r=0}^{n} \binom{n}{r} f^{(r)}(x) g^{(n-r)}(x),$$

where the coefficients $\binom{n}{r}$ are *binomial coefficients*.

For example, to find $h^{(8)}(x)$, when $h(x) = x^2 \sin x$, let $f(x) = x^2$ and $g(x) = \sin x$. Then $f'(x) = 2x$ and $f''(x) = 2$; and $g^{(8)}(x) = \sin x$, $g^{(7)}(x) = -\cos x$ and $g^{(6)}(x) = -\sin x$. So

$$h^{(8)}(x) = x^2 \sin x + \binom{8}{1} 2x(-\cos x) + \binom{8}{2} 2(-\sin x)$$
$$= x^2 \sin x - 16x \cos x - 56 \sin x.$$

length (of a line segment)   The **length** $|AB|$ of the *line segment* AB, and the length $|\overrightarrow{AB}|$ of the *directed line-segment*, is equal to the distance between A and B. It is equal to zero when A and B coincide and is otherwise always positive.

length (of a sequence)   See *sequence*.

length (of a series)   See *series*.

length (of a vector)   See *vector*.

length of the major and **minor axis**   See *ellipse*.

limit from the left and **right**   The statement that $f(x)$ tends to l as x tends to a **from the left** can be written: $f(x) \rightarrow l$ as $x \rightarrow a-$. Another way of writing this is

$$\lim_{x \to a-} f(x) = l.$$

The formal definition says that this is so if, given $\epsilon > 0$, there is a number $\delta > 0$ such that, for all x strictly between $a-\delta$ and a, $f(x)$ lies between $l-\epsilon$ and $l+\epsilon$. In place of $x \rightarrow a-$, some authors use $x \nearrow a$. In the same way, the statement that $f(x)$ tends to l as x tends to a **from the right** can be written: $f(x) \rightarrow l$ as $x \rightarrow a+$. Another way of writing this is

$$\lim_{x \to a+} f(x) = l.$$

The formal definition says that this is so if, given $\epsilon > 0$, there is a number $\delta > 0$ such that, for all x strictly between a and $a+\delta$, $f(x)$ lies between $l-\epsilon$ and $l+\epsilon$. In place of $x \rightarrow a+$, some authors use $x \searrow a$. For example, if $f(x) = x - [x]$, then

$$\lim_{x \to 1-} f(x) = 1, \qquad \lim_{x \to 1+} f(x) = 0.$$

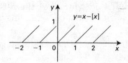

limit (of $f(x)$)   The **limit**, if it exists, of $f(x)$ as x tends to a is a number l with the property that, as x gets closer and closer to a, $f(x)$ gets closer and closer to l. This is written

$$\lim_{x \to a} f(x) = l.$$

Such an understanding may be adequate at an elementary level. It is important to realize that this limit may not equal $f(a)$; indeed, $f(a)$ may not necessarily be defined.

At a more advanced level, the definition just given needs to be made more precise: a formal statement says that $f(x)$ can be made as close to l as we please by restricting x to a sufficiently small neighbourhood of a (but excluding a itself). Thus, it is said that $f(x)$ tends to l as x tends to a, written $f(x) \rightarrow l$ as $x \rightarrow a$, if, given any positive number ϵ (however small), there is a positive number δ (which depends upon ϵ) such that, for all x, except possibly a itself, lying between $a-\delta$ and $a+\delta$, $f(x)$ lies between $l-\epsilon$ and $l+\epsilon$.

Notice that a itself may not be in the domain of f; but there must be a neighbourhood of a, the whole of which (apart possibly from a itself) is in the domain of f. For example, let f be the function defined by

$$f(x) = \frac{\sin x}{x} \qquad (x \neq 0).$$

Then 0 is not in the domain of f, but it can be shown that

$$\lim_{x \to 0} \frac{\sin x}{x} = 1.$$

In the above, l is a real number, but it is also possible that $f(x) \to \pm\infty$, where appropriate formal definitions can be given: it is said that $f(x) \to +\infty$ as $x \to a$ if, given any positive number K (however large), there is a positive number δ (which depends upon K) such that, for all x, except possibly a itself, lying between $a - \delta$ and $a + \delta$, $f(x)$ is greater than K. It is clear, for example, that $1/x^2 \to +\infty$ as $x \to 0$. There is a similar definition for $f(x) \to -\infty$ as $x \to a$.

Sometimes the behaviour of $f(x)$ as x gets indefinitely large is of interest and importance: it is said that $f(x) \to l$ as $x \to \infty$ if, given any positive number ϵ (however small), there is a number X (which depends upon ϵ) such that, for all $x > X$, $f(x)$ lies between $l - \epsilon$ and $l + \epsilon$. This means that $y = l$ is a horizontal *asymptote* for the graph $y = f(x)$. Similar definitions can be given for $f(x) \to l$ as $x \to -\infty$, and for $f(x) \to \pm\infty$ as $x \to \infty$ and $f(x) \to \pm\infty$ as $x \to -\infty$.

limit (of a sequence)   The **limit**, if it exists, of an infinite sequence a_1, a_2, a_3, ... is a number l with the property that a_n gets closer and closer to l as n gets indefinitely large. Such an understanding may be adequate at an elementary level.

At a more advanced level, the statement just given needs to be made more precise: it is said that the sequence a_1, a_2, a_3, ... has the limit l if, given any positive number ϵ (however small), there is a number N (which depends upon ϵ) such that, for all $n > N$, a_n lies between $l - \epsilon$ and $l + \epsilon$. This can be written: $a_n \to l$.

The sequence 0, $\frac{1}{2}$, $\frac{3}{4}$, $\frac{7}{8}$, $\frac{15}{16}$, ..., for example, has the limit 1. To take another example, the sequence -1, $\frac{1}{2}$, $-\frac{1}{3}$, $\frac{1}{4}$, $-\frac{1}{5}$, ... has the limit 0; since this is the sequence whose n-th term is $(-1)^n/n$, this fact can be stated as: $(-1)^n/n \to 0$.

There are, of course, sequences that do not have a limit. These can be classified into different kinds.

(i) A formal definition says that $a_n \to \infty$ if, given any positive number K (however large), there is an integer N (which depends upon K) such that, for all $n > N$, a_n is greater than K. For example, $a_n \to \infty$ for the sequence 1, 4, 9, 16, ..., in which $a_n = n^2$.

(ii) There is a similar definition for $a_n \to -\infty$, and an example is the sequence -4, -5, -6, ..., in which $a_n = -n - 3$.

(iii) If a sequence does not have a limit but is *bounded*, such as the sequence $-\frac{1}{2}$, $\frac{2}{3}$, $-\frac{3}{4}$, $\frac{4}{5}$, ..., in which $a_n = (-1)^n n/(n + 1)$, it may be said to **oscillate finitely**.

(iv) If a sequence is not bounded, but it is not the case that $a_n \to \infty$ or $a_n \to -\infty$ (the sequence 1, 2, 1, 4, 1, 8, 1, ... is an example), the sequence may be said to **oscillate infinitely**.

limit of integration　　In the definite integral

$$\int_a^b f(x)\,dx,$$

the **lower limit** (of **integration**) is a and the **upper limit** (of **integration**) is b.

linear algebra　　The topics of linear equations, matrices, vectors, and of the algebraic structure known as a vector space, are intimately linked, and this area of mathematics is known as **linear algebra**.

linear congruence equation　　See *congruence equation*.

linear differential equation　　A **linear differential equation** is a *differential equation* of the form

$$a_n(x)y^{(n)}(x) + a_{n-1}(x)y^{(n-1)}(x) + \cdots + a_1(x)y'(x) + a_0(x)y(x) = f(x),$$

where $a_0, a_1, \ldots, a_n$ and f are given functions, and $y', \ldots, y^{(n)}$ are *derivatives* of y. See also *linear differential equation with constant coefficients* and *linear first-order differential equation*.

linear differential equation with constant coefficients　　For simplicity, consider a second-order **linear differential equation with constant coefficients**,

$$a\frac{d^2y}{dx} + b\frac{dy}{dx} + cy = f(x),\qquad\qquad\mathbf{1}$$

where a, b and c are given constants and f is a given function. (Higher-order equations can be treated similarly.) Suppose that f is not the zero function. Then the equation

$$a\frac{d^2y}{dx^2} + b\frac{dy}{dx} + cy = 0\qquad\qquad\mathbf{2}$$

is the **homogeneous** equation that corresponds to the **non-homogeneous** equation **1**. The two are connected by the following result.

THEOREM: If $y = G(x)$ is the general solution of **2** and $y = y_1(x)$ is a particular solution of **1**, then $y = G(x) + y_1(x)$ is the general solution of **1**.

Thus the problem of solving **1** is reduced to the problem of finding the **complementary function** (C.F.) $G(x)$, which is the general solution of **2**, and a particular solution $y_1(x)$ of **1**, usually known in this context as a **particular integral** (P.I.).

The complementary function is found by looking for solutions of **2** of the form $y = e^{mx}$ and obtaining the **auxiliary equation** $am^2 + bm + c = 0$. If this equation has distinct real roots m_1 and m_2, the C.F. is $y = Ae^{m_1 x} + Be^{m_2 x}$; if it has one (repeated) root m, the C.F. is $y = (A + Bx)e^{mx}$; if it has non-real roots $\alpha \pm \beta i$, the C.F. is $y = e^{\alpha x}(A\cos\beta x + B\sin\beta x)$.

The most elementary way of obtaining a particular integral is to try something similar in form to $f(x)$. Thus if $f(x) = e^{kx}$, try, as P.I., $y_1(x) = pe^{kx}$. If

$f(x)$ is a polynomial in x, try a polynomial of the same degree. If $f(x) = \cos kx$ or $\sin kx$, try $y_1(x) = p\cos kx + q\sin kx$. In each case, the values of the unknown coefficients are found by substituting the possible P.I. into the equation **1**. If $f(x)$ is the sum of two terms, a P.I. corresponding to each may be found and the two added together.

Using these methods, the general solution of $y'' - 3y' + 2y = 4x + e^{3x}$, for example, is found to be $y = Ae^x + Be^{2x} + 2x + 3 + \frac{1}{2}e^{3x}$.

linear equation   Consider, in turn, **linear equations** in one, two and three variables. A linear equation in one variable x is an equation of the form $ax + b = 0$. If $a \neq 0$, this has the solution $x = -b/a$. A linear equation in two variables x and y is an equation of the form $ax + by + c = 0$. If a and b are not both zero, and x and y are taken as Cartesian coordinates in the plane, the equation is an equation of a *straight line*. A linear equation in three variables x, y and z is an equation of the form $ax + by + cz + d = 0$. If a, b and c are not all zero, and x, y and z are taken as Cartesian coordinates in 3-dimensional space, the equation is an equation of a *plane*. See also *simultaneous linear equations*.

linear first-order differential equation   A **linear first-order differential equation** is of the form

$$\frac{dy}{dx} + P(x)y = Q(x),$$

where P and Q are given functions. One method of solution is to multiply both sides of the equation by an **integrating factor** $\mu(x)$, given by

$$\mu(x) = e^{\int P(x)dx}.$$

This choice is made because then the left-hand side of the equation becomes

$$\mu(x)\frac{dy}{dx} + \mu(x)P(x)y,$$

which is the exact derivative of $\mu(x)y$, and the solution can be found by integration.

linear function   In real analysis, a **linear function** is a function f such that $f(x) = ax + b$ for all x in $\mathbf{R}$, where a and b are real numbers with, normally, $a \neq 0$.

linear interpolation   See *interpolation*.

linear programming   The branch of mathematics known as **linear programming** is concerned with maximizing or minimizing a linear function subject to a number of linear constraints, and has applications in economics, town planning, management in industry, and commerce, for example. In its simplest form, with two variables, the constraints determine a **feasible region**, which is the interior of a polygon in the plane. The **objective function**

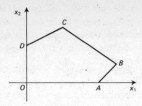

to be maximized or minimized attains its maximum or minimum value at a vertex of the feasible region. For example, consider the problem of maximizing $4x_1 - 3x_2$ subject to $x_1 - 2x_2 \geq -4$, $2x_1 + 3x_2 \leq 13$, $x_1 - x_2 \leq 4$, and $x_1 \geq 0$, $x_2 \geq 0$. The feasible region is the interior of the polygon $OABCD$ shown in the figure, and the objective function $4x_1 - 3x_2$ attains its maximum value of 17 at the point B with coordinates $(5, 1)$.

linearly dependent and **independent**   A set of vectors $\mathbf{u}_1, \mathbf{u}_2, \ldots, \mathbf{u}_r$ is **linearly independent** if $x_1\mathbf{u}_1 + x_2\mathbf{u}_2 + \cdots + x_r\mathbf{u}_r = \mathbf{0}$ holds only if $x_1 = 0$, $x_2 = 0$, $\ldots$, $x_r = 0$. Otherwise, the set is **linearly dependent**. In 3-dimensional space, any set of four or more vectors must be linearly dependent. A set of three vectors is linearly independent if and only if the three are not coplanar. A set of two vectors is linearly independent if and only if the two are not parallel or, in other words, if and only if neither is a scalar multiple of the other.

linear transformation   See *transformation* (of the plane).

line of symmetry   See *symmetrical about a line*.

line segment   If A and B are two points on a straight line, the part of the line between and including A and B is a **line segment**. This may be denoted by AB or BA. (The notation AB may also be used with a different meaning, as a real number, the *measure* of $\overrightarrow{AB}$ on a directed line.) Some authors use 'line segment' to mean what we call a *directed line-segment*.

local maximum (plural: maxima)   For a function f, a **local maximum** is a point c that has a neighbourhood at every point of which, except for c, $f(x) < f(c)$. If f is *differentiable* at a local maximum c, then $f'(c) = 0$; that is, it is a *stationary point*.

local minimum (plural: minima)   For a function f, a **local minimum** is a point c that has a neighbourhood at every point of which, except for c, $f(x) > f(c)$. If f is *differentiable* at a local minimum c, then $f'(c) = 0$; that is, it is a *stationary point*.

locus (plural: loci)   A **locus** (in the plane) is the set of all points in the plane that satisfy some given condition or property. For example, the locus of all points that are a given distance from a fixed point is a circle; the locus of all points equidistant from two given points, A and B, is the perpendicular bisector of AB. If, in a given coordinate system, a locus can be expressed in the form $\{\,(x,y)\mid f(x,y)=0\,\}$, the equation $f(x,y)=0$ is called an **equation** of the locus (in the given coordinate system). The equation may be said to 'represent' the locus.

logarithm   Let a be any positive number, not equal to 1. Then, for any real number x, the meaning of a^x can be defined (see approach **1** to the *exponential function to base a*). The **logarithmic function to base** a, denoted by $\log_a$, is defined as the inverse of this function. So $y = \log_a x$ if and only if $x = a^y$. Thus $\log_a x$ is the index to which a must be raised in order to get x. Since any power a^y of a is positive, x must be positive for $\log_a x$ to be defined, and so the domain of the function $\log_a$ is the set of positive real numbers. (See *inverse function* for a more detailed explanation about the domain of an inverse function.) The value $\log_a x$ is usually called simply the **logarithm** of x to base a. The notation $\log x$ may be used when the base intended is understood. The following properties hold, where x, y and r are real, with $x > 0$ and $y > 0$:

  (i) $\log_a(xy) = \log_a x + \log_a y$.
  (ii) $\log_a(1/x) = -\log_a x$.
  (iii) $\log_a(x/y) = \log_a x - \log_a y$.
  (iv) $\log_a(x^r) = r\log_a x$.
  (v) Logarithms to different bases are related by the formula

$$\log_b x = \frac{\log_a x}{\log_a b}.$$

Logarithms to base 10 are called **common** logarithms. Tables of common logarithms were in the past used for arithmetical calculations. Logarithms to base e are called **natural** or **Napierian** logarithms and the notation ln can be used instead of $\log_e$. However, this presupposes that the value of e has been defined independently. It is preferable to define the *logarithmic function* ln in quite a different way. From this, e can be defined and then the equivalence of ln and $\log_e$ proved.

logarithmic function   The **logarithmic function** ln must be distinguished from the *logarithmic function to base a* (see *logarithm*). Here are two approaches:

  1. Suppose that the value of the number e has already been obtained independently. Then the *logarithm* of x to base e can be defined and denoted by $\log_e x$, and the logarithmic function ln can be taken to be just this function $\log_e$. The problem with this approach is its reliance on a prior definition of e and the difficulty of subsequently proving some of the important properties of ln.

  2. The following is more satisfactory. Let f be the function defined, for $t > 0$, by $f(t) = 1/t$. Then the logarithmic function ln is defined, for $x > 0$, by

$$\ln x = \int_1^x \frac{1}{t}\,dt.$$

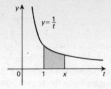

The intention is best appreciated in the case when $x > 1$, for then $\ln x$ gives the area under the graph of f in the interval $[1, x]$. This function $\ln$ is *continuous* and increasing; it is *differentiable* and, from the fundamental relationship between differentiation and integration, its *derived function* is the function f. Thus it has been established that

$$\frac{d}{dx}(\ln x) = \frac{1}{x} \quad (x > 0).$$

From the definition, the following properties can be obtained, where x, y and r are real, with $x > 0$ and $y > 0$:

(i) $\ln(xy) = \ln x + \ln y$.
(ii) $\ln(1/x) = -\ln x$.
(iii) $\ln(x/y) = \ln x - \ln y$.
(iv) $\ln(x^r) = r \ln x$.

With this approach, exp can be defined as the inverse function of $\ln$ and the number e defined as $\exp 1$. Finally, it is shown that $\ln x$ and $\log_e x$ are identical.

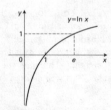

logarithmic function to base a See *logarithm*.

logarithmic plotting   Two varieties of logarithmic graph paper are commonly available. One, known as **semi-log** or **single log** paper, allows a standard scale on the x-axis and a *logarithmic scale* on the y-axis. If given data satisfy an equation $y = ba^x$ (where a and b are constants), exhibiting *exponential growth*, then on this special graph paper the corresponding points lie on a straight line. The other variety is known as **log-log** or **double log** paper and has a logarithmic scale on both axes. In this case, data satisfying $y = bx^m$ (where b and m are constants) produce points that lie on a straight line. Given some experimental data, such **logarithmic plotting** on one variety or the other of logarithmic graph paper can be used to determine what relationship might have given rise to such data.

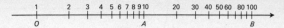

logarithmic scale   A **logarithmic scale** is a method of representing numbers (certainly positive and usually greater than or equal to 1) by points on a line as follows. Suppose that one direction along the line is taken as positive and that the point O is taken as origin. The number x is represented by the point P in such a way that OP is proportional to $\log x$, where logarithms are to base 10. Thus the number 1 is represented by O; and, if the point A represents 10, the point B that represents 100 is such that $OB = 2OA$.

logarithmic spiral   = *equiangular spiral*.

logically equivalent   Two *compound statements* involving the same components are **logically equivalent** if they have the same *truth tables*. This means that, for all possible truth values of the components, the resulting truth values of the two statements are the same. For example, the truth table for the statement $(\neg p) \lor q$ can be completed as follows:

p	q	$\neg p$	$(\neg p) \lor q$
T	T	F	T
T	F	F	F
F	T	T	T
F	F	T	T

By comparing the last column here with the truth table for $p \Rightarrow q$ (see *implication*), it can be seen that $(\neg p) \lor q$ and $p \Rightarrow q$ are logically equivalent.

loop   See *graph*.

lower bound   See *bound*.

lower limit   See *limit of integration*.

lower triangular matrix   See *triangular matrix*.

M

Maclaurin, Colin (1698–1746)   Maclaurin was an notable Scottish mathematician who worked at the universities of Aberdeen and Edinburgh. He did much important work on the calculus, so it is ironic that he is best known for *Maclaurin series*, which are just a special case of the already known *Taylor series*, which were invented by James Gregory and others. This is not a case of plagiarism. Maclaurin emphasized the series in a well-known book and his name stuck.

Maclaurin series (or **expansion**)   Suppose that f is a *real function*, all of whose *derived functions* $f^{(r)}$ $(r = 1, 2, \ldots)$ exist in some interval containing 0. It is then possible to write down the power series

$$f(0) + \frac{f'(0)}{1!}x + \frac{f''(0)}{2!}x^2 + \cdots + \frac{f^{(n)}(0)}{n!}x^n + \cdots .$$

This is the **Maclaurin series** (or **expansion**) for f. For many important functions, it can be proved that the Maclaurin series is convergent, either for all x or for a certain range of values of x, and that for these values the sum of the series is $f(x)$. For these values it is said that the Maclaurin series is a 'valid' expansion of $f(x)$. The Maclaurin series for some common functions, with the values of x for which they are valid, are given in the Table of Series (Appendix 4). The function f, defined by $f(0) = 0$ and $f(x) = e^{-1/x^2}$ for all $x \neq 0$, is notorious in this context. It can be shown that all of its derived functions exist and that $f^{(r)}(0) = 0$ for all r. Consequently, its Maclaurin series is convergent and has sum 0, for all x. This shows, perhaps contrary to expectation, that, even when the Maclaurin series for a function f is convergent, its sum is not necessarily $f(x)$. See also *Taylor's Theorem*.

magnitude (of a vector)   See *vector*. Also, if the vector **a** is given in terms of its components (with respect to the standard vectors **i**, **j** and **k**) in the form $\mathbf{a} = a_1\mathbf{i} + a_2\mathbf{j} + a_3\mathbf{k}$, the magnitude of **a** is given by the formula $|\mathbf{a}| = \sqrt{a_1{}^2 + a_2{}^2 + a_3{}^2}$.

main diagonal   In the $n \times n$ matrix $[a_{ij}]$, the entries a_{11}, a_{22}, ..., a_{nn} form the **main diagonal**.

major arc   See *arc*.

major axis   See *ellipse*.

mantissa   See *floating-point*.

mapping A **mapping** (or **function**) f from S to T, where S and T are non-empty sets, is a rule which associates, with each element of S, a unique element of T. The set S is the **domain** and T is the **codomain** of f. The phrase 'f from S to T' is written '$f: S \to T$'. For s in S, the unique element of T that f associates with s is the **image of s under** f and is denoted by $f(s)$. If $f(s) = t$, it is said that f **maps** s to t, written $f: s \mapsto t$. The subset of T consisting of those elements that are images of elements of S under f, that is, the subset $\{ t \mid t = f(s),$ for some s in $S \}$, is the **image** (or **range**) of f, denoted by $f(S)$. For the mapping $f: S \to T$, the subset $\{ (s, f(s)) \mid s \in S \}$ of the *Cartesian product* $S \times T$ is the *graph* of f. The graph of a mapping has the property that, for each s in S, there is a unique element (s, t) in the graph. Some authors define a mapping from S to T to be a subset of $S \times T$ with this property; then the image of s under this mapping is defined to be the unique t such that (s, t) is in this subset.

mathematical induction The method of proof 'by **mathematical induction**' is based on the following principle:

THE PRINCIPLE OF MATHEMATICAL INDUCTION: Let there be associated, with each positive integer n, a proposition $P(n)$, which is either true or false. If

(i) $P(1)$ is true,
(ii) for all k, $P(k)$ implies $P(k + 1)$,

then $P(n)$ is true for all positive integers n.

This essentially describes a property of the positive integers; either it is accepted as a principle that does not require proof or it is proved as a theorem from some agreed set of more fundamental axioms. The following are typical of results that can be proved by induction:

    1. For all positive integers n, $\displaystyle\sum_{r=1}^{n} r^2 = \frac{1}{6}n(n + 1)(2n + 1)$.

    2. For all positive integers n, the n-th derivative of $\dfrac{1}{x}$ is $(-1)^n \dfrac{n!}{x^{n+1}}$.

    3. For all positive integers n, $(\cos\theta + i\sin\theta)^n = \cos n\theta + i\sin n\theta$.

In each case, it is clear what the proposition $P(n)$ should be, and that (i) can be verified. The method by which the so-called induction step (ii) is proved depends upon the particular result to be established.

    A modified form of the principle is this. Let there be associated, with each integer $n \geq n_0$, a proposition $P(n)$, which is either true or false. If (i) $P(n_0)$ is true, and (ii) for all $k \geq n_0$, $P(k)$ implies $P(k + 1)$, then $P(n)$ is true for all integers $n \geq n_0$. This may be used to prove, for example, that $3^n > n^3$ for all integers $n \geq 4$.

matrix (plural: matrices) A **matrix** is a rectangular array of **entries**, that is, an arrangement with the entries displayed in rows and columns. These entries are elements of some suitable set, either specified or understood. They are often numbers, perhaps integers or real numbers or complex numbers, but they may be, say, polynomials or other expressions. An $m \times n$ matrix has m rows and n columns and can be written as

$$\begin{bmatrix} a_{11} & a_{12} & \cdots & a_{1n} \\ a_{21} & a_{22} & \cdots & a_{2n} \\ \vdots & \vdots & \ddots & \vdots \\ a_{m1} & a_{m2} & \cdots & a_{mn} \end{bmatrix}.$$

Round brackets may be used instead of square brackets. The subscripts are read as though separated by commas: for example, a_{23} is read as 'a, two, three'. The matrix above may be written in abbreviated form as $[a_{ij}]$, where the number of rows and columns is understood and a_{ij} denotes the entry in the i-th row and j-th column. See also *addition* (of matrices), *multiplication* (of matrices) and *inverse matrix*.

matrix of coefficients   For a set of m linear equations in n unknowns x_1, $x_2, \ldots, x_n$:

$$a_{11}x_1 + a_{12}x_2 + \ldots + a_{1n}x_n = b_1,$$
$$a_{21}x_1 + a_{22}x_2 + \ldots + a_{2n}x_n = b_2,$$
$$\ldots$$
$$a_{m1}x_1 + a_{m2}x_2 + \ldots + a_{mn}x_n = b_m,$$

the **matrix of coefficients** is the $m \times n$ matrix $[a_{ij}]$.

matrix of cofactors   For **A**, a square matrix $[a_{ij}]$, the **matrix of cofactors** is the matrix, of the same order, that is obtained by replacing each entry a_{ij} by its *cofactor* A_{ij}. It is used to find the *adjoint* of **A**, and hence the inverse $\mathbf{A}^{-1}$.

maximum   For **maximum value**, see *greatest value*. See also *local maximum*.

mean   The **mean** of the numbers $a_1, a_2, \ldots, a_n$ is equal to

$$\frac{a_1 + a_2 + \cdots + a_n}{n}.$$

This is the number most commonly used as the average. It may be called the **arithmetic mean** to distinguish it from other means such as those described below. When each number a_i is to have weight w_i, the **weighted mean** is equal to

$$\frac{w_1 a_1 + w_2 a_2 + \cdots + w_n a_n}{w_1 + w_2 + \cdots + w_n}.$$

The **geometric mean** of the positive numbers $a_1, \ldots, a_n$ is $\sqrt[n]{a_1 a_2 \ldots a_n}$. Given two positive numbers a and b, suppose that $a < b$. The arithmetic mean m is equal to $\frac{1}{2}(a + b)$ and a, m, b is an arithmetic sequence. The geometric mean g is equal to $\sqrt{ab}$ and a, g, b is a geometric sequence. The arithmetic mean of 3 and 12 is $7\frac{1}{2}$ and the geometric mean is 6. It is a theorem of elementary algebra that, for any positive numbers $a_1, \ldots, a_n$, the arithmetic mean is greater than or equal to the geometric mean; that is,

$$\frac{1}{n}(a_1 + a_2 + \cdots + a_n) \geq \sqrt[n]{a_1 a_2 \ldots a_n}.$$

The **harmonic mean** of positive numbers $a_1, a_2, \ldots, a_n$ is the number h such that $1/h$ is the arithmetic mean of $1/a_1, 1/a_2, \ldots, 1/a_n$. Thus

$$h = \frac{n}{(1/a_1) + \ldots + (1/a_n)}.$$

Mean Value Theorem　　A theorem that has very important consequences in differential calculus is the **Mean Value Theorem**:

THEOREM: Let f be a function that is continuous on $[a, b]$ and differentiable in (a, b). Then there is a number c with $a < c < b$ such that

$$f'(c) = \frac{f(b) - f(a)}{b - a}.$$

The result stated in the theorem can be expressed as a statement about the graph of f: if A, with coordinates $(a, f(a))$, and B, with coordinates $(b, f(b))$, are the points of the graph corresponding to the end-points of the interval, there must be a point C on the graph between A and B at which the tangent is parallel to the chord AB.

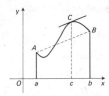

The theorem is normally deduced from *Rolle's Theorem*, which is in fact the special case of the Mean Value Theorem in which $f(a) = f(b)$. A rigorous proof of either theorem relies on the non-elementary result that a *continuous function* on a closed interval attains its bounds. The Mean Value Theorem has immediate corollaries such as the following. With appropriate conditions on f, (i) if $f'(x) = 0$ for all x, then f is a *constant function*; (ii) if $f'(x) > 0$ for all x, then f is *strictly increasing*. The important *Taylor's Theorem* can also be seen as an extension of the Mean Value Theorem.

measure　　Let A and B be two points on a *directed line* and let $\overrightarrow{AB}$ be the *directed line-segment* from A to B. The **measure** AB is defined by

$$AB = \begin{cases} |AB|, & \text{if } \overrightarrow{AB} \text{ is in the positive direction,} \\ -|AB|, & \text{if } \overrightarrow{AB} \text{ is in the negative direction.} \end{cases}$$

Suppose, for example, that a horizontal line has positive direction to the right (like the usual x-axis). Then the definition of measure gives $AB = 2$, if B is 2 units to the right of A, and $AB = -2$, if B is 2 units to the left of A.

The following properties are easily deduced from the definition:

(i) For points A and B on a directed line, $AB = -BA$.

(ii) For points A, B and C on a directed line, $AB + BC = AC$ (established by considering the different possible relative positions of A, B and C).

median   A **median** of a triangle is a line through a vertex and the midpoint of the opposite side. The three medians are concurrent at the *centroid*.

member   = *element*.

Mersenne prime   A **Mersenne prime** is a *prime* of the form $2^p - 1$, where p is a prime. The number of known primes of this form keeps increasing as they are discovered by using computers: 24 are known at present. The largest so far, $2^{19937} - 1$, was announced in 1971. Each Mersenne prime gives rise to an even *perfect number*.

midpoint   Let A and B be points in the plane with Cartesian coordinates (x_1, y_1) and (x_2, y_2). Then, as a special case of the *section formulae*, the midpoint of AB has coordinates $\left(\frac{1}{2}(x_1 + x_2), \frac{1}{2}(y_1 + y_2)\right)$. For points A and B in 3-dimensional space, with Cartesian coordinates (x_1, y_1, z_1) and (x_2, y_2, z_2), the midpoint of AB has coordinates

$$\left(\tfrac{1}{2}(x_1 + x_2), \tfrac{1}{2}(y_1 + y_2), \tfrac{1}{2}(z_1 + z_2)\right).$$

If points A and B have position vectors $\mathbf{a}$ and $\mathbf{b}$, the midpoint of AB has position vector $\frac{1}{2}(\mathbf{a} + \mathbf{b})$.

minimum   For **minimum value** see *least value*. See also *local minimum*.

minor arc   See *arc*.

minor axis   See *ellipse*.

mirror-image   See *reflection* (of the plane).

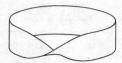

Möbius band (or **strip**)   A **Möbius band** (or **strip**) is a continuous flat loop with one twist in it. Between any two points on it, a continuous line can be drawn on the surface without crossing an edge. Thus the band has only one surface and likewise only one edge.

modulo n, addition and **multiplication**   The word 'modulo' means 'to the modulus'. For any positive integer n, let S be the *complete set of residues* $\{0, 1, 2, \ldots, n-1\}$. Then **addition modulo n** on S is defined as follows. For a and b in S, take the usual sum of a and b as integers, and let r be the element of S to which the result is *congruent* (modulo n); the sum $a + b$ (mod n) is equal to r. Similarly, **multiplication modulo n** is defined by taking ab (mod n) to be equal to s, where s is the element of S to which the usual product of a and b is congruent (modulo n). For example, addition and multiplication modulo 5 are given by the following tables:

+	0	1	2	3	4
0	0	1	2	3	4
1	1	2	3	4	0
2	2	3	4	0	1
3	3	4	0	1	2
4	4	0	1	2	3

×	0	1	2	3	4
0	0	0	0	0	0
1	0	1	2	3	4
2	0	2	4	1	3
3	0	3	1	4	2
4	0	4	3	2	1

modulus of a complex number (plural: moduli)   If z is a *complex number* and $z = x + yi$, the **modulus** of z, denoted by $|z|$ (read as 'mod z'), is equal to $\sqrt{x^2 + y^2}$. (As always, the sign $\sqrt{}$ means the non-negative square root.) If z is represented by the point P in the *complex plane*, the modulus of z equals the distance $|OP|$. Thus $|z| = r$, where (r, θ) are the polar coordinates of P. If z is real, the modulus of z equals the *absolute value* of the real number, so the two uses of the same notation $|\ |$ are consistent and the term 'modulus' may be used for 'absolute value'.

modulus of a congruence   See *congruence*.

monotonic function   A *real function* f is **monotonic** on or over an interval I if it is either increasing on I ($f(x_1) \leq f(x_2)$ whenever $x_1 < x_2$) or decreasing on I ($f(x_1) \geq f(x_2)$ whenever $x_1 < x_2$). Also f is **strictly monotonic** if it is either strictly increasing or strictly decreasing.

monotonic sequence   A sequence $a_1, a_2, a_3, \ldots$ is **monotonic** if it is either increasing ($a_i \leq a_{i+1}$ for all i) or decreasing ($a_i \geq a_{i+1}$ for all i), and **strictly monotonic** if it is either strictly increasing or strictly decreasing.

multiple   See *divides*.

multiple edges   See *graph*.

multiple root   See *root*.

multiplication modulo n   See *modulo n, addition and multiplication*.

multiplication (of complex numbers)   For complex numbers z_1 and z_2, given by $z_1 = a + bi$ and $z_2 = c + di$, the **product** is defined by $z_1 z_2 =$

$(ac - bd) + (ad + bc)i$. In some circumstances, it may be more convenient to write z_1 and z_2 in *polar form*, so that

$$z_1 = r_1 e^{i\theta_1} = r_1(\cos\theta_1 + i\sin\theta_1),$$
$$z_2 = r_2 e^{i\theta_2} = r_2(\cos\theta_2 + i\sin\theta_2).$$

Then $z_1 z_2 = r_1 r_2 e^{i(\theta_1 + \theta_2)} = r_1 r_2 (\cos(\theta_1 + \theta_2) + i\sin(\theta_1 + \theta_2))$. Thus 'you multiply the moduli and add the arguments'.

multiplication (of matrices)   Suppose that matrices $\mathbf{A}$ and $\mathbf{B}$ are *conformable* for multiplication, so that $\mathbf{A}$ has order $m \times n$ and $\mathbf{B}$ has order $n \times p$. Let $\mathbf{A} = [a_{ij}]$ and $\mathbf{B} = [b_{ij}]$. Then **(matrix) multiplication** is defined by taking the **product** $\mathbf{AB}$ to be the $m \times p$ matrix $\mathbf{C}$, where $\mathbf{C} = [c_{ij}]$ and

$$c_{ij} = a_{i1}b_{1j} + a_{i2}b_{2j} + \cdots + a_{in}b_{nj} = \sum_{r=1}^{n} a_{ir}b_{rj}.$$

The product $\mathbf{AB}$ is not defined if $\mathbf{A}$ and $\mathbf{B}$ are not conformable for multiplication. Matrix multiplication is not *commutative*; for example, if

$$\mathbf{A} = \begin{bmatrix} 0 & 1 \\ 0 & 0 \end{bmatrix}, \qquad \mathbf{B} = \begin{bmatrix} 1 & 0 \\ 0 & 0 \end{bmatrix},$$

then $\mathbf{AB} \neq \mathbf{BA}$. Moreover, it is not true that $\mathbf{AB} = \mathbf{O}$ implies that either $\mathbf{A} = \mathbf{O}$ or $\mathbf{B} = \mathbf{O}$, as the same example of $\mathbf{A}$ and $\mathbf{B}$ shows. However, matrix multiplication is associative: $\mathbf{A}(\mathbf{BC}) = (\mathbf{AB})\mathbf{C}$, and the distributive laws hold: $\mathbf{A}(\mathbf{B} + \mathbf{C}) = \mathbf{AB} + \mathbf{AC}$ and $(\mathbf{A} + \mathbf{B})\mathbf{C} = \mathbf{AC} + \mathbf{BC}$. Strictly, in each case, what should be said is that, if $\mathbf{A}$, $\mathbf{B}$ and $\mathbf{C}$ are such that one side of the equation exists, so does the other side and the two sides are equal.

multiplicative group   A *group* in which the operation is called multiplication, usually denoted by ' . ' but with the product $a \cdot b$ normally written as ab, may be called a **multiplicative group**.

multiplicative inverse   See *inverse element*.

multiplicity   See *root*.

mutually disjoint   = *pairwise disjoint*.

mutually prime   = *relatively prime*.

N   See *natural number*.

Napierian logarithm   See *logarithm*.

natural logarithm   See *logarithm*.

natural number   A **natural number** is one of the numbers 1, 2, 3, …; some authors also include 0. The set of natural numbers is often denoted by **N**.

negation   If p is a statement, then the statement 'not p', denoted by $\neg p$, is the **negation** of p. It states, in some suitable wording, the opposite of p. For example, if p is 'It is raining', then $\neg p$ is 'It is not raining'; if p is '2 is not an integer', then $\neg p$ is 'It is not the case that 2 is not an integer' or, in other words, '2 is an integer'. If p is true then $\neg p$ is false, and vice versa. So the *truth table* of $\neg p$ is:

p	$\neg p$
T	F
F	T

negative   See *inverse element*.

negative direction   See *directed line*.

negative (of a matrix)   The **negative** of an $m \times n$ matrix **A**, where $\mathbf{A} = [a_{ij}]$, is the $m \times n$ matrix **C**, where $\mathbf{C} = [c_{ij}]$ and $c_{ij} = -a_{ij}$. It is denoted by $-\mathbf{A}$.

negative (of a vector)   Given a vector **a**, let $\overrightarrow{AB}$ be a *directed line-segment* representing **a**. The **negative** of **a**, denoted by $-\mathbf{a}$, is the vector represented by $\overrightarrow{BA}$. The following properties hold, for all **a**:

(i) $\mathbf{a} + (-\mathbf{a}) = (-\mathbf{a}) + \mathbf{a} = \mathbf{0}$, where **0** is the zero vector.
(ii) $-(-\mathbf{a}) = \mathbf{a}$.

neighbourhood   When considering the *real line*, a **neighbourhood** of the real number a is an open interval $(a - \delta, a + \delta)$, where $\delta > 0$, with its centre at a.

nested multiplication   A polynomial $f(x)$, such as $2x^3 - 7x^2 + 5x + 11$, can be evaluated for $x = h$ by calculating h^2 and h^3, multiplying by appropriate coefficients and summing the terms. But fewer operations are required if the polynomial is rewritten as $((2x - 7)x + 5)x + 11$, and then evaluated. This method, known as **nested multiplication**, is therefore more efficient and is recommended when evaluation is carried out by hand or by computer. A polynomial $a_5x^5 + a_4x^4 + a_3x^3 + a_2x^2 + a_1x + a_0$ of degree 5 would, for example, be rewritten in the form $((((a_5x+a_4)x+a_3)x+a_2)x+a_1)x+a_0$. The steps involved in this evaluation in fact correspond exactly to the calculations that are made in the process of *synthetic division*, in which the remainder gives $f(h)$.

network   A **network** is a *digraph* in which every arc is assigned a **weight** (some non-negative number). In some applications, something may be thought of as flowing or being transported between the vertices of a network, with the weight of each arc giving its 'capacity'. In some other cases, the vertices of a network may represent steps in a process and the weight of the arc joining u and v may give the time that must elapse between step u and step v.

neutral element   An element e is a **neutral element** for a *binary operation* $\circ$ on a set S if, for all a in S, $a \circ e = e \circ a = a$. If the operation is called multiplication, a neutral element is normally called an **identity element** and may be denoted by 1. If the operation is called addition, such an element is normally denoted by 0 and is often called a zero element. However, there is a case for preferring the term 'neutral element', as there is an alternative definition for the term 'zero element' (See *zero element*).

Newton, Isaac (1642–1727)   Born a farmer's son in Lincolnshire, Isaac Newton grew to dominate and revolutionize the mathematics and physics of the seventeenth century. To him we owe the essentials of the calculus, the theory of mechanics, the law of gravity, the theory of planetary motion, the theory of colours, the *binomial series* and many important results in the theory of equations. Numerical analysis would be crippled without *Newton's method*. Assertions about the relative merits of mathematicians of this calibre are always questionable, but since both Gauss and Einstein seem to have conceded top position to Newton we need not argue. A morbid dislike of criticism held Newton back from publishing much of his work. In 1684, Edmond Halley, of the comet, suggested to Newton that he investigate the law of attraction that would yield Kepler's laws of planetary motion. Newton replied immediately that it was the inverse square law — he had worked that out many years earlier. Rather startled by this, Halley set to work to persuade Newton to publish his results. This Newton eventually did in the form of his *Principia*, the single most powerful work in the long history of mathematics. Newton also worked fanatically on biblical chronology and on alchemy. He was a very effective Master of the Mint and carried through a major reform of Britain's currency. His tomb and monument are in Westminster Abbey: 'Buried like a king,' said Voltaire.

Newton quotient   The quotient $(f(a + h) - f(a))/h$ used to determine whether f is *differentiable* at a, and if so to find the *derivative*, may be called the **Newton quotient**.

Newton-Raphson method = *Newton's method*.

Newton's method **Newton's method** is used for finding successive approximations to a root of an equation $f(x) = 0$. Suppose that x_0 is a first approximation, known to be quite close to a root. If the root is in fact $x_0 + h$, where h is 'small', taking the first two terms of Taylor's series gives $f(x_0+h) \approx f(x_0)+hf'(x_0)$. Since $f(x_0+h) = 0$, this gives $h \approx -f(x_0)/f'(x_0)$. Thus x_1, given by

$$x_1 = x_0 - \frac{f(x_0)}{f'(x_0)},$$

is likely to be a better approximation to the root. To see the geometrical significance of the method, Suppose that P_0 is the point $(x_0, f(x_0))$ on the curve $y = f(x)$, as shown on the left below. The value x_1 is given by the point at which the tangent to the curve at P_0 meets the x-axis. It may be possible to repeat the process to get successive approximations x_0, x_1, x_2, ..., where

$$x_{n+1} = x_n - \frac{f(x_n)}{f'(x_n)}.$$

These may be successively better approximations to the root as required, but on the right below is shown the graph of a function, with a value x_0 close to a root, for which x_1 and x_2 do not give successively better approximations.

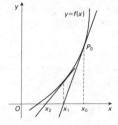

node See *graph* and *tree*.

non-homogeneous linear differential equation See *linear differential equation with constant coefficients.*

non-homogeneous set of linear equations A **non-homogeneous set of m linear equations** in n unknowns x_1, x_2, ..., x_n has the form

$$a_{11}x_1 + a_{12}x_2 + \ldots + a_{1n}x_n = b_1,$$
$$a_{21}x_1 + a_{22}x_2 + \ldots + a_{2n}x_n = b_2,$$
$$\ldots$$
$$a_{m1}x_1 + a_{m2}x_2 + \ldots + a_{mn}x_n = b_m,$$

where b_1, b_2, ..., b_m are not all zero. (Compare with *homogeneous set of linear equations*.) In matrix notation, this set of equations may be written as

$\mathbf{Ax} = \mathbf{b}$, where $\mathbf{A}$ is the $m \times n$ matrix $[a_{ij}]$ and $\mathbf{b}$ ($\neq \mathbf{0}$) and $\mathbf{x}$ are column matrices:

$$\mathbf{b} = \begin{bmatrix} b_1 \\ b_2 \\ \vdots \\ b_m \end{bmatrix}, \qquad \mathbf{x} = \begin{bmatrix} x_1 \\ x_2 \\ \vdots \\ x_m \end{bmatrix}.$$

Such a set of equations may be inconsistent, have a unique solution, or have infinitely many solutions (see *simultaneous linear equations*). For a set consisting of the same number of linear equations as unknowns, the matrix of coefficients $\mathbf{A}$ is a square matrix, and the set of equations has a unique solution, namely $\mathbf{x} = \mathbf{A}^{-1}\mathbf{b}$, if and only if $\mathbf{A}$ is invertible.

non-singular   A square matrix $\mathbf{A}$ is **non-singular** if it is not *singular*; that is, if $\det \mathbf{A} \neq 0$, where $\det \mathbf{A}$ is the determinant of $\mathbf{A}$. See also *inverse matrix*.

norm   See *partition* (of an interval).

normal (to a curve)   Suppose that P is a point on a curve in the plane. Then the **normal** at P is the line through P perpendicular to the tangent at P.

normal (to a plane)   A **normal** to a plane is a line perpendicular to that plane. A normal is perpendicular to any line that lies in the plane.

normal (to a surface)   See *tangent plane*.

normal vector   A **normal vector** to a plane is a vector whose direction is perpendicular to that plane. A normal vector is perpendicular to any vector whose direction lies in the plane.

n-th derivative   See *higher derivative*.

n-th-order partial derivative   See *higher-order partial derivative*.

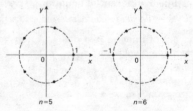

n-th root of unity   An **n-th root of unity** is a complex number z such that $z^n = 1$. The n distinct n-th roots of unity are $e^{i2k\pi/n}$ ($k = 0, 1, \ldots, n-1$), or

$$\cos \frac{2k\pi}{n} + i \sin \frac{2k\pi}{n} \quad (k = 0, 1, \ldots, n-1).$$

They are represented in the *complex plane* by points that lie on the unit circle and are vertices of a regular n-sided polygon. The n-th roots of unity for $n = 5$ and $n = 6$ are shown in the figure. The n-th roots of unity always include the real number 1 and also include the real number -1 if n is even. The non-real n-th roots of unity form pairs of *conjugates*. See also *cube root of unity* and *fourth root of unity*.

n-tuple   An **n-tuple** consists of n objects normally taken in a particular order, denoted, for example, by $(x_1, x_2, \ldots, x_n)$. The notion is a generalization of triple (x_1, x_2, x_3) and quadruple (x_1, x_2, x_3, x_4).

nullity   The **nullity** of a matrix $\mathbf{A}$ is a number relating to the set of solutions of $\mathbf{Ax} = \mathbf{0}$, the corresponding *homogeneous set of linear equations*: it can be defined as the number of *parameters* required when the solutions of the equations are expressed in terms of parameters. In other words, it is the number of unknowns that are free to take arbitrary values. A way of obtaining the solutions in terms of parameters is by transforming the matrix to one in *reduced echelon form*. There is an important connection between the nullity and the *rank* of a matrix: for an $m \times n$ matrix $\mathbf{A}$, the nullity of $\mathbf{A}$ equals n minus the rank of $\mathbf{A}$.

null matrix   = *zero matrix*.

null sequence   A **null sequence** is a sequence whose limit is 0.

null set   = *empty set*.

number line   = *real line*.

numerical analysis   Many mathematical problems, to which answers are required in practical situations, cannot be solved in all generality. The only way may be to use a numerical method; that is, to consider the problem in such a way that, from given data, a solution, or an approximation to one, is obtained essentially by numerical calculations. The subject that derives and analyses such methods is called **numerical analysis**.

numerical integration   The methods of **numerical integration** are used to find approximate values for *definite integrals* and are useful for the following reasons. It may be that there is no analytical method of finding an *antiderivative* of the *integrand*. Possibly, such a method may exist but be very complicated. In another case, the integrand may not be known explicitly; it might be that only its values at certain points within the interval of integration are known. Among the elementary methods of numerical integration are the *trapezium rule* and *Simpson's rule*.

numerical value   = *absolute value*.

O

objective function   See *linear programming*.

oblique   A pair of intersecting lines, to be taken, for example, as coordinate axes, are **oblique** if they are not (or at least not necessarily) perpendicular. Three concurrent lines, similarly, are oblique if they are not mutually perpendicular.

obtuse angle   An angle is **obtuse** if it is greater than a *right angle* and less than two right angles. An **obtuse-angled** triangle is one in which one angle is obtuse.

octagon   An **octagon** is an eight-sided polygon.

octahedron (plural: octahedra)   See *polyhedron*.

octant   In a Cartesian coordinate system in 3-dimensional space, the axial planes divide the rest of the space into eight regions called **octants**. The set of points $\{(x, y, z) \mid x > 0, y > 0, z > 0\}$ may be called the **positive**, or possibly the **first**, **octant**.

odd function   The *real function* f is an **odd function** if $f(-x) = -f(x)$ for all x (in the domain of f). Thus the graph $y = f(x)$ of an odd function is symmetrical about the origin; that is, it has a half-turn symmetry about the origin, because whenever (x, y) lies on the graph so does $(-x, -y)$. For example, f is an odd function when $f(x)$ is defined as any of the following: $2x$, x^3, $x^7 - 8x^3 + 5x$, $1/(x^3 - x)$, $\sin x$, $\tan x$.

one-to-one correspondence   A **one-to-one correspondence** is a *one-to-one mapping* between two sets that is also *onto*. Thus each element of the first set is made to correspond with exactly one element of the second set, and vice versa. Such a correspondence is also called a *bijection*.

one-to-one mapping   A *mapping* $f: S \to T$ is **one-to-one** if, whenever s_1 and s_2 are distinct elements of S, their images $f(s_1)$ and $f(s_2)$ are distinct elements of T. So f is one-to-one if $f(s_1) = f(s_2)$ implies $s_1 = s_2$.

only if   See *condition, necessary and sufficient*.

onto mapping   A *mapping* $f: S \to T$ is **onto** if every element of the codomain T is the image under f of at least one element of the domain S. So f is onto if the image (or range) $f(S)$ is the whole of T.

open disc　　See *disc*.

open half-plane　　See *half-plane*.

open interval　　The **open interval** (a, b) is the set

$$\{ x \mid x \in \mathbf{R} \text{ and } a < x < b \}.$$

For **open interval determined by** I, see *interval*.

operation　　An **operation** on a set S is a rule that associates with some number of elements of S a resulting element. If this resulting element is always also in S then S is said to be **closed under** the operation. An operation that associates with one element of S a resulting element is called a *unary operation*; and one that associates with two elements of S a resulting element is a *binary operation*.

ordered pair　　An **ordered pair** consists of two objects considered in a particular order. Thus, if $a \neq b$, the ordered pair (a, b) is not the same as the ordered pair (b, a). See *Cartesian product*.

order (of a differential equation)　　See *differential equation*.

order (of a group)　　The **order** of a *group* G is the number of elements in G.

order (of a matrix)　　An $m \times n$ matrix is said to have **order** $m \times n$ (read as 'm by n'). An $n \times n$ matrix may be called a square matrix of order n.

order (of a partial derivative)　　See *higher-order partial derivative*.

order (of a root)　　See *root*.

ordinary differential equation　　See *differential equation*.

ordinate　　The **ordinate** is the y-coordinate in a Cartesian coordinate system in the plane.

origin　　See *coordinates* (on a line), *coordinates* (in the plane) and *coordinates* (in 3-dimensional space).

orthocentre　　The **orthocentre** of a triangle is the point at which the *altitudes* are concurrent. The orthocentre lies on the *Euler line* of the triangle.

orthogonal curves　　Two curves, or straight lines, are **orthogonal** if they intersect at right angles.

orthogonal matrix　　A square matrix $\mathbf{A}$ is **orthogonal** if $\mathbf{A}^T \mathbf{A} = \mathbf{I}$, where $\mathbf{A}^T$ is the *transpose* of $\mathbf{A}$. The following properties hold:

(i) If $\mathbf{A}$ is orthogonal, $\mathbf{A}^{-1} = \mathbf{A}^T$ and so $\mathbf{A}\mathbf{A}^T = \mathbf{I}$.
(ii) If $\mathbf{A}$ is orthogonal, $\det \mathbf{A} = \pm 1$.

(iii) If **A** and **B** are orthogonal matrices of the same order, then **AB** is orthogonal.

orthogonal vectors   Two non-zero vectors are **orthogonal** if their directions are perpendicular. Thus non-zero vectors **a** and **b** are orthogonal if and only if $\mathbf{a} \cdot \mathbf{b} = 0$.

orthonormal   An **orthonormal** set of vectors is a set of mutually orthogonal unit vectors. In 3-dimensional space, three mutually orthogonal unit vectors form an orthonormal basis. The standard orthonormal basis in a Cartesian coordinate system consists of the unit vectors **i**, **j** and **k** along the three coordinate axes.

oscillate finitely and **infinitely**   See *limit* (of a sequence).

P

pairwise disjoint   Sets $A_1, A_2, \ldots, A_n$ are said to be **pairwise disjoint** if $A_i \cap A_j = \emptyset$ for all i and j, with $i \neq j$. The term can also be applied to an infinite collection of sets.

parabola   A **parabola** is a *conic* with eccentricity equal to 1. Thus it is the locus of all points P such that the distance from P to a fixed point F (the **focus**) is equal to the distance from P to a fixed line l (the **directrix**). It is obtained as a plane section of a cone in the case when the plane is parallel to a generator of the cone (see *conic*). A line through the focus perpendicular to the directrix is the **axis** of the parabola, and the point where the axis cuts the parabola is the **vertex**. It is possible to take the vertex as origin, the axis of the parabola as the x-axis, the tangent at the vertex as the y-axis and the focus as the point $(a, 0)$. In this coordinate system, the directrix has equation $x = -a$ and the parabola has equation $y^2 = 4ax$. When investigating the properties of a parabola, it is normal to choose this convenient coordinate system.

Different values of a give parabolas of different sizes, but all parabolas are the same shape. For any value of t, the point $(at^2, 2at)$ satisfies $y^2 = 4ax$, and conversely any point of the parabola has coordinates $(at^2, 2at)$ for some value of t. Thus $x = at^2, y = 2at$ may be taken as *parametric equations* for the parabola $y^2 = 4ax$.

One important property of a parabola is this. For a point P on the parabola, let α be the angle between the tangent at P and a line through P

parallel to the axis of the parabola, and let β be the angle between the tangent at P and a line through P and the focus, as shown in the figure; then $\alpha = \beta$. This is the basis of the parabolic reflector: if a source of light is placed at the focus of a parabolic reflector, each ray of light is reflected parallel to the axis, so producing a parallel beam of light.

parabolic cylinder   A **parabolic cylinder** is a *cylinder* in which the fixed curve is a *parabola* and the fixed line to which the generators are parallel is perpendicular to the plane of the parabola. It is a *quadric* and in a suitable coordinate system has equation

$$\frac{x^2}{a^2} = \frac{2y}{b}.$$

paraboloid   See *elliptic paraboloid* and *hyperbolic paraboloid*.

parallelepiped   A **parallelepiped** (a word commonly misspelt) is a *polyhedron* with six faces, each of which is a parallelogram.

parallelogram   A **parallelogram** is a quadrilateral in which (i) both pairs of opposite sides are parallel, and (ii) the lengths of opposite sides are equal. Either property, (i) or (ii), in fact implies the other. The area of a parallelogram equals 'base times height'. That is to say, if one pair of parallel sides, of length b, are a distance h apart, the area equals bh. Alternatively, if the other pair of sides have length a and θ is the angle between adjacent sides, the area equals $ab \sin \theta$.

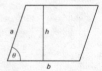

parallelogram law   See *addition* (of vectors).

parameter   A **parameter** is a variable that is to take different values, thereby giving different values to certain other variables. For example, a parameter t could be used to write the solutions of the equation $5x_1 + 4x_2 = 7$ as $x_1 = 3 - 4t$, $x_2 = -2 + 5t$ ($t \in \mathbf{R}$). See also *parametric equations* (of a line in space) and *parametrization*.

parametric equations (of a curve)   See *parametrization*.

parametric equations (of a line in space)   Given a line in 3-dimensional space, let (x_1, y_1, z_1) be coordinates of a point on the line and l, m, n be *direction ratios* of a direction along the line. Then the line consists of all points P whose coordinates (x, y, z) are given by

$$x = x_1 + tl, \quad y = y_1 + tm, \quad z = z_1 + tn,$$

for some value of the *parameter t*. These are **parametric equations** for the line. They are most easily established by using the *vector equation* of the line and taking components. If none of l, m, n is zero, the equations can be written

$$\frac{x - x_1}{l} = \frac{y - y_1}{m} = \frac{z - z_1}{n} \quad (= t),$$

which can be considered another form of the parametric equations, or called the equations of the line in 'symmetric form'. If, say, $n = 0$ and l and m are both non-zero, the equations are written

$$\frac{x - x_1}{l} = \frac{y - y_1}{m}, \quad z = z_1.$$

If, say, $m = n = 0$, they become $y = y_1$, $z = z_1$.

parametrization (of a curve)   A **parametrization** of a curve is a method of associating, with every value of a *parameter t* in some interval I (or some other subset of $\mathbf{R}$), a point $P(t)$ on the curve, such that every point of the curve corresponds to some value of t. Often this is done by giving the x- and y-coordinates of P as functions of t, so that the coordinates of P may be written as $(x(t), y(t))$. The equations that give x and y as functions of t are **parametric equations** for the curve. For example, $x = at^2$, $y = 2at$ ($t \in \mathbf{R}$) are parametric equations for the parabola $y^2 = 4ax$; and $x = a\cos\theta$, $y = b\sin\theta$ ($\theta \in [0, 2\pi)$) are parametric equations for the ellipse

$$\frac{x^2}{a^2} + \frac{y^2}{b^2} = 1.$$

The gradient dy/dx of the curve at any point can be found, if $x'(t) \neq 0$, from $dy/dx = y'(t)/x'(t)$.

parity   The **parity** of an integer is its attribute of being even or odd. Thus, it can be said that 6 and 14 have the same parity (both are even), whereas 7 and 12 have opposite parity.

partial derivative   Suppose that f is a real function of n variables x_1, x_2, ..., x_n, so that its value at a typical point is $f(x_1, \ldots, x_n)$. If

$$\frac{f(x_1 + h, x_2, \ldots, x_n) - f(x_1, x_2, \ldots, x_n)}{h}$$

tends to a limit as $h \to 0$, this limit is the **partial derivative** of f, at the point $(x_1, \ldots, x_n)$, with respect to x_1; it is denoted by $f_1(x_1, \ldots, x_n)$ or $\partial f/\partial x_1$ (read as 'partial df by dx_1'). For a particular function, this partial derivative may be found using the normal rules of differentiation, by differentiating as though the function were a function of x_1 only and treating x_2, ..., x_n as constants. The other partial derivatives,

$$\frac{\partial f}{\partial x_2}, \ldots, \frac{\partial f}{\partial x_n},$$

are defined similarly. The partial derivatives may also be denoted by f_{x_1}, f_{x_2}, ..., f_{x_n}. For example, if $f(x, y) = xy^3$, then the partial derivatives are $\partial f / \partial x$, or f_x, and $\partial f / \partial y$, or f_y; and $f_x = y^3$, $f_y = 3xy^2$. With the value of f at (x, y) denoted by $f(x, y)$, the notation f_1 and f_2 is also used for the partial derivatives f_x and f_y, and this can be extended to functions of more variables. See also *higher-order partial derivative*.

partial differential equation   See *differential equation*.

partial differentiation   **Partial differentiation** is the process of obtaining one of the *partial derivatives* of a function of more than one variable. The partial derivative $\partial f / \partial x_i$ is said to be obtained from f by 'differentiating partially with respect to x_i'.

partial fractions   Suppose that $f(x)/g(x)$ defines a *rational function*, so that $f(x)$ and $g(x)$ are polynomials, and suppose that the degree of $f(x)$ is less than the degree of $g(x)$. In general, $g(x)$ can be factorized into a product of some different linear factors, each to some index, and some different irreducible quadratic factors, each to some index. Then the original expression $f(x)/g(x)$ can be written as a sum of terms: corresponding to each $(x - \alpha)^n$ in $g(x)$, there are terms

$$\frac{A_1}{x - \alpha} + \frac{A_2}{(x - \alpha)^2} + \cdots + \frac{A_n}{(x - \alpha)^n},$$

and corresponding to each $(ax^2 + bx + c)^n$ in $g(x)$, there are terms

$$\frac{B_1 x + C_1}{ax^2 + bx + c} + \frac{B_2 x + C_2}{(ax^2 + bx + c)^2} + \cdots + \frac{B_n x + C_n}{(ax^2 + bx + c)^n},$$

where the real numbers denoted here by capital letters are uniquely determined. The expression $f(x)/g(x)$ is said to have been written in **partial fractions**. The method, which sounds complicated when stated in general, as above, is more easily understood from examples:

$$\frac{3}{(x - 1)(x + 2)} = \frac{A}{x - 1} + \frac{B}{x + 2},$$

$$\frac{3x^2 + 2x + 1}{(x - 1)^3} = \frac{A}{x - 1} + \frac{B}{(x - 1)^2} + \frac{C}{(x - 1)^3},$$

$$\frac{3x + 2}{(x - 1)(x^2 + x + 1)^2} = \frac{A}{x - 1} + \frac{Bx + C}{x^2 + x + 1} + \frac{Dx + E}{(x^2 + x + 1)^2},$$

$$\frac{3x + 2}{(x - 1)^2(x^2 + x + 1)} = \frac{A}{x - 1} + \frac{B}{(x - 1)^2} + \frac{Cx + D}{x^2 + x + 1}.$$

The values for the numbers A, B, C, ... are found by first multiplying both sides of the equation by the denominator $g(x)$. In the last example, this gives

$$3x + 2 = A(x - 1)(x^2 + x + 1) + B(x^2 + x + 1) + (Cx + D)(x - 1)^2.$$

This has to hold for all values of x, so the coefficients of corresponding powers of x on the two sides can be equated, and this determines the unknowns.

In some cases, setting x equal to particular values (in this example, $x = 1$) may determine some of the unknowns more quickly. The method of partial fractions is used in the integration of rational functions.

partial product   When an infinite product

$$\prod_{r=1}^{\infty} a_r$$

is formed from a sequence $a_1, a_2, a_3, \ldots$, the product $a_1 a_2 \ldots a_n$ of the first n terms is called the n-th **partial product**.

partial sum   The n-th **partial sum** s_n of a series $a_1 + a_2 + \cdots$ is the sum of the first n terms; thus $s_n = a_1 + a_2 + \cdots + a_n$.

particle   A **particle** is a small object considered as having mass but idealized as having no size.

particular integral   See *linear differential equation with constant coefficients*.

particular solution   See *differential equation*.

partition (of an interval)   Let $[a, b]$ be a closed interval. A set of $n+1$ points $x_0, x_1, \ldots, x_n$ such that

$$a = x_0 < x_1 < x_2 < \cdots < x_{n-1} < x_n = b$$

is a **partition** of the interval $[a, b]$. A partition divides the interval into n subintervals $[x_i, x_{i+1}]$. The **norm** of the partition P is equal to the length of the largest subinterval and is denoted by $\|P\|$. Such partitions are used in defining the Riemann integral of a function over $[a, b]$ (see *integral*).

partition (of a set)   A **partition** of a set S is a collection of non-empty subsets of S such that every element of S belongs to exactly one of the subsets in the collection. Thus S is the union of these subsets and any two distinct subsets are disjoint. Given a partition of a set S, an *equivalence relation* $\sim$ on S can be obtained by defining $a \sim b$ if a and b belong to the same subset in the partition. It is an important fact that, conversely, from any equivalence relation on S a partition of S can be obtained.

Pascal, Blaise (1623–1662)   Pascal is known to the world at large as the author of the *Pensées* and as a religious thinker. However, he was just as active as a mathematician and physicist. He did important work in hydrostatics (hence the unit of pressure called the pascal), and his discussions with Fermat about the de Méré problem initiated the theory of probability. *Pascal's triangle*, the diagram for binomial coefficients, was not original to him but he did use it in his probability calculations. He also joined in the work on finding the areas of curved figures, work which was soon to lead to the calculus.

Pascal's main contribution was to find the area of a cycloidal arch; this he did to take his mind off the pain of a toothache. Students of geometry may know of Pascal's 'Mystic Hexagram'.

Pascal's triangle   Below are shown the first seven rows of the arrangement of numbers known as **Pascal's triangle**. In general, the n-th row consists of the *binomial coefficients* $\binom{n}{r}$, or ^nC_r, with $r = 0, 1, \ldots, n$. With the numbers set out in this fashion, it can be seen how the number $\binom{n+1}{r}$ is equal to the sum of the two numbers $\binom{n}{r-1}$ and $\binom{n}{r}$, which are situated above it to the left and right. For example, $\binom{7}{3}$ equals 21, and is the sum of $\binom{6}{2}$, which equals 6, and $\binom{6}{3}$, which equals 15.

$$
\begin{array}{ccccccccccccc}
 & & & & & 1 & & 1 & & & & & \\
 & & & & 1 & & 2 & & 1 & & & & \\
 & & & 1 & & 3 & & 3 & & 1 & & & \\
 & & 1 & & 4 & & 6 & & 4 & & 1 & & \\
 & 1 & & 5 & & 10 & & 10 & & 5 & & 1 & \\
1 & & 6 & & 15 & & 20 & & 15 & & 6 & & 1 \\
\end{array}
$$

$$1 \quad 7 \quad 21 \quad 35 \quad 35 \quad 21 \quad 7 \quad 1$$

path (in a graph)   Let u and v be vertices in a *graph*. A path from u to v is traced out by travelling from u to v along edges. In a precise definition, it is normal to insist that, in a path, no edge is used more than once and no vertex is visited more than once. Thus a **path** is defined as a sequence v_0, e_1, v_1, $\ldots$, e_k, v_k of alternately vertices and edges (where e_i is an edge joining v_{i-1} and v_i), with all the edges different and all the vertices different; this is a path from v_0 to v_k.

Peano, Guiseppe (1858–1932)   Peano is known for his axiomatization of the integers which was an important development in the formal analysis of 'ordinary' arithmetic. He was also the first person to produce examples of so-called space-filling curves.

pentagon   A **pentagon** is a five-sided polygon.

pentagram   A **pentagram** is the plane figure shown above, formed by joining alternate points situated at the vertices of a regular *pentagon*.

percentage error   The **percentage error** is the *relative* error expressed as a percentage. When 1·9 is used as an approximation for 1·875, the relative error equals $0·025/1·875$ (or $0·025/1·9) = 0·013$, to 2 significant figures. So the percentage error is 1·3%, to 2 significant figures.

perfect number   An integer is called a **perfect number** if it is equal to the sum of its positive divisors (not including itself). Thus, 6 is a perfect number, since its positive divisors (not including itself) are 1, 2 and 3, and $1+2+3 = 6$; so too are 28 and 496, for example. At present, there are 24 known perfect numbers, all even. If $2^p - 1$ is prime (so that it is a *Mersenne prime*), then $2^{p-1}(2^p - 1)$ is perfect; moreover, these are the only even perfect numbers. It is not known if there are any odd perfect numbers; none has been found, but it has not been proved that one cannot exist.

perimeter   The **perimeter** of a plane figure is the length of its boundary. Thus, the perimeter of a rectangle of length L and width W is $2L + 2W$. The perimeter of a circle is the length of its circumference.

period, periodic   If, for some value p, $f(x + p) = f(x)$ for all x, the real function f is **periodic** and has **period** p. For example, $\cos x$ is periodic with period 2π, since $\cos(x + 2\pi) = \cos x$ for all x; or, using degrees, $\cos x°$ is periodic with period 360, since $\cos(x + 360)° = \cos x°$ for all x. Some authors restrict the term 'period' to being the smallest positive value of p with this property.

period (of oscillation)   Suppose that $x = A\sin(\omega t + \alpha)$, where A (> 0), ω and α are constants. This may, for example, give the displacement x of a particle, moving in a straight line, at time t. The particle is thus oscillating about the origin. The **period** is the time taken for one complete oscillation and is equal to $2\pi/\omega$.

permutation   At an elementary level, a **permutation** of n objects can be thought of as an arrangement or a re-arrangement of the n objects. The number of permutations of n objects is equal to $n!$. The number of 'permutations of n objects taken r at a time' is denoted by ^nP_r and equals $n(n-1)\ldots(n-r+1)$, which equals $n!/(n - r)!$. For example, there are 12 permutations of A, B, C, D taken two at a time: AB, AC, AD, BA, BC, BD, CA, CB, CD, DA, DB, DC. Suppose that n objects are of k different kinds, with r_1 alike of one kind, r_2 alike of a second kind, and so on. Then the number of distinct permutations of the n objects equals

$$\frac{n!}{r_1!r_2!\ldots r_k!},$$

where $r_1 + r_2 + \cdots + r_k = n$. For example, the number of different anagrams of the word '*CHEESES*' is $7!/3!2!$, which equals 420. At a more advanced level, a **permutation** of a set X is defined as a *one-to-one onto mapping* from X to X.

perpendicular lines   In coordinate geometry of the plane, a useful necessary and sufficient condition that two lines, with gradients m_1 and m_2, are **perpendicular** is that $m_1 m_2 = -1$. (This is taken to include the cases when $m_1 = 0$ and m_2 is infinite, and vice versa.)

perpendicular planes   Two planes in 3-dimensional space are **perpendicular** if *normals* to the two planes are perpendicular. If $\mathbf{n}_1$ and $\mathbf{n}_2$ are vectors normal to the planes, this is so if $\mathbf{n}_1 \cdot \mathbf{n}_2 = 0$.

phase   Suppose that $x = A\sin(\omega t + \alpha)$, where A (> 0), ω and α are constants. This may, for example, give the displacement x of a particle, moving in a straight line, at time t. The particle is thus oscillating about the origin. The constant α is the **phase**. Two particles oscillating like this with the same *amplitude* and *period* (of oscillation) but with different phases are executing the same motion apart from a shift in time.

pi   For circles of all sizes, the length of the circumference divided by the length of the diameter is the same, and this number is the value of π. It is equal to $3\cdot14159265$ to 8 decimal places. Sometimes π is taken to be equal to $\frac{22}{7}$, but it must be emphasized that this is only an approximation. The decimal expansion of π is neither finite nor recurring, for it was shown in 1761 by Lambert, using continued fractions, that π is *irrational*. In 1882, Lindemann proved that π is *transcendental*. The number appears in some contexts that seem to have no connection with the definition relating to a circle:

$$\frac{\pi}{4} = 1 - \frac{1}{3} + \frac{1}{5} - \frac{1}{7} + \cdots, \qquad \frac{\pi^2}{6} = 1 + \frac{1}{2^2} + \frac{1}{3^2} + \frac{1}{4^2} + \cdots,$$

$$\frac{\pi}{2} = \frac{2}{1} \cdot \frac{2}{3} \cdot \frac{4}{3} \cdot \frac{4}{5} \cdot \frac{6}{5} \cdot \frac{6}{7} \cdot \frac{8}{7} \cdot \frac{8}{9} \cdots = \prod_{n=1}^{\infty} \frac{4n^2}{4n^2 - 1} \quad \textbf{(Wallis's Product)}.$$

Pigeonhole Principle   The following observation is known as the **Pigeonhole Principle**: If m objects are distributed into n boxes, with $m > n$, then at least one box receives at least two objects. This can be applied in some obvious ways; for example, if you take any 13 people, then at least two of them have birthdays that fall in the same month. It also has less trivial applications.

pivot, pivot operation   Each step in *Gaussian* or *Gauss-Jordan elimination* consists of making one of the entries a_{ij} of the matrix equal to 1 and using this to produce zeros elsewhere in the j-th column. This process is known as a **pivot operation**, with a_{ij} as **pivot**. The pivot, of course, must be non-zero. This corresponds to solving one of the equations for one of the unknowns x_j and substituting this into the other equations.

planar graph   A *graph* is **planar** if it can be drawn in such a way that no two edges cross. The *complete graph* K_4 is planar, for example, as either

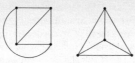

drawing of it in the figure shows. The complete graph K_5 and the complete bipartite graph $K_{3,3}$, for example, are not planar.

plane (in Cartesian coordinates)   A **plane** is represented by a linear equation, in other words, by an equation of the form $ax + by + cz + d = 0$, where the constants a, b and c are not all zero. Here a, b and c are *direction ratios* of a direction *normal* to the plane. See also *vector equation of a plane*.

Platonic solid   See *polyhedron*.

Poincaré, Henri (1854–1912)   As Hardy said, mathematical fame, once earned, is long-lasting. Raymond Poincaré, President of France, was Henri's cousin and not vice versa. Poincaré is commonly regarded as the last mathematician to be active over the entire field of mathematics. He moved from one area of mathematics to another, making major contributions to most of them — a conqueror rather than a colonist. Within pure mathematics, Poincaré is seen as one of the main founders of topology and the discoverer of automorphic functions. In applied mathematics, he is remembered for his theoretical work on the qualitative aspects of celestial mechanics, which was probably the most important work in that area since Laplace and Lagrange. Connecting and motivating both was his qualitative theory of differential equations. Not the least of Poincaré's achievements was a stream of books, popular in both senses, on mathematics and science. These books are still most strongly recommended to any aspiring young mathematician or scientist.

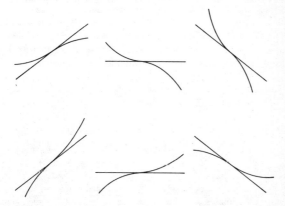

point of inflexion   A **point of inflexion** is a point on a graph $y = f(x)$ at which the *concavity* changes. Thus, there is a point of inflexion at a if, for some $\delta > 0$, $f''(x)$ exists and is positive in the open interval $(a - \delta, a)$ and $f''(x)$ exists and is negative in the open interval $(a, a + \delta)$, or vice versa.

If the change (as x increases) is from concave up to concave down, the graph and its tangent at the point of inflexion look like one of the cases shown in the first row of the figure. If the change is from concave down to concave up, the graph and its tangent look like one of the cases shown in the second row. The middle diagram in each row shows a point of inflexion that is also a *stationary point*, since the tangent is horizontal.

If f'' is continuous at a, then, for $y = f(x)$ to have a point of inflexion at a, it is necessary that $f''(a) = 0$, and so this is the usual method of finding possible points of inflexion. However, the condition $f''(a) = 0$ is not sufficient to ensure that there is a point of inflexion at a; it is necessary to show that $f''(x)$ is positive to one side of a and negative to the other side. Thus if $f(x) = x^4$ then $f''(0) = 0$; but $y = x^4$ does not have a point of inflexion at 0 since $f''(x)$ is positive to both sides of 0. Finally, there may be a point of inflexion at a point where $f''(x)$ does not exist, for example at the origin on the curve $y = x^{1/3}$.

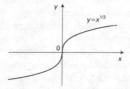

polar coordinates　　Suppose that a point O in the plane is chosen as origin, and let Ox be a directed line through O, with a given unit of length. For any point P in the plane, let $r = |OP|$ and let θ be the angle (in radians) that OP makes with Ox, the angle being given a positive sense anti-clockwise from Ox. The angle θ satisfies $0 \le \theta < 2\pi$. Then (r, θ) are the **polar coordinates** of P. (The point O gives no corresponding value for θ, but is simply said to correspond to $r = 0$.) If P has polar coordinates (r, θ), then $(r, \theta + 2k\pi)$, where k is an integer, may also be permitted as polar coordinates of P.

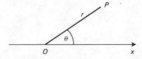

Suppose that Cartesian coordinates are taken with the same origin and the same unit of length, with positive x-axis along the directed line Ox. Then the Cartesian coordinates (x, y) of a point P can be found from (r, θ), by $x = r\cos\theta$, $y = r\sin\theta$. Conversely, the polar coordinates can be found from the Cartesian coordinates as follows: $r = \sqrt{x^2 + y^2}$, and θ is such that

$$\cos\theta = \frac{x}{\sqrt{x^2 + y^2}}, \quad \sin\theta = \frac{y}{\sqrt{x^2 + y^2}}.$$

(It is true that, when $x \neq 0$, $\theta = \tan^{-1}(y/x)$, but this is not sufficient to determine θ.) In certain circumstances, authors may allow r to be negative, in which case the polar coordinates $(-r, \theta)$ give the same point as $(r, \theta + \pi)$.

polar equation   An equation of a curve in *polar coordinates* is usually written in the form $r = f(\theta)$. **Polar equations** of some common curves are given in the following table:

Curve		Polar equation	
circle	$x^2 + y^2 = 1$	$r = 1$	
half-line	$y = x, \ x > 0$	$\theta = \pi/4$	
line	$x = 1$	$r = \sec \theta$	$(-\tfrac{1}{2}\pi < \theta < \tfrac{1}{2}\pi)$
line	$y = 1$	$r = \operatorname{cosec} \theta$	$(0 < \theta < \pi)$
circle	$x^2 + y^2 - 2ax = 0 \ (a > 0)$	$r = 2a \cos \theta$	$(-\tfrac{1}{2}\pi < \theta \leq \tfrac{1}{2}\pi)$
circle	$x^2 + y^2 - 2by = 0 \ (b > 0)$	$r = 2b \sin \theta$	$(0 \leq \theta < \pi)$
cardioid	See *cardioid*	$r = 2a(1 + \cos \theta)$	$(-\pi < \theta \leq \pi)$
conic	See *conic*	$l/r = 1 + e \cos \theta$	$(\cos \theta \neq -1/e)$

polar form of a complex number   For a complex number z, let $r = |z|$ and $\theta = \arg z$. Then $z = r(\cos \theta + i \sin \theta)$, and this is the **polar form** of z. It may also be written $z = re^{i\theta}$.

polygon   A **polygon** is a plane figure bounded by some number of straight sides. This definition would include polygons like the one shown on the left below, but often figures of this sort are intended to be excluded and it is implicitly assumed that a polygon is to be *convex*. Thus a (convex) polygon is a plane figure consisting of a finite region bounded by some finite number of straight lines, in the sense that the region lies entirely on one side of each line. The **exterior angles** of the polygon shown on the right below are those marked, and the sum of the exterior angles is always equal to 360°. The sum of the interior angles of an n-sided (convex) polygon equals $2n - 4$ right angles. In a regular (convex) polygon, all the sides have equal length and the interior angles have equal size; and the vertices lie on a circle.

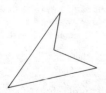
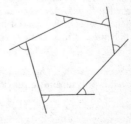

polyhedron (plural: polyhedra)   A **polyhedron** is a solid figure bounded by some number of plane polygonal faces. This definition would include the one shown on the left below and it may well be that figures such as this are to be excluded from consideration. So it is often assumed that a polyhedron is *convex*. Thus a (convex) polyhedron is a finite region bounded by some number of planes, in the sense that the region lies entirely on one side of each plane. Each edge of the polyhedron joins two vertices and each edge is the common edge of two faces. A (convex) polyhedron is regular if all its faces are alike and all its vertices are alike. More precisely, this means that (i) all the faces are regular polygons and have the same number p of edges, and (ii) the same number q of edges meet at each vertex. (Notice that the polyhedron shown on the right below, with 6 triangular faces, satisfies (i) but is not regular because it does not satisfy (ii).)

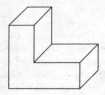

There are five regular convex polyhedra, known as the **Platonic solids**:

(i) the regular *tetrahedron*, with 4 triangular faces ($p = 3$, $q = 3$),

(ii) the *cube*, with 6 square faces ($p = 4$, $q = 3$),

(iii) the regular **octahedron**, with 8 triangular faces ($p = 3$, $q = 4$),

(iv) the regular **dodecahedron**, with 12 five-sided faces ($p = 5$, $q = 3$),

(v) the regular **icosahedron**, with 20 triangular faces ($p = 3$, $q = 5$).

polynomial   Let $a_0, a_1, \ldots, a_n$ be real numbers. Then

$$a_n x^n + a_{n-1} x^{n-1} + \cdots + a_1 x + a_0$$

is a **polynomial** in x (with real coefficients). When $a_0, a_1, \ldots, a_n$ are not all zero, it can be assumed that $a_n \neq 0$ and the polynomial has **degree** n. For example, $x^2 - \sqrt{2}x + 5$ and $3x^4 + \frac{7}{2}x^2 - x$ are polynomials of degrees 2 and 4 respectively. The number a_r is the **coefficient** of x^r (for $r = 1, 2, \ldots, n$) and a_0 is the **constant term**. A polynomial can be denoted by $f(x)$ (so that f is a *polynomial function*), and then $f(-1)$, for example, denotes the value of the polynomial when x is replaced by -1. In the same way, it is possible to consider polynomials in x, or more commonly in z, with complex coefficients, such as $z^2 + 2(1-i)z + (15 + 6i)$, and the same terminology is used.

polynomial equation   An equation $f(x) = 0$, where $f(x)$ is a polynomial, can be called a **polynomial equation**.

polynomial function   In real analysis, a **polynomial function** is a function f defined by a formula $f(x) = a_n x^n + a_{n-1} x^{n-1} + \cdots + a_1 x + a_0$ for all x in **R**, where $a_0, a_1, \ldots, a_n$ are real numbers. See also *polynomial*; terminology applying to a polynomial is also used to apply to the corresponding polynomial function.

position ratio   If A and B are two given points and P is a point on the line through A and B, the ratio $AP : PB$ may be called the **position ratio** of P.

position vector   Suppose that a point O is chosen as origin (in the plane, or in 3-dimensional space). Given any point P, the **position vector p** of the point P is the *vector* represented by the directed line-segment $\overrightarrow{OP}$. Authors who call $\overrightarrow{OP}$ a vector call this the position vector of P.

positive direction   See *directed line*.

post-multiplication   When the product **AB** of matrices **A** and **B** is formed (see *multiplication* (of matrices)), **A** is said to be **post-multiplied** by **B**.

power   When a real number a is raised to the *index* p to give a^p, the result is a **power** of a. The same index notation is used in other contexts, for example to give a power $\mathbf{A}^p$ of a square matrix (see *power* (of a matrix)) or a power g^p of an element g in a multiplicative group. When a^p is formed, p is sometimes called the power but it is more correctly called the index to which a is raised.

power (of a matrix)   If **A** is a square matrix, then **AA**, **AAA**, **AAAA**, ... are defined and these **powers** of **A** are denoted by $\mathbf{A}^2$, $\mathbf{A}^3$, $\mathbf{A}^4$, ... For all positive integers p and q, (i) $\mathbf{A}^p\mathbf{A}^q = \mathbf{A}^{p+q} = \mathbf{A}^q\mathbf{A}^p$, and (ii) $(\mathbf{A}^p)^q = \mathbf{A}^{pq}$. By definition, $\mathbf{A}^0 = \mathbf{I}$. Moreover, if **A** is *invertible*, then $\mathbf{A}^2$, $\mathbf{A}^3$, ... are invertible, and it can be shown that $(\mathbf{A}^{-1})^p$ is the inverse of $\mathbf{A}^p$, that is, $(\mathbf{A}^{-1})^p = (\mathbf{A}^p)^{-1}$. So either of these is denoted by $\mathbf{A}^{-p}$. Thus, when **A** is invertible, $\mathbf{A}^p$ has been defined for all integers (positive, zero and negative) and properties (i) and (ii) above hold for *all* integers p and q.

power series   A series $a_0 + a_1x + a_2x^2 + a_3x^3 + \cdots + a_nx^n + \cdots$, in ascending powers of x, with coefficients a_0, a_1, a_2, ..., is a **power series** in x. For example, the *geometric series* $1 + x + x^2 + \cdots + x^n + \cdots$ is a power series; this has a sum to infinity (see *series*) only if $-1 < x < 1$. Further examples of power series are given in Appendix 4. Notice that it is necessary to say for what values of x each series has the given sum. This is the case with any power series.

power set   The set of all subsets of a set S is the **power set** of S, denoted by $\mathcal{P}(S)$. Suppose that S has n elements a_1, a_2, ..., a_n, and let A be a subset of S. For each element a_i of S, there are two possibilities: either $a_i \in A$ or not. Considering all n elements leads to 2^n possibilities in all. Consequently S has 2^n subsets, that is, $\mathcal{P}(S)$ has 2^n elements. If $S = \{a,b,c\}$, the 8 $(= 2^3)$ elements of $\mathcal{P}(S)$ are $\emptyset$, $\{a\}$, $\{b\}$, $\{c\}$, $\{a,b\}$, $\{a,c\}$, $\{b,c\}$ and $\{a,b,c\}$.

pre-multiplication   When the product **AB** of matrices **A** and **B** is formed (see *multiplication* (of matrices)), **B** is said to be **pre-multiplied** by **A**.

prime   A positive integer p is a **prime**, or a **prime number**, if $p \neq 1$ and its only positive divisors are 1 and itself.

prime decomposition   See *Unique Factorization Theorem*.

prime factorization, prime representation   = *prime decomposition*.

Prime Number Theorem   For a positive real number x, let $\pi(x)$ be the number of *primes* less than or equal to x. The **Prime Number Theorem** says that, as $x \to \infty$,

$$\frac{\pi(x)}{x/\ln x} \to 1.$$

In other words, for large values of x, $\pi(x)$ is approximately equal to $x/\ln x$. This gives, in a sense, an idea of what proportion of integers are prime. Proved first in 1896 by Hadamard and de la Vallée Poussin independently, all proofs are either extremely complicated or based on advanced mathematical ideas.

prime to each other   = *relatively prime*.

primitive (*n*-th root of unity)   An *n-th root of unity* z is **primitive** if every *n*-th root of unity is a power of z. For example, i is a primitive fourth root of unity but -1 is a fourth root of unity that is not primitive.

principal axes   A set of **principal axes** of a *quadric* is a set of axes of a coordinate system in which the quadric has equation in *canonical form*.

principal value   See *argument*.

Principle of Mathematical Induction   See *mathematical induction*.

prism   A **prism** is a convex *polyhedron* with two faces that are congruent convex polygons that lie in parallel planes in such a way that, with edges joining corresponding vertices, the remaining faces are parallelograms. A **right-regular prism** is one in which the two 'end' faces are regular polygons and the remaining faces are rectangular.

product (of complex numbers)   See *multiplication* (of complex numbers).

product (of matrices)   See *multiplication* (of matrices).

product notation   For a finite sequence a_1, a_2, ..., a_n, the product $a_1 a_2 \ldots a_n$ may be denoted, using the capital Greek letter pi, by

$$\prod_{r=1}^{n} a_r.$$

(The letter r used here could equally well be replaced by any other letter.)
For example,

$$\prod_{r=1}^{9}\left(1 - \frac{1}{r+1}\right) = \left(1 - \frac{1}{2}\right)\left(1 - \frac{1}{3}\right)\cdots\left(1 - \frac{1}{10}\right).$$

Similarly, from an infinite sequence $a_1, a_2, \ldots$, an *infinite product* $a_1a_2a_3\ldots$
can be formed and it is denoted by

$$\prod_{r=1}^{\infty} a_r.$$

This notation is also used for the value of the infinite product if it exists. For
example:

$$\prod_{r=2}^{\infty}\left(1 - \frac{1}{r^2}\right) = \frac{1}{2}.$$

product rule (for differentiation)   See *differentiation*.

product set   = *Cartesian product*.

progression   = finite *sequence*.

projection (of a line on a plane)   Given a line l and a plane p, the locus of
all points N in the plane p such that N is the projection on p of some point
on l is a straight line, the **projection** of l on p.

projection (of a point on a line)   Given a line l and a point P not on l, the
projection of P on l is the point N on l such that PN is perpendicular to l.
The length $|PN|$ is the distance from P to l. The point N is called the **foot
of the perpendicular** from P to l.

projection (of a point on a plane)   Given a plane p and a point P not in p,
the **projection** of P on p is the point N in p such that PN is perpendicular
to p. The length $|PN|$ is the distance from P to p. The point N is called the
foot of the perpendicular from P to p.

projection (of a vector on a vector)   See *vector projection* (of a vector on
a vector).

proof by contradiction   A *direct proof* of a statement q is a logically
correct argument establishing the truth of q. A **proof by contradiction**
assumes that q is false and derives the truth of some statement r and of its
negation $\neg r$. This contradiction shows that the initial assumption cannot hold,
hence establishing the truth of q. A more complicated example is a proof that
'if p then q'. A proof by contradiction assumes that p is true and that q is
false and derives the truth of some statement r and of its negation $\neg r$. This

contradiction shows that the initial assumptions cannot both hold, and so a valid proof has been given that if p is true then q is true.

proper subset   Let A be a subset of B. Then A is a **proper subset** of B if A is not equal to B itself. Thus there is some element of B not in A. The subset A is then said to be **properly** (or **strictly**) **included** in B and this is written $A \subset B$. Some authors use $A \subset B$ to mean $A \subseteq B$ (see *subset*), but they then have no easy means of indicating proper inclusion.

properly included   See *proper subset*.

proposition   = *statement*.

pure imaginary   A *complex number* is **pure imaginary** if its real part is zero.

pyramid   A **pyramid** is a convex *polyhedron* with one face (the **base**) a convex polygon and all the vertices of the base joined by edges to one other vertex (the **apex**); thus the remaining faces are all triangular. A **right-regular pyramid** is one in which the base is a regular polygon and the remaining faces are isosceles triangles.

Pythagoras (died about 497 BC)   Pythagoras was an early Greek philosopher and mystic. He and his school seem to have been the first people to take mathematics seriously as a study in its own right as opposed to being a collection of formulae for practical calculation. They are credited with the discovery of the well-known *Pythagoras' Theorem* on right-angled triangles. The Pythagoreans were also much involved with figurate numbers, for semi-philosophical reasons. It is said that they regarded whole numbers as the fundamental constituents of reality. This view was shattered by the discovery of *irrational numbers*.

Pythagoras' Theorem   The most well-known theorem in geometry is probably **Pythagoras' Theorem**, which gives the relationship between the lengths of the sides of a right-angled triangle:

THEOREM: In a right-angled triangle, the square on the hypotenuse is equal to the sum of the squares on the other two sides.

Thus, if the hypotenuse, the side opposite the right angle, has length c and the other two sides have lengths a and b then $a^2 + b^2 = c^2$. One elegant proof is

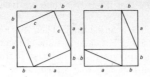

obtained by dividing up a square of side $a + b$ in two different ways as shown, and equating areas.

Pythagorean triple   A **Pythagorean triple** is a set of three positive integers a, b and c such that $a^2 + b^2 = c^2$ (see *Pythagoras' Theorem*). If $\{a, b, c\}$ is a Pythagorean triple, then so is $\{ka, kb, kc\}$ for any positive integer k. Pythagorean triples that have *greatest common divisor* equal to 1 include the following: $\{3, 4, 5\}$, $\{5, 12, 13\}$, $\{8, 15, 17\}$, $\{7, 24, 25\}$ and $\{20, 21, 29\}$.

Q

Q   See *rational number*.

quadrant   In a Cartesian coordinate system in the plane, the axes divide the rest of the plane into four regions called **quadrants**. By convention, they are usually numbered as follows: the first quadrant is $\{\,(x,y) \mid x > 0,\ y > 0\,\}$, the second is $\{\,(x,y) \mid x < 0,\ y > 0\,\}$, the third is $\{\,(x,y) \mid x < 0,\ y < 0\,\}$, the fourth is $\{\,(x,y) \mid x > 0,\ y < 0\,\}$.

quadratic equation   A **quadratic equation** in the unknown x is an equation of the form $ax^2 + bx + c = 0$, where a, b and c are given real numbers, with $a \neq 0$. This may be solved by *completing the square* or by using the formula

$$x = \frac{-b \pm \sqrt{b^2 - 4ac}}{2a},$$

which is established by completing the square. If $b^2 > 4ac$, there are two distinct real roots; if $b^2 = 4ac$, there is a single real root (which it may be convenient to treat as two equal or coincident roots); and, if $b^2 < 4ac$, the equation has no real roots, but there are two complex roots:

$$x = -\frac{b}{2a} \pm i\frac{\sqrt{4ac - b^2}}{2a}.$$

If α and β are the roots of the quadratic equation $ax^2 + bx + c = 0$, then $\alpha + \beta = -b/a$ and $\alpha\beta = c/a$. Thus a quadratic equation with given numbers α and β as its roots is $x^2 - (\alpha + \beta)x + \alpha\beta = 0$.

quadratic function   In real analysis, a **quadratic function** is a *real function* f such that $f(x) = ax^2 + bx + c$ for all x in $\mathbf{R}$, where a, b and c are real numbers, with $a \neq 0$. (In some situations, $a = 0$ may be permitted.) The graph $y = f(x)$ of such a function is a *parabola* with its axis parallel to the y-axis, with its vertex downwards if $a > 0$ and upwards if $a < 0$. The graph cuts the x-axis where $ax^2 + bx + c = 0$, so the points (if any) are given by the roots (if real) of this *quadratic equation*. The position of the vertex can be determined by completing the square or by finding the *stationary point* of the function using differentiation. If the graph cuts the x-axis in two points, the x-coordinate of the vertex is midway between these two points. In this way the graph of the quadratic function can be sketched and information can be deduced.

quadrature   A method of **quadrature** is a numerical method that finds an approximation to the area of a region with a curved boundary; the area of the region may then be found by some kind of limiting process.

quadric   A **quadric**, or **quadric surface**, is a locus in 3-dimensional space that can be represented in a Cartesian coordinate system by a polynomial equation in x, y and z of the second degree, that is, an equation of the form

$$ax^2 + by^2 + cz^2 + 2fyz + 2gzx + 2hxy + 2ux + 2vy + 2wz + d = 0,$$

where the constants a, b, c, f, g, h are not all zero. When the equation represents a non-empty locus, it can be reduced by translation and rotation of axes to one of the following **canonical forms** and hence classified:

(i) *Ellipsoid:* $\dfrac{x^2}{a^2} + \dfrac{y^2}{b^2} + \dfrac{z^2}{c^2} = 1.$

(ii) *Hyperboloid of one sheet:* $\dfrac{x^2}{a^2} + \dfrac{y^2}{b^2} - \dfrac{z^2}{c^2} = 1.$

(iii) *Hyperboloid of two sheets:* $\dfrac{x^2}{a^2} + \dfrac{y^2}{b^2} - \dfrac{z^2}{c^2} = -1.$

(iv) *Elliptic paraboloid:* $\dfrac{x^2}{a^2} + \dfrac{y^2}{b^2} = \dfrac{2z}{c}.$

(v) *Hyperbolic paraboloid:* $\dfrac{x^2}{a^2} - \dfrac{y^2}{b^2} = \dfrac{2z}{c}.$

(vi) *Quadric cone:* $\dfrac{x^2}{a^2} + \dfrac{y^2}{b^2} = \dfrac{z^2}{c^2}.$

(vii) *Elliptic cylinder:* $\dfrac{x^2}{a^2} + \dfrac{y^2}{b^2} = 1.$

(viii) *Hyperbolic cylinder:* $\dfrac{x^2}{a^2} - \dfrac{y^2}{b^2} = 1.$

(ix) *Parabolic cylinder:* $\dfrac{x^2}{a^2} = \dfrac{2y}{b}.$

(x) *Pair of non-parallel planes:* $\dfrac{x^2}{a^2} = \dfrac{y^2}{b^2}$ (that is, $y = \pm\dfrac{b}{a}x$).

(xi) *Pair of parallel planes:* $\dfrac{x^2}{a^2} = 1$ (that is, $x = \pm a$).

(xii) *Plane:* $\dfrac{x^2}{a^2} = 0$ (that is, $x = 0$).

(xiii) *Line:* $\dfrac{x^2}{a^2} + \dfrac{y^2}{b^2} = 0$ (that is, $x = y = 0$).

(xiv) Point: $\dfrac{x^2}{a^2} + \dfrac{y^2}{b^2} + \dfrac{z^2}{c^2} = 0$ (that is, $x = y = z = 0$).

Forms (i), (ii), (iii), (iv) and (v) are the non-*degenerate* quadrics.

quadric cone   A **quadric cone** is a *quadric* whose equation in a suitable coordinate system is

$$\frac{x^2}{a^2} + \frac{y^2}{b^2} = \frac{z^2}{c^2}.$$

Sections by planes parallel to the xy-plane are ellipses (circles if $a = b$), and sections by planes parallel to the other axial planes are hyperbolas.

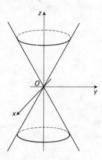

quadrilateral   A **quadrilateral** is a *polygon* with four sides.

quantifier   The two expressions 'For all ...' and 'There exists ...' are called **quantifiers**. A phrase such as 'For all x' or 'There exists x' may stand in front of a sentence involving a symbol x and thereby create a statement that makes sense and is either true or false. There are different ways in English of expressing the same sense as 'For all x', but it is sometimes useful to standardize the language to this particular form. This is known as a **universal quantifier** and is written in symbols as '$\forall x$'. Similarly, 'There exists x' may be used as the standard form to replace any phrase with this meaning, and is an **existential quantifier**, written in symbols as '$\exists x$'.

For example, the statements, 'If x is any number greater than 3 then x is positive' and 'There is a real number satisfying $x^2 = 2$', can be written in the more standard form: 'For all x, if x is greater than 3 then x is positive', and 'There exists x such that x is real and $x^2 = 2$'. These can be written, using the symbols of mathematical logic, as: $(\forall x)(x > 3 \Rightarrow x > 0)$, and $(\exists x)(x \in \mathbf{R} \wedge x^2 = 2)$.

quartic equation, quartic polynomial   A **quartic polynomial** is a polynomial of degree four; a **quartic equation** is a polynomial equation of degree four.

quintic equation, quintic polynomial　A **quintic polynomial** is a polynomial of degree five; a **quintic equation** is a polynomial equation of degree five.

quotient rule (for differentiation)　See *differentiation*.

quotient　See *Division Algorithm*.

R

R   See *real number*.

radian   In elementary work, angles are measured in degrees, where one revolution measures 360°. In more advanced work, it is essential that angles are measured differently. Suppose that a circle centre O meets two lines through O at A and B. Take the length of arc AB divided by the length of OA. This value is independent of the radius of the circle and depends only upon the size of $\angle AOB$. So the value is called the size of $\angle AOB$, measured in **radians**.

The angle measures 1 radian when the length of the arc AB equals the length of OA. This happens when $\angle AOB$ is about 57°. More accurately, 1 radian = 57·296° = 57° 17′ 45″, approximately. Since the length of the circumference of a circle of radius r is $2\pi r$, one revolution measures 2π radians. Consequently, $x° = \pi x/180$ radians. In much theoretical work, particularly involving calculus, radian measure is essential. When *trigonometric functions* are evaluated with a calculator, it is essential to be sure that the correct measure is being used.

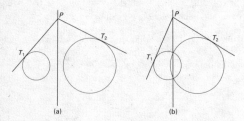

(a)   (b)

radical axis   The **radical axis** of two circles is the straight line containing all points P such that the lengths of the tangents from P to the two circles are equal. If the circles intersect in two points, the radical axis is the straight line through the two points of intersection. For the circles with equations, $x^2 + y^2 + 2g_1 x + 2f_1 y + c_1 = 0$ and $x^2 + y^2 + 2g_2 x + 2f_2 y + c_2 = 0$, the radical axis has equation $2(g_1 - g_2)x + 2(f_1 - f_2)y + (c_1 - c_2) = 0$.

radius (plural: radii)   See *circle*.

radius vector   Suppose that a point O is taken as origin in the plane. If a point P in the plane has *position vector* **p**, then **p** may also be called the **radius vector**, particularly when P is a typical point on a certain curve or when P is thought of as a point moving in the plane.

range   See *function* and *mapping*.

rank   Let **A** be an $m \times n$ matrix. The **column rank** of **A** is the largest number of elements in a *linearly independent* set of columns of **A**. The **row rank** of **A** is the largest number of elements in a linearly independent set of rows of **A**. It can be shown that elementary row operations on a matrix do not change the column rank or the row rank. Consequently, the column rank and row rank of **A** are equal, both being equal to the number of non-zero rows in the matrix in *reduced echelon form* to which **A** can be transformed. This common value is the **rank** of **A**. It can also be shown that the rank of **A** is equal to the number of rows and columns in the largest square submatrix of **A** that has non-zero determinant. An $n \times n$ matrix is *invertible* if and only if it has rank n.

rate of change   Suppose that the quantity y is a function of the quantity x, so that $y = f(x)$. If f is *differentiable*, the **rate of change** of y with respect to x is the derivative dy/dx or $f'(x)$. The rate of change is often with respect to time t. Suppose, now, that x denotes the *displacement* of a particle, at time t, on a directed line with origin O. Then the velocity is dx/dt or $\dot{x}$, the rate of change of x with respect to t, and the acceleration is d^2x/dt^2 or $\ddot{x}$, the rate of change of the velocity with respect to t.

rational function   In real analysis, a **rational function** is a *real function f* such that, for x in the domain, $f(x) = g(x)/h(x)$, where $g(x)$ and $h(x)$ are polynomials, which may be assumed to have no common factor of degree greater than or equal to 1. The domain is usually taken to be the whole of **R**, with any zeros of the denominator $h(x)$ omitted.

rational number   A **rational number** is a number that can be written in the form a/b, where a and b are integers, with $b \neq 0$. The set of all rational numbers is usually denoted by **Q**. A real number is rational if and only if, when expressed as a decimal, it has a finite or *recurring* expansion. For example,

$$\frac{5}{4} = 1{\cdot}25, \qquad \frac{2}{3} = 0{\cdot}\dot{6}, \qquad \frac{20}{7} = 2{\cdot}\dot{8}5714\dot{2}.$$

A famous proof, attributed to Pythagoras, shows that $\sqrt{2}$ is not rational, and e and π are also known to be irrational.

The same rational number can be expressed as a/b in different ways; for example, $\frac{2}{3} = \frac{6}{9} = \frac{-4}{-6}$. In fact, $a/b = c/d$ if and only if $ad = bc$. But a rational number can be expressed uniquely as a/b if it is insisted that a and b have *greatest common divisor* 1 and that $b > 0$. Accepting the different forms for

the same rational number, the explicit rules for addition and multiplication
are that

$$\frac{a}{b} + \frac{c}{d} = \frac{ad + bc}{bd}, \qquad \frac{a}{b} \cdot \frac{c}{d} = \frac{ac}{bd}.$$

The set of rational numbers is closed under addition, subtraction, multiplication and division (not allowing division by zero). Indeed, all the axioms for a
field can be seen to hold.

A more rigorous approach sets up the field **Q** of rational numbers as follows. Consider the set of all *ordered pairs* (a, b), where a and b are integers,
with $b \neq 0$. Introduce an *equivalence relation* $\sim$ on this set, by defining:
$(a, b) \sim (c, d)$ if $ad = bc$, and let $[(a, b)]$ be the *equivalence class* containing (a, b). The intuitive approach above suggests that addition and multiplication between equivalence classes should be defined by

$$[(a, b)] + [(c, d)] = [(ad + bc, bd)], \qquad [(a, b)][(c, d)] = [(ac, bd)],$$

where it is necessary, in each case, to verify that the class on the right-hand
side is independent of the choice of elements (a, b) and (c, d) taken an *representatives* of the equivalence classes on the left-hand side. It can then be
shown that the set of equivalence classes, with this addition and multiplication, form a field **Q**, whose elements, according to this approach, are called
rational numbers.

real axis   In the *complex plane*, the x-axis is called the **real axis**; its points
represent the real numbers.

real function   A **real function** f is a function from the set **R** of real
numbers (or a subset of **R**) to **R**. Thus, for every real number x in the
domain, a corresponding real number $f(x)$ is defined. In analysis, a function
$f \colon S \to \mathbf{R}$ is often defined by giving a formula for $f(x)$, without specifying the
domain S (see *function*). In that case, it is usual to assume that the domain
is the largest possible subset S of **R**. For example, if $f(x) = 1/(x - 2)$, the
domain would be taken to be $\mathbf{R} \setminus \{2\}$, that is, the set of all real numbers not
equal to 2; if $f(x) = \sqrt{9 - x^2}$, the domain would be the closed interval $[-3, 3]$.

real line   On a horizontal straight line, choose a point O as origin, and a
point A, to the right of O, such that $|OA|$ is equal to 1 unit. Each positive
real number x can be represented by a point on the line to the right of O,
whose distance from O equals x units, and each negative number by a point
on the line to the left of O. The origin represents zero. The line is called the
real line when its points are taken in this way to represent the real numbers.

real number   The numbers generally used in mathematics, in scientific
work and in everyday life are the **real numbers**. They can be pictured as
points of a line, with the integers equally spaced along the line and a real
number b to the right of the real number a if $a < b$. The set of real numbers is
usually denoted by **R**. It contains such numbers as 0, $\frac{1}{2}$, -2, $4{\cdot}75$, $\sqrt{2}$ and π.

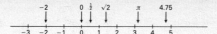

Indeed, **R** contains all the rational numbers but also numbers such as $\sqrt{2}$ and π that are irrational. Every real number has an expression as an infinite *decimal*.

The set of real numbers, with the familiar addition and multiplication, form a *field* and, since there is a notion of 'less than' that satisfies certain basic axioms, **R** is called an 'ordered' field. However, a statement of a complete set of axioms that characterize **R** will not be attempted here. There are too a number of rigorous approaches that, assuming the existence of the field **Q** of *rational numbers*, construct a system of real numbers with the required properties.

real part   A *complex number* z may be written $x + yi$, where x and y are real, and then x is the **real part** of z. It is denoted by $\operatorname{Re} z$ or $\Re z$.

reciprocal   The *multiplicative inverse* of a quantity may, when the operation of multiplication is *commutative*, be called its **reciprocal**. Thus the reciprocal of 2 is $\frac{1}{2}$, the reciprocal of $3x + 4$ is $1/(3x + 4)$ and the reciprocal of $\sin x$ is $1/\sin x$.

reciprocal rule (for differentiation)   See *differentiation*.

rectangular coordinate system   See *coordinates* (in the plane).

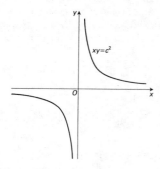

rectangular hyperbola   A *hyperbola* whose asymptotes are perpendicular is a **rectangular hyperbola**. With the origin at the centre and the coordinate x-axis along the transverse axis, it has equation $x^2 - y^2 = a^2$. Instead, the coordinate axes can be taken along the asymptotes in such a way that the two branches of the hyperbola are in the first and third quadrants. This coordinate system can be obtained from the other by a rotation of axes. The rectangular hyperbola then has equation of the form $xy = c^2$. For example, $y = 1/x$ is a rectangular hyperbola. For $xy = c^2$, it is customary to take $c > 0$ and to use, as *parametric equations*, $x = ct, y = c/t$ $(t \neq 0)$.

recurring decimal   See *decimal*.

reduced echelon form   Suppose that a row of a matrix is called zero if all its entries are zero. Then a matrix is in **reduced echelon form** if

(i) all the zero rows come below the non-zero rows,

(ii) the first non-zero entry in each non-zero row is 1 and occurs in a column to the right of the leading 1 in the row above,

(iii) the leading 1 in each non-zero row is the only non-zero entry in the column that it is in.

(If (i) and (ii) hold, the matrix is in *echelon form*.) For example, these two matrices are in reduced echelon form:

$$\begin{bmatrix} 1 & 6 & 0 & 0 & 2 \\ 0 & 0 & 1 & 0 & -3 \\ 0 & 0 & 0 & 1 & 5 \end{bmatrix}, \qquad \begin{bmatrix} 1 & 0 & -1 & 4 & 2 \\ 0 & 1 & 2 & -3 & 5 \\ 0 & 0 & 0 & 0 & 0 \end{bmatrix}.$$

Any matrix can be transformed to a matrix in reduced echelon form using elementary row operations, by a method known as *Gauss-Jordan elimination*. For any matrix, the reduced echelon form to which it can be transformed is unique. The solutions of a set of linear equations can be immediately obtained from the reduced echelon form to which the augmented matrix has been transformed. A set of linear equations is said to be in reduced echelon form if its augmented matrix is in reduced echelon form.

reduced set of residues   For a positive integer n, the number of positive integers, less than n, *relatively prime* to n, is denoted by $\phi(n)$ (see *Euler's function*). A **reduced set of residues** modulo n is a set of $\phi(n)$ integers, one *congruent* (modulo n) to each of the positive integers less than n, relatively prime to n. Thus $\{1, 5, 7, 11\}$ is a reduced set of residues modulo 12, and so is $\{1, -1, 5, -5\}$.

reduction formula   Let I_n be some quantity that is dependent upon the integer n (≥ 0). It may be possible to establish some general formula, expressing I_n in terms of some of the quantities I_{n-1}, I_{n-2}, ... Such a formula is a **reduction formula** and can be used to evaluate I_n for a particular value of n. The method is useful in integration. For example, if

$$I_n = \int_0^{\pi/2} \sin^n x \, dx,$$

it can be shown, by integration by parts, that $I_n = ((n-1)/n)I_{n-2}$ ($n \geq 2$). It is easy to see that $I_0 = \pi/2$, and then the reduction formula can be used, for example, to find that

$$I_6 = \frac{5}{6}I_4 = \frac{5}{6}\cdot\frac{3}{4}I_2 = \frac{5}{6}\cdot\frac{3}{4}\cdot\frac{1}{2}I_0 = \frac{5}{6}\cdot\frac{3}{4}\cdot\frac{1}{2}\cdot\frac{\pi}{2} = \frac{5\pi}{32}.$$

reflection (of the plane)   Let l be a line in the plane. Then the **mirror-image** of a point P is the point P' such that PP' is perpendicular to l and

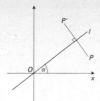

l cuts PP' at its midpoint. The **reflection** of the plane in the line l is the transformation of the plane that maps each point P to its mirror-image P'. Suppose that the line l passes through the origin O and makes an angle α with the x-axis. If P has polar coordinates (r, θ), its mirror-image P' has polar coordinates $(r, 2\alpha - \theta)$. In terms of Cartesian coordinates, reflection in the line l maps P with coordinates (x, y) to P' with coordinates (x', y'), where

$$x' = x \cos 2\alpha + y \sin 2\alpha,$$
$$y' = x \sin 2\alpha - y \cos 2\alpha.$$

reflexive relation   A *binary relation* $\sim$ on a set S is **reflexive** if $a \sim a$ for all a in S.

regular graph   A *graph* is **regular** if all its vertices have the same *degree*. It is r**-regular** or **regular of degree** r if every vertex has degree r.

regular polygon   See *polygon*.

regular polyhedron   See *polyhedron*.

relation   A **relation** on a set S is usually a *binary relation* on S, though the notion can be extended to involve more than two elements. An example of a **ternary relation**, involving three elements, is 'a lies between b and c', where a, b and c are real numbers.

relative complement   If the set A is included in the set B, the *difference set* $B \setminus A$ is the (**relative**) **complement** of A in B, or the **complement of A relative to** B.

relative error   Let x be an approximation to a value X and let $X = x + e$. The **relative error** is $|e/X|$. When $1 \cdot 9$ is used as an approximation for $1 \cdot 875$, the relative error equals $0 \cdot 025 / 1 \cdot 875 = 0 \cdot 013$, to 3 decimal places. (This may be expressed as a *percentage error* of $1 \cdot 3\%$.) Notice, in this example, that $0 \cdot 025 / 1 \cdot 9 = 0 \cdot 013$, to 3 decimal places, too. In general, when e is small, it does not make much difference if the relative error is taken as $|e/x|$, instead of $|e/X|$; this has to be done if the exact value is not known but only the approximation. The relative error may be a more helpful figure than the absolute error. An absolute error of $0 \cdot 025$ in a value of $1 \cdot 9$, as above, may be acceptable. But the same absolute error in a value of $0 \cdot 2$, say, would give a relative error of $0.025/0.2 = 0.125$ (a percentage error of $12\frac{1}{2}\%$), which would probably be considered quite serious.

relatively prime   Integers a and b are **relatively prime** if their *greatest common divisor* is 1. Similarly, any number of integers $a_1, a_2, \ldots, a_n$ are relatively prime if their g.c.d. is 1.

Remainder Theorem   The following result about polynomials is called the **Remainder Theorem**:

THEOREM: If a polynomial $f(x)$ is divided by $x - h$, then the remainder is equal to $f(h)$.

It is proved as follows. Divide the polynomial $f(x)$ by $x - h$ to get a quotient $q(x)$ and a remainder which will be a constant r. This means that $f(x) = (x - h)q(x) + r$. Replacing x by h in this equation gives $r = f(h)$, proving the theorem. An important consequence of the Remainder Theorem is the *Factor Theorem*.

repeated root   See *root*.

repeating decimal   See *decimal*.

representation (of a vector)   When the directed line-segment $\overrightarrow{AB}$ represents the *vector* **a**, then $\overrightarrow{AB}$ is a **representation** of **a**.

representative   Given an *equivalence relation* on a set, any one of the *equivalence classes* can be specified by giving one of the elements in it. The particular element a used can be called a **representative** of the class and the class can be denoted by $[a]$.

residue class (modulo n)   The **residue classes** modulo n are the *equivalence classes* for the *equivalence relation* of *congruence* modulo n. So, two integers are in the same class if they have the same remainder upon division by n. If $[a]$ denotes the residue class modulo n containing a, the residue classes modulo n can be taken as $[0], [1], [2], \ldots, [n-1]$. The sum and product of residue classes can be defined by

$$[a] + [b] = [a + b], \qquad [a][b] = [ab],$$

where it is necessary to show that the definitions here do not depend upon which *representatives* a and b are chosen for the two classes. With this addition and multiplication, the set, denoted by $\mathbf{Z}_n$, of residue classes modulo n forms a *ring* (in fact, a commutative ring with identity). If n is composite, the ring $\mathbf{Z}_n$ has *divisors of zero*, but when p is prime $\mathbf{Z}_p$ is a *field*.

restriction (of mapping)   A mapping $g: S_1 \rightarrow T_1$ is a **restriction** of the mapping $f: S \rightarrow T$ if $S_1 \subseteq S$, $T_1 \subseteq T$ and $g(s_1) = f(s_1)$ for all s_1 in S_1. Thus a restriction is obtained by taking, perhaps, a subset of the domain or codomain or both, but otherwise following the same rule for defining the mapping.

rhombus   A **rhombus** is a quadrilateral all of whose sides have the same length. A rhombus is both a *kite* and a *parallelogram*.

Riemann, Bernhard (1826–1866)   The German mathematician Riemann was a major figure in nineteenth-century mathematics. In many ways, he was the intellectual successor of Gauss. He is remembered for the Cauchy-Riemann equations, Riemann surfaces, Riemannian geometry, Riemann's differential equation, the *Riemann integral*, the Riemann zeta function and the Riemann hypothesis. These make up a major body of work. In geometry, Riemann started the development of those tools that Einstein would eventually use to describe the universe and that the twentieth century would turn into the theory of manifolds. His basic geometrical ideas were presented in his famous inaugural lecture to the faculty at Göttingen. The audience included Gauss himself, then in the last year of his long life. Riemann did much significant work in analysis, at a time when the subject was gaining precision after the formal orgies of the eighteenth century. He is known to many mathematics students for his definition of the integral. He left mathematics one of its outstanding problems in the Riemann hypothesis: that the Riemann zeta function has all its complex zeros on the line $\Re z = \frac{1}{2}$. If proved, this would tell us a lot about the distribution of the prime numbers and would be one of the most remarkable interactions of analysis and arithmetic.

Riemann integral, Riemann sum   See *integral*.

right angle   A **right angle** is a quarter of a complete revolution. It is equal to 90° or $\pi/2$ radians.

right-circular   See *cone* and *cylinder*.

right derivative   See *left, and right, derivative*.

right-handed system   Let Ox, Oy and Oz be three mutually perpendicular directed lines, intersecting at the point O. In the order Ox, Oy, Oz, they form a **right-handed system** if a person standing with his head in the positive z-direction and facing the positive y-direction would have the positive x-direction to his right. Putting it another way, when seen from a position facing the positive z-direction, a rotation from the positive x-direction to the positive y-direction passes through a right angle clockwise. Following the normal practice, the figures in this book that use a Cartesian coordinate system for 3-dimensional space have Ox, Oy and Oz forming a right-handed system.

The three directed lines Ox, Oy and Oz (in that order) form a **left-handed system** if, taken in the order Oy, Ox, Oz, they form a right-handed system. If the direction of any one of three lines of a right-handed system is reversed, the three directed lines form a left-handed system.

Similarly, an ordered set of three oblique directed lines may be described as forming a right- or left-handed system. Three vectors, in a given order, form a right- or left-handed system if directed line-segments representing them define directed lines that do so.

right-regular   See *prism* and *pyramid*.

ring   Sets of entities with two operations, often called addition and multiplication, occur in different situations in mathematics and sometimes share many of the same properties. It is useful to recognize these similarities, by identifying certain of the common characteristics. One such set of properties is specified in the definition of a ring: a **ring** is a set R, closed under two operations called addition and multiplication, denoted in the usual way, such that

1. for all a, b and c in R, $a + (b + c) = (a + b) + c$,
2. for all a and b in R, $a + b = b + a$,
3. there is an element 0 in R such that $a + 0 = a$ for all a in R,
4. for each a in R, there is an element $-a$ in R such that $a + (-a) = 0$,
5. for all a, b and c in R, $a(bc) = (ab)c$,
6. for all a, b and c in R, $a(b + c) = ab + ac$ and $(a + b)c = ac + bc$.

The element guaranteed by **3** is a *neutral element* for addition. It can be shown that in a ring this element is unique and has the extra property that $a0 = 0$ for all a in R, so it is usually called the *zero element*. Also, for each a, the element $-a$ guaranteed by **4** is unique and is the *negative* of a.

The ring is a **commutative ring** if it is true that

7. for all a and b in R, $ab = ba$,

and it is a **commutative ring with identity** if also

8. there is an element 1 ($\neq 0$) such that $a1 = a$ for all a in R.

If certain further properties are added, the definitions of an *integral domain* and a *field* are obtained. So any integral domain and any field is a ring. Further examples of rings (which are not integral domains or fields) are the set of 2×2 real matrices and the set of all even integers, each with the appropriate addition and multiplication. Another example of a ring is $\mathbf{Z}_n$, the set $\{0, 1, 2, \ldots, n - 1\}$ with addition and multiplication modulo n.

A ring may be denoted by $\langle R, +, \times \rangle$ and another ring by, say, $\langle R', \oplus, \otimes \rangle$ when it is necessary to distinguish the operations in one ring from the operations in the other. But it is sufficient to refer simply to the ring R when the operations intended are clear.

Rolle's Theorem   The following result, known as **Rolle's Theorem**, concerns the existence of *stationary points* of a function f:

THEOREM: Let f be a function which is continuous on $[a, b]$ and differentiable in (a, b), such that $f(a) = f(b)$. (Some authors require $f(a) = f(b) = 0$.) Then there is a number c with $a < c < b$ such that $f'(c) = 0$.

The result stated in the theorem can be expressed as a statement about the graph of f: with appropriate conditions on f, between any two points on the graph $y = f(x)$ that are level with each other, there must be a stationary point, that is, a point at which the tangent is horizontal. The theorem, is in fact, a special case of the *Mean Value Theorem*; however, it is normal to establish Rolle's Theorem first and deduce the Mean Value Theorem from it.

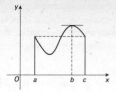

A rigorous proof relies on the non-elementary result that a *continuous function* on a closed interval attains its bounds.

root   Let $f(x) = 0$ be an equation involving the indeterminate x. A **root** of the equation is a value h such that $f(h) = 0$. Such a value is also called a **zero** of the function f. Some authors use 'root' and 'zero' interchangeably.

If $f(x)$ is a polynomial, then $f(x) = 0$ is a polynomial equation. By the *Factor Theorem*, h is a root of this equation if and only if $x - h$ is a factor of $f(x)$. The value h is a **simple root** if $x - h$ is a factor but $(x - h)^2$ is not a factor of $f(x)$; and h is a root of **order** (or **multiplicity**) n if $(x - h)^n$ is a factor but $(x - h)^{n+1}$ is not. A root of order 2 is a **double root**; a root of order 3 is a **triple root**. A root of order n, where $n \geq 2$, is a **multiple** (or **repeated**) **root**.

If h is a double root of the polynomial equation $f(x) = 0$, then close to $x = h$ the graph $y = f(x)$ looks something like one of the diagrams in the first row below. If h is a triple root, then the graph looks like one of the diagrams in the second row below. The value h is a root of order at least n if and only if $f(h) = 0$, $f'(h) = 0$, ..., $f^{(n-1)}(h) = 0$.

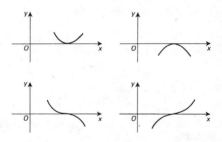

If α and β are the roots of the quadratic equation $ax^2 + bx + c = 0$, with $a \neq 0$, then $\alpha + \beta = -b/a$ and $\alpha\beta = c/a$. If α, β and γ are the roots of the cubic equation $ax^3 + bx^2 + cx + d = 0$, with $a \neq 0$, then $\alpha + \beta + \gamma = -b/a$, $\beta\gamma + \gamma\alpha + \alpha\beta = c/a$ and $\alpha\beta\gamma = -d/a$. Similar results hold for polynomial equations of higher degree.

root (of a tree)   See *tree*.

root of unity   See *n-th root of unity*.

rotational symmetry   A plane figure has **rotational symmetry** about a point O if the figure appears the same when it is rotated about O through some positive angle less than one complete revolution. For example, an equilateral triangle and, indeed, any regular polygon, has rotational symmetry about its centre.

rotation of axes (in the plane)   Suppose that a Cartesian coordinate system has a given x-axis and y-axis with origin O and given unit length, so that a typical point P has coordinates (x, y). Consider taking a new coordinate system with the same origin O and the same unit length, with X-axis and Y-axis, such that a rotation through an angle α (with the positive direction taken anti-clockwise) carries the x-axis to the X-axis and the y-axis to the Y-axis. With respect to the new coordinate system, the point P has coordinates (X, Y). Then the old and new coordinates in such a **rotation of axes** are related by

$$x = X \cos \alpha - Y \sin \alpha,$$
$$y = X \sin \alpha + Y \cos \alpha.$$

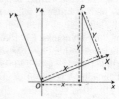

In matrix notation, these equations become

$$\begin{bmatrix} x \\ y \end{bmatrix} = \begin{bmatrix} \cos \alpha & -\sin \alpha \\ \sin \alpha & \cos \alpha \end{bmatrix} \begin{bmatrix} X \\ Y \end{bmatrix}$$

and, conversely,

$$\begin{bmatrix} X \\ Y \end{bmatrix} = \begin{bmatrix} \cos \alpha & \sin \alpha \\ -\sin \alpha & \cos \alpha \end{bmatrix} \begin{bmatrix} x \\ y \end{bmatrix}.$$

For example, in a rotation of axes through an angle of $-\pi/4$ radians, the coordinates are related by

$$x = \frac{1}{\sqrt{2}}(X + Y), \qquad y = \frac{1}{\sqrt{2}}(-X + Y),$$

and the curve with equation $x^2 - y^2 = 2$ has equation $XY = 1$ in the new coordinate system.

rotation (of the plane)   A **rotation** of the plane about the origin O through an angle α is the *transformation* of the plane in which O is mapped to itself, and a point P with polar coordinates (r, θ) is mapped to the point P' with polar coordinates $(r, \theta + \alpha)$. In terms of Cartesian coordinates, P with coordinates (x, y) is mapped to P' with coordinates (x', y'), where

$$x' = x \cos \alpha - y \sin \alpha,$$
$$y' = x \sin \alpha + y \cos \alpha.$$

rounding   Suppose that a number has more digits than can be conveniently handled or stored. In **rounding** (as opposed to *truncation*), the original number is replaced by the number, with the required number of digits, that is closest to it. Thus, when rounding to 1 decimal place, the number $1 \cdot 875$ becomes $1 \cdot 9$ and the number $1 \cdot 845$ becomes $1 \cdot 8$. It is said that the number is accordingly **rounded up** or **rounded down**. When the original is precisely at a halfway point (for example, if $1 \cdot 85$ is to be rounded to 1 decimal place), it may be rounded up (to $1 \cdot 9$) or rounded down (to $1 \cdot 8$). Some authors like to recommend a particular way of deciding which to do. See also *decimal places* and *significant figures*.

rounding error   = *round-off error*.

round-off error   When a number X is rounded to a certain number of digits to obtain an approximation x, the *error* is called the **round-off error**. For some authors this is $X - x$ and for some it is $x - X$. For example, if $1 \cdot 875$ is rounded to 1 decimal place, or to 2 significant figures, to give $1 \cdot 9$, the round-off error is either $0 \cdot 025$ or $-0 \cdot 025$. When a number is rounded to k decimal places, the round-off error lies between $\pm 5 \times 10^{-(k+1)}$; for example, when rounding to 3 decimal places, the round-off error lies between $\pm 0 \cdot 0005$. For some authors, the error is $|X - x|$ (see *absolute value*) and so, for them, it is always greater than or equal to zero.

row matrix   A **row matrix** is a *matrix* with exactly one row, that is, a $1 \times n$ matrix of the form $[\, a_1 \quad a_2 \quad \ldots \quad a_n \,]$. Given an $m \times n$ matrix, it may be useful to treat its rows as individual row matrices.

row operation   See *elementary row operation*.

row rank   See *rank*.

row vector   = *row matrix*.

Russell's paradox   By using the notation of set theory, a set can be defined as the set of all x that satisfy some property. Now it is clearly possible for a set not to belong to itself: any set of numbers, say, does not belong to itself because to belong to itself it would have to be a number. But it is also possible to have a set that does belong to itself: for example, the set of all sets belongs to itself. In 1901, Bertrand Russell drew attention to what has become known as **Russell's paradox**, by considering the set R, defined by $R = \{\, x \mid x \notin x \,\}$. If $R \in R$ then $R \notin R$; and if $R \notin R$ then $R \in R$. The paradox points out the danger of the unrestricted use of abstraction, and various solutions have been proposed to avoid the paradox.

saddle-point   Suppose that a surface has equation $z = f(x, y)$, with, as usual, the z-axis vertically upwards. A point P on the surface is a **saddle-point** if the *tangent plane* at P is horizontal and if P is a local minimum on the curve obtained by one vertical cross-section and a local maximum on the curve obtained by another vertical cross-section. It is so called because the central point on the seat of a horse's saddle has this property. The *hyperbolic paraboloid*, for example, has a saddle-point at the origin. See also *stationary point* (in two variables).

scalar (for matrices)   When working with *matrices*, the entries must belong to some particular set S. An element of S may be called a **scalar** to emphasize that it is not a matrix. For example, the occasion may arise when a matrix **A** is to be multiplied by a scalar k to form $k\mathbf{A}$, or when a certain row of a matrix is to be multiplied by a scalar.

scalar (for vectors)   When working with *vectors*, a quantity that is a real number, in other words, *not* a vector, is called a **scalar**.

scalar multiple (of a matrix)   Let **A** be an $m \times n$ matrix, with $\mathbf{A} = [a_{ij}]$, and k a scalar. The **scalar multiple** $k\mathbf{A}$ is the $m \times n$ matrix **C**, where $\mathbf{C} = [c_{ij}]$ and $c_{ij} = ka_{ij}$. Multiplication by scalars has the following properties:

   (i) $(h + k)\mathbf{A} = h\mathbf{A} + k\mathbf{A}$.
   (ii) $k(\mathbf{A} + \mathbf{B}) = k\mathbf{A} + k\mathbf{B}$.
   (iii) $h(k\mathbf{A}) = (hk)\mathbf{A}$.
   (iv) $0\mathbf{A} = \mathbf{O}$, the zero matrix.
   (v) $(-1)\mathbf{A} = -\mathbf{A}$, the negative of **A**.

scalar multiple (of a vector)   Let **a** be a non-zero vector and k a non-zero scalar. The **scalar multiple** of **a** by k, denoted by $k\mathbf{a}$, is the vector whose magnitude is $|k||\mathbf{a}|$ and whose direction is that of **a**, if $k > 0$, and that of $-\mathbf{a}$, if $k < 0$. Also, $k\mathbf{0}$ and $0\mathbf{a}$ are defined to be **0**, for all k and **a**. Multiplication by scalars has the following properties:

   (i) $(h + k)\mathbf{a} = h\mathbf{a} + k\mathbf{a}$.
   (ii) $k(\mathbf{a} + \mathbf{b}) = k\mathbf{a} + k\mathbf{b}$.
   (iii) $h(k\mathbf{a}) = (hk)\mathbf{a}$.
   (iv) $1\mathbf{a} = \mathbf{a}$.
   (v) $(-1)\mathbf{a} = -\mathbf{a}$, the negative of **a**.

scalar product   For vectors **a** and **b**, the **scalar product** $\mathbf{a} \cdot \mathbf{b}$ is defined by $\mathbf{a} \cdot \mathbf{b} = |\mathbf{a}||\mathbf{b}| \cos \theta$, where θ is the angle, in radians with $0 \leq \theta \leq \pi$, between

a and **b**. This is a scalar quantity, that is, a real number, not a vector. The scalar product has the following properties:

(i) $\mathbf{a} \cdot \mathbf{b} = \mathbf{b} \cdot \mathbf{a}$.

(ii) For non-zero vectors **a** and **b**, $\mathbf{a} \cdot \mathbf{b} = 0$ if and only if **a** is perpendicular to **b**.

(iii) $\mathbf{a} \cdot \mathbf{a} = |\mathbf{a}|^2$; the scalar product $\mathbf{a} \cdot \mathbf{a}$ may be written $\mathbf{a}^2$.

(iv) $\mathbf{a} \cdot (\mathbf{b} + \mathbf{c}) = \mathbf{a} \cdot \mathbf{b} + \mathbf{a} \cdot \mathbf{c}$, the distributive law.

(v) $\mathbf{a} \cdot (k\mathbf{b}) = (k\mathbf{a}) \cdot \mathbf{b} = k(\mathbf{a} \cdot \mathbf{b})$.

(vi) If the vectors **a** and **b** are given in terms of their components (with respect to the standard vectors **i**, **j** and **k**) as $\mathbf{a} = a_1\mathbf{i} + a_2\mathbf{j} + a_3\mathbf{k}$, $\mathbf{b} = b_1\mathbf{i} + b_2\mathbf{j} + b_3\mathbf{k}$, then $\mathbf{a} \cdot \mathbf{b} = a_1b_1 + a_2b_2 + a_3b_3$.

scalar projection (of a vector on a vector)   See *vector projection* (of a vector on a vector).

scalar triple product   For vectors **a**, **b** and **c**, the *scalar product*, $\mathbf{a} \cdot (\mathbf{b} \times \mathbf{c})$, of **a** with the vector $\mathbf{b} \times \mathbf{c}$ (see *vector product*), is called a **scalar triple product**. It is a scalar quantity and is denoted by $[\mathbf{a}, \mathbf{b}, \mathbf{c}]$. It has the following properties:

(i) $[\mathbf{a}, \mathbf{b}, \mathbf{c}] = -[\mathbf{a}, \mathbf{c}, \mathbf{b}]$.

(ii) $[\mathbf{a}, \mathbf{b}, \mathbf{c}] = [\mathbf{b}, \mathbf{c}, \mathbf{a}] = [\mathbf{c}, \mathbf{a}, \mathbf{b}]$.

(iii) The vectors **a**, **b** and **c** are coplanar if and only if $[\mathbf{a}, \mathbf{b}, \mathbf{c}] = 0$.

(iv) If the vectors are given in terms of their components (with respect to the standard vectors **i**, **j** and **k**) as $\mathbf{a} = a_1\mathbf{i} + a_2\mathbf{j} + a_3\mathbf{k}$, $\mathbf{b} = b_1\mathbf{i} + b_2\mathbf{j} + b_3\mathbf{k}$, $\mathbf{c} = c_1\mathbf{i} + c_2\mathbf{j} + c_3\mathbf{k}$, then

$$[\mathbf{a}, \mathbf{b}, \mathbf{c}] = a_1(b_2c_3 - b_3c_2) + a_2(b_3c_1 - b_1c_3) + a_3(b_1c_2 - b_2c_1)$$

$$= \begin{vmatrix} a_1 & a_2 & a_3 \\ b_1 & b_2 & b_3 \\ c_1 & c_2 & c_3 \end{vmatrix}.$$

(v) Let $\overrightarrow{OA}$, $\overrightarrow{OB}$ and $\overrightarrow{OC}$ represent **a**, **b** and **c** and let P be the parallelepiped with OA, OB and OC as three of its edges. The *absolute value* of $[\mathbf{a}, \mathbf{b}, \mathbf{c}]$ gives the volume of the parallelepiped P. (If **a**, **b** and **c** form a right-handed system, $[\mathbf{a}, \mathbf{b}, \mathbf{c}]$ is positive; and if **a**, **b** and **c** form a left-handed system, $[\mathbf{a}, \mathbf{b}, \mathbf{c}]$ is negative.)

scientific notation   A number is said to be in **scientific notation** when it is written as a number between 1 and 10, times a power of 10, that is to say, as $a \times 10^n$, where $1 \le a < 10$ and n is an integer. Thus 634·8 and 0·00234 are written in scientific notation as $6·348 \times 10^2$ and $2·34 \times 10^{-3}$. The notation is particularly useful for very large and very small numbers.

secant   See *trigonometric function*.

sech   See *hyperbolic function*.

second derivative   See *higher derivative*.

second-order partial derivative   See *higher-order partial derivative*.

section formula (in vectors)   Let A and B be two points with *position vectors* **a** and **b**, and P a point on the line through A and B, such that $AP : PB = m : n$. Then P has position vector **p**, given by the **section formula**

$$\mathbf{p} = \frac{1}{m+n}(m\mathbf{b} + n\mathbf{a}).$$

It is possible to choose m and n such that $m + n = 1$ and thus to suppose, changing notation, that $AP : PB = k : 1 - k$. Then $\mathbf{p} = (1 - k)\mathbf{a} + k\mathbf{b}$.

section formulae (in the plane)   Let A and B be two points with Cartesian coordinates (x_1, y_1) and (x_2, y_2), and P a point on the line through A and B, such that $AP : PB = m : n$. Then the **section formulae** give the coordinates of P as

$$\left(\frac{mx_2 + nx_1}{m+n}, \frac{my_2 + ny_1}{m+n}\right).$$

If, instead, P is a point on the line such that $AP : PB = k : 1 - k$, its coordinates are $((1 - k)x_1 + kx_2, (1 - k)y_1 + ky_2)$.

section formulae (in 3-dimensional space)   Let A and B be two points with Cartesian coordinates (x_1, y_1, z_1) and (x_2, y_2, z_2), and P a point on the line through A and B. If $AP : PB = m : n$, the **section formulae** give the coordinates of P as

$$\left(\frac{mx_2 + nx_1}{m+n}, \frac{my_2 + ny_1}{m+n}, \frac{mz_2 + nz_1}{m+n}\right),$$

and, if P is a point on the line such that $AP : PB = k : 1 - k$, its coordinates are $((1 - k)x_1 + kx_2, (1 - k)y_1 + ky_2, (1 - k)z_1 + kz_2)$.

sector   A **sector** of a circle, with centre O, is the region bounded by an arc AB of the circle and the two radii OA and OB. The area of a sector is equal to $\frac{1}{2}r^2\theta$, where r is the radius and θ is the angle in radians.

segment   A **segment** of a circle is the region bounded by an arc AB of the circle and the chord AB.

selection   The number of **selections** of n objects taken r at a time, that is, the number of ways of selecting r objects out of n, is denoted by ^nC_r and is equal to

$$\frac{n!}{r!(n-r)!}.$$

(See *binomial coefficient*, where the alternative notation $\binom{n}{r}$ is defined.) For example, from four objects A, B, C and D, there are six ways of selecting two: AB, AC, AD, BC, BD, CD. The property that $^{n+1}C_r = {}^nC_{r-1} + {}^nC_r$ can be seen displayed in *Pascal's triangle*.

semi-vertical angle   See *cone*.

separable first-order differential equation   The first-order differential equation $dy/dx = f(x,y)$ is **separable** if the function f can be expressed as the product of a function of x and a function of y. The differential equation then has the form $dy/dx = g(x)h(y)$ and its solution is given by the equation

$$\int \frac{1}{h(y)}\, dy = \int g(x)\, dx + c,$$

where c is an arbitrary constant.

sequence   A **finite sequence** consists of n terms a_1, a_2, ..., a_n, one corresponding to each of the integers 1, 2, ..., n, where n, some positive integer, is the **length** of the sequence. An **infinite sequence** consists of terms a_1, a_2, a_3, ..., one corresponding to each positive integer. Sometimes, it is more convenient to denote the terms of a sequence by a_0, a_1, a_2, ... See also *limit* (of a sequence).

series   A **finite series** is written as $a_1 + a_2 + \ldots + a_n$, where a_1, a_2, ..., a_n are n numbers called the **terms** in the series, and n, some positive integer, is the **length** of the series. The **sum** of the series is simply the sum of the n terms. For certain finite series, such as *arithmetic series* and *geometric series*, the sum of the series is given by a known formula. The following can also be established:

$$\sum_{r=1}^{n} r^2 = 1^2 + 2^2 + \cdots + n^2 = \tfrac{1}{6}n(n+1)(2n+1),$$

$$\sum_{r=1}^{n} r^3 = 1^3 + 2^3 + \cdots + n^3 = \tfrac{1}{4}n^2(n+1)^2.$$

An **infinite series** is written as $a_1 + a_2 + a_3 + \ldots$, with terms a_1, a_2, ..., one corresponding to each positive integer. Let s_n be the sum of the first n terms of such a series. If the sequence s_1, s_2, s_3, ... has a limit s, then the value s is called the **sum** (or **sum to infinity**) of the infinite series. Otherwise, the infinite series has no sum. See also *arithmetic series*, *geometric series*, *binomial series*, *Taylor series* and *Maclaurin series*.

set   A **set** is any well-defined collection of objects. It may be possible to define a set by listing the elements: $\{a, e, i, o, u\}$ is the set consisting of the vowels of the alphabet, $\{1, 2, \ldots, 100\}$ is the set of the first 100 positive integers. The meaning of $\{1, 2, 3, \ldots\}$ is also clear: it is the set of all positive integers. It may be possible to define a set as consisting of all elements, from some universal set, that satisfy some property. Thus the set of all real numbers greater than 1 can be written as either $\{x \mid x \in \mathbf{R} \text{ and } x > 1\}$ or $\{x : x \in \mathbf{R} \text{ and } x > 1\}$, both of which are read as 'the set of x such that x belongs to $\mathbf{R}$ and x is greater than 1'. The same set is sometimes written as $\{x \in \mathbf{R} \mid x > 1\}$.

sheet   See *hyperboloid of one sheet* and *hyperboloid of two sheets*.

sieve of Eratosthenes   All the *primes* up to some given number N can be found by a method called the **sieve of Eratosthenes**. List all the positive integers from 2 up to N. Leave the first number, 2, but delete all its multiples; leave the next remaining number, 3, but delete all its multiples; leave the next remaining number, 5, but delete all its multiples, and so on. The integers not deleted when the process ends are the primes.

significant figures   To count the number of **significant figures** in a given number, start with the first non-zero digit from the left and, moving to the right, count all the digits thereafter, counting final zeros if they are to the right of the decimal point. For example, $1 \cdot 2048$, $1 \cdot 2040$, $0 \cdot 012048$, $0 \cdot 0012040$ and $1204 \cdot 0$ all have 5 significant figures. In *rounding* or *truncation* of a number to n significant figures, the original is replaced by a number with n significant figures.

Note that final zeros to the left of the decimal point may or may not be significant: the number 1204000 has at least 4 significant figures, but without more information there is no way of knowing whether or not any more figures are significant. When 1203960 is rounded to 5 significant figures to give 1204000, an explanation that this has 5 significant figures is required. This could be made clear by writing it in *scientific notation*: $1 \cdot 2040 \times 10^6$.

To say that $a = 1 \cdot 2048$ to 5 significant figures means that the exact value of a becomes $1 \cdot 2048$ after rounding to 5 significant figures; that is to say, $1 \cdot 20475 \leq a \leq 1 \cdot 20485$.

similar (figures)   Two geometrical figures are **similar** if they are of the same shape but not necessarily of the same size. This includes the case when one is a mirror-image of the other, so the three triangles shown are all similar. For two similar triangles, there is a correspondence between their vertices such that corresponding angles are equal and the ratios of corresponding sides are equal. In the figure, $\angle A = \angle P$, $\angle B = \angle Q$, $\angle C = \angle R$ and $QR/BC = RP/CA = PQ/AB = 3/2$.

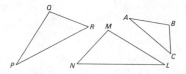

simple graph   A **simple graph** is a graph with no loops or multiple edges. See *graph*.

simple harmonic motion   Suppose that a particle is moving in a straight line so that its displacement x at time t is given by $x = A\sin(\omega t + \alpha)$, where A (> 0), ω and α are constants. Then the particle is executing **simple harmonic motion**, with *amplitude* A, *period* $2\pi/\omega$ and *phase* α. This equation gives the general solution of the differential equation $\ddot{x} + \omega^2 x = 0$.

simple interest   Suppose that a sum of money P (measured in £, say) is invested with interest of i per cent a year. When simple interest is given, the interest due each year is $(i/100)P$ and so, after n years, the amount becomes

$$P\left(1 + \frac{ni}{100}\right).$$

When points are plotted on graph paper to show how the amount increases, they lie on a straight line. Most banks and building societies in fact do not operate in this way but use the method of *compound interest*.

simple root   See *root*.

Simpson's rule   An approximate value can be found for the definite integral

$$\int_a^b f(x)\,dx,$$

using the values of $f(x)$ at equally spaced values of x between a and b, as follows. Divide $[a, b]$ into n equal subintervals of length h by the *partition*

$$a = x_0 < x_1 < x_2 < \cdots < x_{n-1} < x_n = b,$$

where $x_{i+1} - x_i = h = (b - a)/n$. Denote $f(x_i)$ by f_i and let P_i be the point (x_i, f_i). The *trapezium rule* uses the line segment P_iP_{i+1} as an approximation to the curve. Instead, take an arc of a certain parabola (in fact, the graph of a polynomial function of degree two) through the points P_0, P_1 and P_2, an arc of a parabola through P_2, P_3 and P_4, similarly, and so on. Thus n must be even. The resulting **Simpson's rule** gives

$$\tfrac{1}{3}h(f_0 + 4f_1 + 2f_2 + 4f_3 + 2f_4 + \cdots + 2f_{n-2} + 4f_{n-1} + f_n)$$

as an approximation to the value of the integral. This approximation has an *error* that is roughly proportional to $1/n^4$. In general, Simpson's rule can be expected to be much more accurate than the trapezium rule, for a given value of n.

simultaneous linear equations   The solution of a set of m linear equations in n unknowns can be investigated by the method of *Gaussian elimination* that transforms the augmented matrix to *echelon form*. The number of non-zero rows in the echelon form cannot be greater than the number of unknowns, and three cases can be distinguished:

   (i) If the echelon form has a row with all its entries zero except for a non-zero entry in the last place, the set of equations is inconsistent.
   (ii) If case (i) does not occur and, in the echelon form, the number of non-zero rows is equal to the number of unknowns, the set of equations has a unique solution.

(iii) If case (i) does not occur and, in the echelon form, the number of non-zero rows is less than the number of unknowns, the set of equations has infinitely many solutions.

When the set of equations is consistent, that is, in cases (ii) and (iii), the solution or solutions can be found either from the echelon form using *back substitution* or by using *Gauss-Jordan elimination* to find the *reduced echelon form*. When there are infinitely many solutions, they can be expressed in terms of *parameters* that replace those unknowns free to take arbitrary values.

sine See *trigonometric function*.

sine rule See *triangle*.

singleton A **singleton** is a set containing just one element.

singular A square matrix $\mathbf{A}$ is **singular** if $\det \mathbf{A} = 0$, where $\det \mathbf{A}$ is the determinant of $\mathbf{A}$. A singular matrix is not invertible (see *inverse matrix*).

sinh See *hyperbolic function*.

skew lines Two straight lines in 3-dimensional space that do not intersect and are not parallel are called **skew lines**.

skew-symmetric matrix Let $\mathbf{A}$ be the square matrix $[a_{ij}]$. Then the matrix $\mathbf{A}$ is **skew-symmetric** if $\mathbf{A}^T = -\mathbf{A}$ (see *transpose*), that is to say, if $a_{ij} = -a_{ji}$ for all i and j. It follows that in a skew-symmetric matrix the entries in the main diagonal are all zero: $a_{ii} = 0$ for all i.

slant asymptote See *asymptote*.

slant height See *cone*.

slope = *gradient* (of a straight line).

small circle A **small circle** is a circle on the surface of a sphere that is not a *great circle*. It is the curve of intersection obtained when a sphere is cut by a plane not through the centre of the sphere.

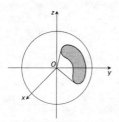

solid angle The 3-dimensional analogue of the 2-dimensional concept of angle is that of **solid angle**. Just as an angle is bounded by two lines, a solid angle is bounded by the generators of a cone.

A solid angle is measured in **steradians**: this is defined to be the area of the intersection of the solid angle with a sphere of unit radius. Thus the 'complete' solid angle at a point measures 4π steradians (comparable with one complete revolution measuring 2π radians).

solid of revolution   Suppose that a suitable plane curve is rotated through one revolution about some line in the same plane. The 3-dimensional region obtained is a **solid of revolution**. See also *volume of a solid of revolution*.

solution   A **solution** of a set of equations is an element, belonging to some appropriate *universal set*, specified or understood, that satisfies the equations. For a set of equations in n unknowns, a solution may be considered to be an n-tuple $(x_1, x_2, \ldots, x_n)$, or a column matrix

$$\begin{bmatrix} x_1 \\ x_2 \\ \vdots \\ x_n \end{bmatrix},$$

such that $x_1, x_2, \ldots, x_n$ satisfy the equations.

solution set   The **solution set** of a set of equations is the set consisting of all the solutions. It may be considered as a subset of some appropriate *universal set*, specified or understood.

spanning set   See *basis*.

speed   In mathematics, it is useful to distinguish between *velocity* and speed. First, when considering motion of a particle in a straight line, specify a positive direction so that it is a *directed line*. Then the velocity of the particle is positive if it is moving in the positive direction and negative if it moving in the negative direction. The **speed** of the particle is the *absolute value* of its velocity. In more advanced work, when the velocity is a vector **v**, the **speed** is the magnitude $|\mathbf{v}|$ of the velocity.

sphere   The **sphere**, with centre C and radius r, is the locus of all points (in 3-dimensional space) whose distance from C is equal to r. If C has Cartesian coordinates (a, b, c), this sphere has equation

$$(x - a)^2 + (y - b)^2 + (z - c)^2 = r^2.$$

The equation $x^2 + y^2 + z^2 + 2ux + 2vy + 2wz + d = 0$ represents a sphere provided $u^2 + v^2 + w^2 - d > 0$ and it is then an equation of the sphere with centre $(-u, -v, -w)$ and radius $\sqrt{u^2 + v^2 + w^2 - d}$.

The volume of a sphere of radius r is equal to $\frac{4}{3}\pi r^3$ and the surface area equals $4\pi r^2$.

spherical cap   See *zone*.

spherical polar coordinates   Suppose that three mutually perpendicular directed lines Ox, Oy and Oz, intersecting at the point O, and forming a right-handed system, are taken as coordinate axes (see *coordinates* (in 3-dimensional space)). For any point P, let M be the projection of P on the xy-plane. Let $r = |OP|$, let θ be the angle $\angle zOP$ in radians ($0 \le \theta \le \pi$) and let ϕ be the angle $\angle xOM$ in radians ($0 \le \phi < 2\pi$). Then (r, θ, ϕ) are the **spherical polar coordinates** of P. (The point O gives no value for θ or ϕ but is simply said to correspond to $r = 0$.) The value $\phi + 2k\pi$, where k is an integer, may be allowed in place of ϕ. The Cartesian coordinates (x, y, z) of P can be found from r, θ and ϕ by $x = r\sin\theta\cos\phi$, $y = r\sin\theta\sin\phi$, $z = r\cos\theta$. Spherical polar coordinates may be useful in treating problems involving spheres, for a sphere with centre at the origin then has equation $r = $ constant.

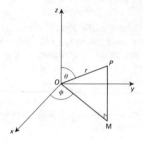

spiral   See *Archimedean spiral* and *equiangular spiral*.

square matrix   A *matrix* with the same number of rows and columns is called a **square matrix**.

square root   A **square root** of a real number a is a number x such that $x^2 = a$. If a is negative, there is no such real number. If a is positive, there are two such numbers, one positive and one negative. For $a \ge 0$, the notation $\sqrt{a}$ is used to denote quite specifically the non-negative square root of a.

squaring the circle   One of the problems that the Greek geometers attempted (like the *duplication of the cube* and the *trisection of an angle*) was to find a construction, with ruler and pair of compasses, to obtain a square whose area was equal to that of a given circle. This is equivalent to a geometrical construction to obtain a length of $\sqrt{\pi}$ from a given unit length. Now constructions of the kind envisaged can give only lengths that are algebraic numbers (and not even all algebraic numbers at that: for instance, $\sqrt[3]{2}$ cannot be obtained). So the proof by Lindemann in 1882 that π is *transcendental* established the impossibility of squaring the circle.

standard form (of a number)   = *scientific notation*.

statement   In mathematics, the fundamental property of a **statement** is that it makes sense and is either true or false. For example, 'There is a real number x such that $x^2 = 2$' makes sense and is true; the statement 'If x and y are positive integers then $x - y$ is a positive integer' makes sense and is false. In contrast, '$x = 2$' is not a statement.

stationary point (in one variable)   A **stationary point** is a point on the graph $y = f(x)$ at which f is *differentiable* and $f'(x) = 0$. The term is also used for the number c such that $f'(c) = 0$. The corresponding value $f(c)$ is a **stationary value**. A stationary point c can be classified as one of the following, depending upon the behaviour of f in the neighbourhood of c:

(i) a *local maximum*, if $f'(x) > 0$ to the left of c and $f'(x) < 0$ to the right of c,

(ii) a *local minimum*, if $f'(x) < 0$ to the left of c and $f'(x) > 0$ to the right of c,

(iii) neither local maximum nor minimum.

The case (iii) can be subdivided to distinguish between the following two cases. It may be that $f'(x)$ has the same sign to the left and to the right of c, in which case c is a horizontal *point of inflexion*; or it may be that there is an interval at every point of which $f'(x)$ equals zero and c is an end-point or interior point of this interval.

stationary point (in two variables)   A point P on the surface $z = f(x, y)$ is a **stationary point** if the *tangent plane* at P is horizontal. This is so if $\partial f / \partial x = 0$ and $\partial f / \partial y = 0$. Now let

$$r = \frac{\partial^2 f}{\partial x^2}, \qquad s = \frac{\partial^2 f}{\partial x \partial y}, \qquad t = \frac{\partial^2 f}{\partial y^2}.$$

If $rt > s^2$ and $r < 0$, the stationary point is a local maximum (all the vertical cross-sections through P have a local maximum at P). If $rt > s^2$ and $r > 0$, the stationary point is a local minimum (all the vertical cross-sections through P have a local minimum at P). If $rt < s^2$, the stationary point is a *saddle-point*.

stationary value   See *stationary point*.

steradian   A **steradian** is a unit for measuring *solid angles*.

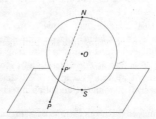

stereographic projection   Suppose that a sphere, centre O, touches a plane at the point S, and let N be the opposite end of the diameter through S.

If P is any point (except N) on the sphere, the line NP meets the plane in a corresponding point P'. Conversely, each point in the plane determines a point on the sphere, so there is a *one-to-one correspondence* between the points of the sphere (except N) and the points of the plane. This means of mapping sphere to plane is **stereographic projection**. Circles (great or small) not through N on the sphere's surface are mapped to circles in the plane; circles (great or small) through N are mapped to straight lines. The angles at which curves intersect are preserved by the projection.

straight line (in the plane)   A **straight line** in the plane is represented in Cartesian coordinates by a linear equation, that is, an equation of the form $ax + by + c = 0$, where the constants a and b are not both zero. A number of different forms are useful for obtaining an equation of a given line.

(i) The equation $y = mx + c$ represents the line with gradient m that cuts the y-axis at the point $(0, c)$. The value c may be called the **intercept**.

(ii) The line through a given point (x_1, y_1) with gradient m has equation $y - y_1 = m(x - x_1)$.

(iii) The line through the two points (x_1, y_1) and (x_2, y_2) has, if $x_2 \neq x_1$, equation

$$y - y_1 = \frac{y_2 - y_1}{x_2 - x_1}(x - x_1),$$

and has equation $x = x_1$, if $x_2 = x_1$.

(iv) The line that meets the coordinate axes at the points $(p, 0)$ and $(0, q)$, where $p \neq 0$ and $q \neq 0$, has equation $x/p + y/q = 1$.

straight line (in 3-dimensional space)   A **straight line** in 3-dimensional space can be specified as the intersection of two planes. Thus a straight line is given, in general, by two *linear equations*, $a_1 x + b_1 y + c_1 z + d_1 = 0$ and $a_2 x + b_2 y + c_2 z + d_2 = 0$. (If these equations represent identical or parallel planes, they do not define a straight line.) Often it is more convenient to obtain *parametric equations* for the line, which can also be written in 'symmetric form'. See also *vector equation* (of a line).

strictly decreasing   See *decreasing function* and *decreasing sequence*.

strictly included   See *proper subset*.

strictly increasing   See *increasing function* and *increasing sequence*.

strictly monotonic   See *monotonic function* and *monotonic sequence*.

subdivision (of an interval)   = *partition* (of an interval).

subfield   Let F be a *field* with operations of addition and multiplication. If S is a subset of F that forms a field with the same operations, then S is a **subfield** of F. For example, the set **Q** of rational numbers forms a subfield of the field **R** of real numbers.

subgroup   Let G be a *group* with a given operation. If H is a subset of G that forms a group with the same operation, then H is a **subgroup** of G. For example, $\{1, i, -1, -i\}$ forms a subgroup of the group of all non-zero complex numbers with multiplication.

submatrix   A **submatrix** of a *matrix* $\mathbf{A}$ is obtained from $\mathbf{A}$ by deleting from $\mathbf{A}$ some number of rows and some number of columns. For example, suppose that $\mathbf{A}$ is a 4×4 matrix and that $\mathbf{A} = [a_{ij}]$. Deleting the first and third rows and the second column gives the submatrix

$$\begin{bmatrix} a_{21} & a_{23} & a_{24} \\ a_{41} & a_{43} & a_{44} \end{bmatrix}.$$

subring   Let R be a *ring* with operations of addition and multiplication. If S is a subset of R that forms a ring with the same operations, then S is a **subring** of R. For example, the set $\mathbf{Z}$ of all integers forms a subring of the ring $\mathbf{R}$ of all real numbers, and the set of all even integers forms a subring of $\mathbf{Z}$.

subset   The set A is a **subset** of the set B if every element of A is an element of B. When this is so, A is **included** in B, written $A \subseteq B$, and B **includes** A, written $B \supseteq A$. The following properties hold:

  (i)   For all sets A, $\varnothing \subseteq A$ and $A \subseteq A$.
  (ii) For all sets A and B, $A = B$ if and only if $A \subseteq B$ and $B \subseteq A$.
  (iii) For all sets A, B and C, if $A \subseteq B$ and $B \subseteq C$ then $A \subseteq C$.

See also *proper subset*.

substitution   See *integration*.

subtraction (of matrices)   For matrices $\mathbf{A}$ and $\mathbf{B}$ of the same order, the operation of **subtraction** is defined by taking $\mathbf{A} - \mathbf{B}$ to mean $\mathbf{A} + (-\mathbf{B})$, where $-\mathbf{B}$ is the *negative* of $\mathbf{B}$. Thus if $\mathbf{A} = [a_{ij}]$ and $\mathbf{B} = [b_{ij}]$, then $\mathbf{A} - \mathbf{B} = \mathbf{C}$, where $\mathbf{C} = [c_{ij}]$ and $c_{ij} = a_{ij} - b_{ij}$.

sum (of a series)   See *series*.

sum (of matrices)   See *addition* (of matrices).

summation notation   The finite series $a_1 + a_2 + \cdots + a_n$ can be written, using the capital Greek letter sigma, as

$$\sum_{r=1}^{n} a_r.$$

Similarly, for example,

$$1^2 + 2^2 + \cdots + 10^2 = \sum_{r=1}^{10} r^2, \qquad 1 + x + x^2 + \cdots + x^{n-1} = \sum_{r=0}^{n-1} x^r.$$

(The letter 'r' used here could equally well be replaced by any other letter.)
In a similar way, the infinite series $a_1 + a_2 + \cdots$ can be written as

$$\sum_{r=1}^{\infty} a_r.$$

The infinite series may not have a sum to infinity (see *series*), but if it does
the same abbreviation is also used to denote the sum to infinity. For example,
the harmonic series

$$\sum_{r=1}^{\infty} \frac{1}{r}$$

is the infinite series $1 + \frac{1}{2} + \frac{1}{3} + \frac{1}{4} + \cdots$ and has no sum to infinity. But, for
$-1 < x < 1$, the geometric series $1 + x + x^2 + x^3 + \cdots$ has sum $1/(1 - x)$, and
this can be written

$$\sum_{r=0}^{\infty} x^r = \frac{1}{1 - x} \quad (-1 < x < 1).$$

sum to infinity   See *series* and *geometric series*.

supremum (plural: suprema)   See *bound*.

surface of revolution   Suppose that a suitable plane curve is rotated
through one revolution about some line in the same plane. The surface of the
3-dimensional figure obtained is a **surface of revolution**. See also *area of a
surface of revolution*.

surjection   = *onto mapping*.

surjective mapping   A *mapping* is **surjective** if it is *onto*.

symmetrical about a line   A plane figure is **symmetrical about the
line** l if, whenever P is a point of the figure, so too is P', where P' is the
mirror-image of P in the line l. The line l is called a **line of symmetry**;
and the figure is said to have **bilateral symmetry** or to be symmetrical by
reflection in the line l. The letter 'A', for example, is symmetrical about the
vertical line down the middle.

symmetrical about a point   A plane figure is **symmetrical about the
point** O if, whenever P is a point of the figure, so too is P', where O is the
midpoint of $P'P$. The point O is called a **centre of symmetry**; and the figure
is said to have **half-turn symmetry** about O because the figure appears the
same when rotated through half a revolution about O. The letter 'S', for
example, is symmetrical about the point at its centre.

symmetric difference   For sets A and B (subsets of some *universal set*),
the **symmetric difference**, denoted by $A + B$, is the set $(A \setminus B) \cup (B \setminus A)$.

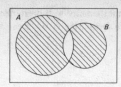

The notation $A \bigtriangleup B$ is also used. The set is represented by the shaded regions of the *Venn diagram* shown above. The following properties hold, for all A, B and C (subsets of some universal set E):

(i) $A + A = \varnothing$, $A + \varnothing = A$, $A + A' = E$, $A + E = A'$.

(ii) $A + B = (A \cup B) \setminus (A \cap B) = (A \cup B) \cap (A' \cup B')$.

(iii) $A + B = B + A$, the commutative law.

(iv) $(A + B) + C = A + (B + C)$, the associative law.

(v) $A \cap (B + C) = (A \cap B) + (A \cap C)$, the operation $\cap$ is distributive over the operation $+$.

symmetric group   For any set X, a permutation of X is a *one-to-one onto mapping* from X to X. If X has n elements, there are $n!$ permutations of X and the set of all of these, with *composition* of mappings as the operation, forms a *group* called the **symmetric group** of degree n, denoted by S_n.

symmetric matrix   Let $\mathbf{A}$ be the square matrix $[a_{ij}]$. Then $\mathbf{A}$ is **symmetric** if $\mathbf{A}^T = \mathbf{A}$ (see *transpose*); that is, if $a_{ij} = a_{ji}$ for all i and j.

symmetric relation   A *binary relation* $\sim$ on a set S is **symmetric** if, for all a and b in S, whenever $a \sim b$ then $b \sim a$.

symmetry (of a graph)   Two particular **symmetries** that a given graph $y = f(x)$ may have are symmetry about the y-axis, if f is an *even function*, and symmetry about the origin, if f is an *odd function*.

synthetic division   A method, known as **synthetic division**, of finding the quotient and remainder when a polynomial $f(x)$ is divided by a factor $x - h$, involves laying out the numbers in the form of a table. The rule to remember is that, at each step, 'you multiply and then add'. To divide $ax^3 + bx^2 + cx + d$ by $x - h$, set up a table as follows:

h	a	b	c	d
	0	...	...	...
	...	...	...	...

Working from the left, each total, written below the line, is multiplied by h and entered above the line in the next column. The two numbers in that column are added to form the next total:

h	a	b	c	d
	0	ah	...	...
	a	$ah + b$	...	...

The last total is equal to the remainder and the other numbers below the line give the coefficients of the quotient. By the *Remainder Theorem*, the remainder equals $f(h)$.

For example, suppose that $2x^3 - 7x^2 + 5x + 11$ is to be divided by $x - 2$. The resulting table is:

2	2	−7	5	11
	0	4	−6	−2
	2	−3	−1	9

So the remainder equals 9 and the quotient is $2x^2 - 3x - 1$. The calculations here in fact correspond exactly to those that are made when the polynomial is evaluated for $x = 2$ by *nested multiplication*, to obtain $f(2) = 9$.

tangent   See *trigonometric function*.

tangent line   See *tangent plane*.

tangent plane   Let P be a point on a smooth surface. The tangent at P to any curve through P on the surface is called a **tangent line** at P and the tangent lines are all perpendicular to a line through P called the **normal** to the surface at P. The tangent lines all lie in the plane through P perpendicular to this normal, and this plane is called the **tangent plane** at P. (A precise definition of 'smooth' cannot be given here. A tangent plane does *not* exist, however, at a point on the edge of a cube or at the vertex of a (double) cone, for example.)

At a point P on the surface, it may be that all the points near P (apart from P itself) lie on one side of the tangent plane at P. On the other hand, this may not be so: there may be some points close to P on one side of the tangent plane and some on the other. In this case, the tangent plane cuts the surface in two curves that intersect at P. This is what happens at a *saddle-point*.

tangent (to a curve)   Let P be a point on a (plane) curve. Then the **tangent** to the curve at P is the line through P that touches the curve at P. The gradient of the tangent at P is equal to the gradient of the curve at P.

tanh   See *hyperbolic function*.

tautology   A **tautology** is a *compound statement* that is true for all possible truth values of its components. For example, $p \Rightarrow (q \Rightarrow p)$ is a tautology, and this can be seen by calculating its *truth table*.

Taylor, Brook (1685–1731)   Taylor was the British mathematician who gave his name to *Taylor series*, the expansion of an arbitrary function in powers of the variable. The series was discovered by James Gregory, among others.

Taylor polynomial, Taylor series (or **expansion**)   See *Taylor's Theorem*.

Taylor's Theorem   Applied to a suitable function f, **Taylor's Theorem** gives a polynomial, called a **Taylor polynomial**, of any required degree, that is an approximation to $f(x)$.

THEOREM: Let f be a function such that, in an interval I, the derived functions $f^{(r)}$ $(r = 1, \ldots, n)$ are continuous, and suppose that $a \in I$. Then, for all x in I,

$$f(x) = f(a) + \frac{f'(a)}{1!}(x-a) + \frac{f''(a)}{2!}(x-a)^2 + \cdots + \frac{f^{(n-1)}(a)}{(n-1)!}(x-a)^{n-1} + R_n,$$

where various forms for the **remainder** R_n are available.

Two possible forms for R_n are

$$R_n = \frac{1}{(n-1)!} \int_a^x f^{(n)}(t)(x-t)^{n-1}\, dt \quad \text{and} \quad R_n = \frac{f^{(n)}(c)}{n!}(x-a)^n,$$

where c lies between a and x. By taking $x = a + h$, where h is small (positive or negative), the formula

$$f(a+h) = f(a) + \frac{f'(a)}{1!}h + \frac{f''(a)}{2!}h^2 + \cdots + \frac{f^{(n-1)}(a)}{(n-1)!}h^{n-1} + R_n$$

is obtained, where the second form of the remainder now becomes

$$R_n = \frac{f^{(n)}(a+k)}{n!}h^n,$$

and k lies between 0 and h. This enables $f(a+h)$ to be determined up to a certain degree of accuracy, the remainder R_n giving the *error*. Suppose now that, for the function f, Taylor's Theorem holds for all values of n, and that $R_n \to 0$ as $n \to \infty$; then an infinite series can be obtained whose sum is $f(x)$. In such a case, it is customary to write

$$f(x) = f(a) + \frac{f'(a)}{1!}(x-a) + \frac{f''(a)}{2!}(x-a)^2 + \cdots.$$

This is the **Taylor series** (or **expansion**) for f at (or about) a. The special case with $a = 0$ is the *Maclaurin series* for f.

techniques of integration   See *integration*.

term   See *sequence* and *series*.

terminating decimal   See *decimal*.

ternary relation   See *relation*.

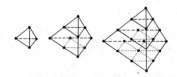

tetrahedral number   A **tetrahedral number** is an integer of the form $\frac{1}{6}n(n+1)(n+2)$, where n is a positive integer. This number equals the sum of the first n *triangular numbers*. The first few tetrahedral numbers are 1, 4, 10 and 20 and the reason for the name can be seen from the figure above.

tetrahedron (plural: tetrahedra)   A **tetrahedron** is a solid figure bounded by four triangular faces, and has four vertices and six edges. A regular tetrahedron has equilateral triangles as its faces and so all its edges have the same length.

third derivative   See *higher derivative*.

Thom, René (1923–)   Thom is a French mathematician best known for his theory of morphogenesis, popularly known as catastrophe theory. This is one of the few serious attempts to apply mathematics to the shapes and processes of living things. Most previous attempts have tried, naturally, to be quantitative in the tradition of applied mathematics. They are defeated by the sheer complexity of nature. Thom's theory has the strength of being both qualitative and rigorous.

torus (plural: tori)   Suppose that a circle of radius a is rotated through one revolution about a line, in the plane of the circle, a distance b from the centre of the circle, where $b > a$. The resulting surface or solid is called a **torus**, the shape of a 'doughnut' or 'anchor ring'. The surface area of such a torus is equal to $4\pi^2 ab$ and its volume equals $2\pi^2 a^2 b$.

trace   The **trace** of a square *matrix* is the sum of the entries in the *main diagonal*.

transcendental number   A **transcendental number** is a real number that is not a root of a polynomial equation with integer coefficients. In other words, a number is transcendental if it is not *algebraic*. In 1873, Hermite showed that e is transcendental; and it was shown by Lindemann, in 1882, that π is transcendental.

transformation (of the plane)   Let S be the set of points in the plane. A **transformation** of the plane is a *one-to-one mapping* from S to S. The most important transformations of the plane are the **linear transformations**, which are those that, in terms of Cartesian coordinates, can be represented by linear equations. For a linear transformation T, there are constants a, b, c, d, h and k such that T maps the point P with coordinates (x, y) to the point P' with coordinates (x', y'), where

$$x' = ax + by + h,$$
$$y' = cx + dy + k.$$

When $h = k = 0$, the origin O is a **fixed point**, since T maps O to itself, and then the transformation can be written $\mathbf{x}' = \mathbf{A}\mathbf{x}$, where

$$\mathbf{x} = \begin{bmatrix} x \\ y \end{bmatrix}, \qquad \mathbf{x}' = \begin{bmatrix} x' \\ y' \end{bmatrix}, \qquad \mathbf{A} = \begin{bmatrix} a & b \\ c & d \end{bmatrix}.$$

Examples of such transformations are *rotations* about O, *reflections* in lines through O and *dilatations* from O. *Translations* are examples of linear transformations in which O is not a fixed point.

transitive relation A *binary relation* $\sim$ on a set S is **transitive** if, for all a, b and c in S, whenever $a \sim b$ and $b \sim c$ then $a \sim c$.

translation of axes (in the plane) Suppose that a Cartesian coordinate system has a given x-axis and y-axis with origin O and given unit length, so that a typical point P has coordinates (x, y). Let O' be the point with coordinates (h, k), and consider a new coordinate system with X-axis and Y-axis parallel and similarly directed to the x-axis and y-axis, with the same unit length, with origin at O'. With respect to the new coordinate system, the point P has coordinates (X, Y). The old and new coordinates in such a **translation of axes** are related by $x = X + h$, $y = Y + k$, or, put another way, $X = x - h$, $Y = y - k$.

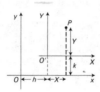

This procedure is useful for investigating, for example, a curve with equation $9x^2 + 4y^2 - 18x + 16y - 11 = 0$. Completing the square in x and y gives $9(x-1)^2 + 4(y+2)^2 = 36$, and so, with respect to a new coordinate system with origin at the point $(1, -2)$, the curve has the simple equation $9X^2 + 4Y^2 = 36$.

translation of axes (in 3-dimensional space) Just like a translation of axes in the plane, a **translation of axes** in 3-dimensional space can be made, to a new origin with coordinates (h, k, l), with new axes parallel and similarly directed to the old. The old coordinates (x, y, z) and new coordinates (X, Y, Z) are related by $x = X + h$, $y = Y + k$, $z = Z + l$, or, to put it another way, $X = x - h$, $Y = y - k$, $Z = z - l$.

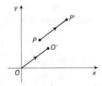

translation (of the plane) A **translation** of the plane is a *transformation* of the plane in which a point P with coordinates (x, y) is mapped to the point P' with coordinates (x', y'), where $x' = x + h$, $y' = y + k$. Thus the origin O is mapped to the point O' with coordinates (h, k) and the point P is mapped to the point P', where the *directed line-segment* $\overrightarrow{PP'}$ has the same direction and length as $\overrightarrow{OO'}$.

transpose   The **transpose** of an $m \times n$ matrix is the $n \times m$ matrix obtained by interchanging the rows and columns. The transpose of $\mathbf{A}$ is denoted by $\mathbf{A}^T$, $\mathbf{A}^t$ or $\mathbf{A}'$. Thus if $\mathbf{A} = [a_{ij}]$ then $\mathbf{A}^T = [a'_{ij}]$, where $a'_{ij} = a_{ji}$; that is,

$$\mathbf{A} = \begin{bmatrix} a_{11} & a_{12} & \cdots & a_{1n} \\ a_{21} & a_{22} & \cdots & a_{2n} \\ \vdots & \vdots & \ddots & \vdots \\ a_{m1} & a_{m2} & \cdots & a_{mn} \end{bmatrix}, \qquad \mathbf{A}^T = \begin{bmatrix} a_{11} & a_{21} & \cdots & a_{m1} \\ a_{12} & a_{22} & \cdots & a_{m2} \\ \vdots & \vdots & \ddots & \vdots \\ a_{1n} & a_{2n} & \cdots & a_{mn} \end{bmatrix}.$$

The following properties hold, for matrices $\mathbf{A}$ and $\mathbf{B}$ of appropriate orders:

(i) $(\mathbf{A}^T)^T = \mathbf{A}$.
(ii) $(\mathbf{A} + \mathbf{B})^T = \mathbf{A}^T + \mathbf{B}^T$.
(iii) $(k\mathbf{A})^T = k\mathbf{A}^T$.
(iv) $(\mathbf{AB})^T = \mathbf{B}^T \mathbf{A}^T$.

transverse axis   See *hyperbola*.

trapezium (plural: trapezia)   A **trapezium** is a quadrilateral with two parallel sides. If the parallel sides have lengths a and b and the distance between them is h, the area of the trapezium equals $\frac{1}{2}h(a+b)$.

trapezium rule   An approximate value can be found for the definite integral

$$\int_a^b f(x)\,dx,$$

using the values of $f(x)$ at equally spaced values of x between a and b, as follows. Divide $[a, b]$ into n equal subintervals of length h by the partition

$$a = x_0 < x_1 < x_2 < \cdots < x_{n-1} < x_n = b,$$

where $x_{i+1} - x_i = h = (b-a)/n$. Denote $f(x_i)$ by f_i and let P_i be the point (x_i, f_i). If the line segment $P_i P_{i+1}$ is used as an approximation to the curve $y = f(x)$ between x_i and x_{i+1}, the area under that part of the curve is approximately the area of the trapezium shown in the figure below, which equals $\frac{1}{2}h(f_i + f_{i+1})$. By adding up the areas of such trapezia between a and b, the resulting **trapezium rule** gives

$$\frac{1}{2}h(f_0 + 2f_1 + 2f_2 + \cdots + 2f_{n-1} + f_n)$$

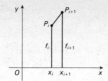

as an approximation to the value of the integral. This approximation has an *error* that is roughly proportional to $1/n^2$; when the number of subintervals is doubled, the error is roughly divided by 4. *Simpson's rule* is significantly more accurate.

trapezoidal rule   = *trapezium rule.*

Travelling Salesman Problem   The following mathematical problem is derived from a real-life situation. There are a certain number of towns, with routes between them, each route, from town i to town j, being assigned a value c_{ij}, giving the distance from town i to town j. The **Travelling Salesman Problem** is to find how to visit all the towns, returning to the starting point, in a way that minimizes the total distance travelled. (Alternatively, c_{ij} can be the cost of travelling, or the time taken to travel, from town i to town j, and the total cost or time is to be minimized.) Theoretically, the problem can be solved by considering all the possible routes. But if there are n towns, the number to be considered is $(n-1)!/2$ and, for all but the smallest values of n, this is impossible even for a large computer. What is sought is a manageable algorithm that works in what is considered to be a reasonable time. Such algorithms are known that find a way for which the total distance travelled is close to, but not necessarily quite equal to, the minimum.

tree   A **cycle** in a *graph* is a sequence v_0, e_1, v_1, ..., e_k, v_k $(k \geq 1)$ of alternately vertices and edges (where e_i is an edge joining v_{i-1} and v_i), with all the edges different and all the vertices different, except that $v_0 = v_k$. Then a **tree** is a connected graph with no cycles. It can be shown that a connected simple graph with n vertices is a tree if and only if it has $n - 1$ edges. The figure above shows all the trees with up to five vertices.

Particularly in applications, one of the vertices (which may be called **nodes**) of a tree may be designated as the **root** and the tree may be drawn with the vertices at different levels indicating their distance from the root. A rooted tree in which every vertex (except the root, of degree 2) has degree either 1 or 3, such as the one shown above, is called a **binary tree**.

triangle   Using the properties of angles made when one line cuts a pair of parallel lines, it is proved, as illustrated on the left below, that the angles of a triangle ABC add up to 180°. By considering separate areas, illustrated on the right below, it can be shown that the area of the triangle is half that of the rectangle shown, and so the area of a triangle is 'half base times height'.

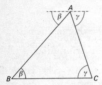 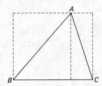

If now A, B and C denote the angles of the triangle and a, b and c the lengths of the sides opposite them, the following results hold:

(i) The area of the triangle equals $\frac{1}{2}bc \sin A$.

(ii) The **sine rule**:

$$\frac{a}{\sin A} = \frac{b}{\sin B} = \frac{c}{\sin C} = 2R,$$

where R is the radius of the *circumcircle*.

(iii) The **cosine rule**: $a^2 = b^2 + c^2 - 2bc \cos A$, or, in another form,

$$\cos A = \frac{b^2 + c^2 - a^2}{2bc}.$$

(iv) **Hero's formula**: Let $s = \frac{1}{2}(a+b+c)$. Then the area of the triangle equals $\sqrt{s(s-a)(s-b)(s-c)}$.

triangle inequality (for complex numbers)   If z_1 and z_2 are complex numbers, $|z_1 + z_2| \leq |z_1| + |z_2|$. This result is known as the **triangle inequality**

because it follows from the fact that $|OQ| \leq |OP_1| + |P_1Q|$, where P_1, P_2 and Q represent z_1, z_2 and $z_1 + z_2$ in the *complex plane*.

triangle inequality (for points in the plane)   For points A, B and C in the plane, $|AC| \leq |AB| + |BC|$. This result, the **triangle inequality**, says that the length of one side of a triangle is less than or equal to the sum of the lengths of the other two sides.

triangle inequality (for vectors)   Let $|\mathbf{a}|$ denote the length of the vector $\mathbf{a}$. For vectors $\mathbf{a}$ and $\mathbf{b}$, $|\mathbf{a} + \mathbf{b}| \leq |\mathbf{a}| + |\mathbf{b}|$. This result is known as the **triangle inequality**, since it is equivalent to saying that the length of one side of a triangle is less than or equal to the sum of the lengths of the other two sides.

triangular matrix   A **triangular matrix** is a square matrix that is either lower triangular or upper triangular; it is **lower triangular** if all the entries above the main diagonal are zero, and **upper triangular** if all the entries below the main diagonal are zero.

triangular number   A **triangular number** is an integer that is of the form $\frac{1}{2}n(n+1)$, where n is a positive integer. The first few triangular numbers are 1, 3, 6, 10 and 15 and the reason for the name can be seen from the figure.

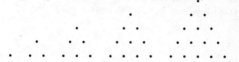

trigonometric function   Though the distinction tends to be overlooked, the **trigonometric functions** are different, depending upon whether degrees or radians are used.

USING DEGREES. The basic trigonometric functions, **cosine, sine** and **tangent**, are first introduced by using a right-angled triangle, but $\cos\theta°$, $\sin\theta°$ and $\tan\theta°$ can also be defined when θ is larger than 90 and when θ is negative. Let P be a point (not at O) with Cartesian coordinates (x, y). Suppose that OP makes an angle of $\theta°$ with the positive x-axis and that $|OP| = r$. Then the following are the definitions: $\cos\theta° = x/r$, $\sin\theta° = y/r$, and (when $x \neq 0$) $\tan\theta° = y/x$. It follows that $\tan\theta° = \sin\theta° / \cos\theta°$, and that $\cos^2 \theta° + \sin^2 \theta° = 1$. Some of the most frequently required values are:

θ	0	30	45	60	90
$\cos \theta°$	1	$\dfrac{\sqrt{3}}{2}$	$\dfrac{1}{\sqrt{2}}$	$\dfrac{1}{2}$	0
$\sin \theta°$	0	$\dfrac{1}{2}$	$\dfrac{1}{\sqrt{2}}$	$\dfrac{\sqrt{3}}{2}$	1
$\tan \theta°$	0	$\dfrac{1}{\sqrt{3}}$	1	$\sqrt{3}$	not defined

The point P may be in any of the four quadrants. By considering the signs of x and y, the quadrants in which the different functions take positive values can be found and are shown in the figure below. The following are useful for calculating values, when P is in quadrants 2, 3 or 4:

$$\cos(180 - \theta)° = -\cos\theta°, \qquad \sin(180 - \theta)° = \sin\theta°,$$
$$\cos(180 + \theta)° = -\cos\theta°, \qquad \sin(180 + \theta)° = -\sin\theta°,$$
$$\cos(-\theta)° = \cos\theta°, \qquad \sin(-\theta)° = -\sin\theta°.$$

The functions cosine and sine are periodic, of period 360; that is to say, $\cos(360 + \theta)° = \cos\theta°$ and $\sin(360 + \theta)° = \sin\theta°$. The function tangent is periodic, of period 180; that is, $\tan(180 + \theta)° = \tan\theta°$.

2 sin positive	1 all positive
3 tan positive	4 cos positive

USING RADIANS. For more advanced work, it is essential that angles are always measured in *radians*. It is necessary to introduce new trigonometric functions $\cos x$, $\sin x$ and $\tan x$, where now x is a real number. These agree with the former functions, if x is treated as being the measure in radians of the angle formerly measured in degrees. For example, since π radians $= 180°$,

$$\cos\pi = \cos 180° = -1, \quad \sin\frac{\pi}{3} = \sin 60° = \frac{\sqrt{3}}{2}, \quad \tan\frac{\pi}{4} = \tan 45° = \frac{1}{\sqrt{2}}.$$

The functions cos and sin are periodic with period 2π, and tan has period π.

It is important to distinguish between the functions $\cos x$ and $\cos x°$. They are different functions, but are related since $\cos x° = \cos(\pi x/180)$. The same applies to sin and tan. Sometimes authors do not make the distinction and use the notation $\cos A$, for example, where A is an angle measured in

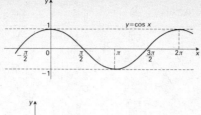

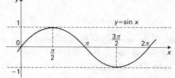

degrees or radians. This is what has been done in the Table of Trigonometric Formulae (Appendix 5).

The other trigonometric functions, **cotangent**, **secant** and **cosecant**, are defined as follows:

$$\cot x = \frac{\cos x}{\sin x}, \qquad \sec x = \frac{1}{\cos x}, \qquad \operatorname{cosec} x = \frac{1}{\sin x},$$

where, in each case, values of x that make the denominator zero must be excluded from the domain. The basic identities satisfied by the trigonometric functions will be found in the Table of Trigonometric Formulae (Appendix 5).

In order to find the derivatives of the trigonometric functions, it is first necessary to show that

$$\lim_{x \to 0} \frac{\sin x}{x} = 1.$$

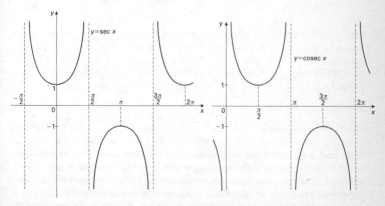

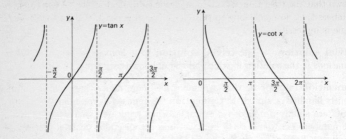

In view of the essentially geometric definition of $\sin x$, a geometric method has to be used. By considering (when $0 < x < \pi/2$) the areas of $\triangle OBQ$, sector OAB and $\triangle OAP$, where $\angle OAB$ measures x radians, it can be shown that

$$\cos x < \frac{\sin x}{x} < \frac{1}{\cos x}.$$

After dealing also with $x < 0$, the required limit can be deduced. Hence it can be shown that

$$\frac{d}{dx}(\sin x) = \cos x, \qquad \frac{d}{dx}(\cos x) = -\sin x.$$

The derivatives of the other trigonometric functions are found from these, by using the rules for differentiation, and are given in the Table of Derivatives (Appendix 2).

triple product (of vectors)   See *scalar triple product* and *vector triple product*.

triple root   See *root*.

trisection of an angle   One of the problems that the Greek geometers attempted (like the *duplication of the cube* and the *squaring of the circle*) was to find a construction, with ruler and compasses, to trisect any angle, that is, to divide it into three equal parts. (The construction for bisecting an angle is probably familiar.) Now constructions of the kind envisaged can give only lengths belonging to a class of numbers obtained, essentially, by addition, subtraction, multiplication, division and the taking of square roots. It can be shown that the trisection of certain angles is equivalent to the construction of numbers that do not belong to this class. So, in general, the trisection of an angle is impossible.

trivial solution The **trivial solution** to a *homogeneous set of linear equations* is the solution in which all the unknowns are equal to zero.

truncation Suppose that a number has more digits than can be conveniently handled or stored. In **truncation** (as opposed to *rounding*), the extra digits are simply dropped; for example, when truncated to 1 decimal place, the numbers 1·875 and 1·845 both become 1·8. See also *decimal places* and *significant figures*.

truth table The *truth value* of a *compound statement* can be determined from the truth values of its components. A table that gives, for all possible truth values of the components, the resulting truth values of the compound statement is a **truth table**. The truth table for $\neg p$ is

p	$\neg p$
T	F
F	T

and combined truth tables for $p \wedge q$, $p \vee q$ and $p \Rightarrow q$ are as follows:

p	q	$p \wedge q$	$p \vee q$	$p \Rightarrow q$
T	T	T	T	T
T	F	F	T	F
F	T	F	T	T
F	F	F	F	T

From these, any other truth table can be completed. For example, the final column below, giving the truth table for the compound statement $(p \wedge q) \vee (\neg r)$, is found by first completing columns for $p \wedge q$ and $\neg r$:

p	q	r	$p \wedge q$	$\neg r$	$(p \wedge q) \vee (\neg r)$
T	T	T	T	F	T
T	T	F	T	T	T
T	F	T	F	F	F
T	F	F	F	T	T
F	T	T	F	F	F
F	T	F	F	T	T
F	F	T	F	F	F
F	F	F	F	T	T

truth value The meaning of **truth value** is apparent from the following usage: if a statement is true, its truth value is T (or *TRUE*); if the statement is false, its truth value is F (or *FALSE*).

turning point   A **turning point** is a point on a graph $y = f(x)$ at which $f'(x) = 0$ and $f'(x)$ changes sign. A turning point is either a *local maximum* or a *local minimum*. Some authors use 'turning point' as equivalent to *stationary point*.

U

unary operation   A **unary operation** on a set S is a rule that associates with any element of S a resulting element. If this resulting element is always also in S, then it is said that S is **closed under** the operation. The following are examples of unary operations: the rule that associates with each integer a its negative $-a$; the rule that associates with each non-zero real number a its inverse $1/a$; and the rule that associates with any subset A of a universal set E its complement A'.

union   The **union** of sets A and B (subsets of a *universal set*) is the set consisting of all objects that belong to A or B (or both), and it is denoted by $A \cup B$ (read as 'A **union** B'). Thus the term 'union' is used for both the resulting set and the operation, a *binary operation* on the set of all subsets of a universal set. The following properties hold:

  (i) For all A, $A \cup A = A$, $A \cup \emptyset = A$.
  (ii) For all A and B, $A \cup B = B \cup A$; that is, $\cup$ is commutative.
  (iii) For all A, B and C, $(A \cup B) \cup C = A \cup (B \cup C)$; that is, $\cup$ is associative.

In view of (iii), the union $A_1 \cup A_2 \cup \cdots \cup A_n$ of more than two sets can be written without brackets, and it may also be denoted by

$$\bigcup_{i=1}^{n} A_i.$$

Unique Factorization Theorem   The process of writing any positive integer as the product of its prime factors is probably familiar; it may be taken as self-evident that this can be done in only one way. Known as the **Unique Factorization Theorem**, this result of elementary number theory can be proved from basic axioms about the integers.

THEOREM: Any positive integer ($\neq 1$) can be expressed as a product of primes. This expression is unique except for the order in which the primes occur.

Thus, any positive integer n ($\neq 1$) can be written as $p_1^{\alpha_1} p_2^{\alpha_2} \ldots p_r^{\alpha_r}$, where p_1, p_2, ..., p_r are primes satisfying $p_1 < p_2 < \cdots < p_r$ and α_1, α_2, ..., α_r are positive integers. This is the **prime decomposition** of n. For example, writing $360 = 2^3 \times 3^2 \times 5$ shows the prime decomposition of 360.

unit circle   In the plane, the **unit circle** is the circle of radius 1 with its centre at the origin. In Cartesian coordinates, it has equation $x^2 + y^2 = 1$. In the *complex plane*, it represents those complex numbers z such that $|z| = 1$.

unit matrix   = *identity matrix*.

unit vector   A **unit vector** is vector with magnitude, or length, equal to 1. For any non-zero vector **a**, a unit vector in the direction of **a** is **a**/|**a**|. The row vector $[\,a_1 \quad a_2 \quad \ldots \quad a_n\,]$ or the column vector

$$\begin{bmatrix} a_1 \\ a_2 \\ \vdots \\ a_n \end{bmatrix}$$

may be called a unit vector if $\sqrt{a_1{}^2 + a_2{}^2 + \cdots + a_n{}^2} = 1$.

universal quantifier   See *quantifier*.

universal set   In a particular piece of work, it may be convenient to fix the **universal set** E, a set to which all the objects to be discussed belong. Then all the sets considered are subsets of E.

upper bound   See *bound*.

upper limit   See *limit of integration*.

upper triangular matrix   See *triangular matrix*.

V

valency   = *degree* (of a vertex of a graph).

value   See *constant function, function* and *infinite product*.

vector   In physics or engineering, the term 'vector' is used to describe a physical quantity like velocity or force that has a magnitude and a direction. Sometimes there may also be a specified point of application, but generally in mathematics that is not of concern. Thus a vector is to be 'something' that has magnitude and direction.

One approach is to define a **vector** to be an *ordered pair* consisting of a positive real number, the **magnitude**, or **length**, and a direction in space. The vectors **a** and **b** are said to be equal if they have the same magnitude and the same direction. The **zero vector 0** that has magnitude 0 and no direction is also allowed.

Another way is to make use of the well-defined notion of *directed line-segment* and define a **vector** to be the collection of all directed line-segments with a given length and a given direction. If $\overrightarrow{AB}$ is a directed line-segment in the collection that is the vector **a**, it is said that $\overrightarrow{AB}$ **represents a**. If $\overrightarrow{AB}$ and $\overrightarrow{CD}$ represent the same vector, then $\overrightarrow{AB}$ and $\overrightarrow{CD}$ are parallel and have the same length. The **magnitude**, or **length**, $|\mathbf{a}|$ of the vector **a** is the length of any of the directed line-segments that represent **a**. According to this definition, two vectors are **equal** if they are the same collection of directed line-segments. It is also necessary to permit directed line-segments of length zero and define the **zero vector 0** to be the collection of all these.

In the first approach, the connection with directed line-segments is made by saying that a directed line-segment $\overrightarrow{AB}$ **represents** the vector **a** if the length and direction of $\overrightarrow{AB}$ are equal to the magnitude and direction of **a**. Some authors write $\overrightarrow{AB} = \mathbf{a}$ if $\overrightarrow{AB}$ represents the vector **a**, and then, if $\overrightarrow{AB} = \mathbf{a}$ and $\overrightarrow{CD} = \mathbf{a}$, they go on to write $\overrightarrow{AB} = \overrightarrow{CD}$. Some authors actually use the word 'vector' for what we prefer to call a directed line-segment. They then write $\overrightarrow{AB} = \overrightarrow{CD}$ if $\overrightarrow{AB}$ and $\overrightarrow{CD}$ have the same length and the same direction.

vector equation (of a line)   Given a line in space, let **a** be the *position vector* of a point A on the line and **u** any vector with direction along the line. Then the line consists of all points P whose position vector **p** is given by $\mathbf{p} = \mathbf{a} + t\mathbf{u}$ for some value of t. This is a **vector equation** of the line.

It is established by noting that P lies on the line if and only if $\mathbf{p} - \mathbf{a}$ has the direction of $\mathbf{u}$ or its negative, which is equivalent to $\mathbf{p} - \mathbf{a}$ being a scalar multiple of $\mathbf{u}$. If, instead, the line is specified by two points A and B on it, with position vectors $\mathbf{a}$ and $\mathbf{b}$, then the line has vector equation $\mathbf{p} = (1 - t)\mathbf{a} + t\mathbf{b}$. This is obtained by setting $\mathbf{u} = \mathbf{b} - \mathbf{a}$ in the previous form.

vector equation (of a plane)   Given a plane in 3-dimensional space, let $\mathbf{a}$ be the *position vector* of a point A in the plane and $\mathbf{n}$ a *normal vector* to the plane. Then the plane consists of all points P whose position vector $\mathbf{p}$ satisfies $(\mathbf{p} - \mathbf{a}) \cdot \mathbf{n} = 0$. This is a **vector equation** of the plane. It may also be written $\mathbf{p} \cdot \mathbf{n} = $ constant. By supposing that $\mathbf{p}$ has components x, y, z, that $\mathbf{a}$ has components x_1, y_1, z_1, and that $\mathbf{n}$ has components l, m, n, the first form of the equation becomes $l(x - x_1) + m(y - y_1) + n(z - z_1) = 0$ and the second form becomes the standard linear equation $lx + my + nz = $ constant.

vector product   Let $\mathbf{a}$ and $\mathbf{b}$ be non-zero non-parallel vectors and let θ be the angle between them (θ in radians, with $0 < \theta < \pi$). The **vector product** $\mathbf{a} \times \mathbf{b}$ of $\mathbf{a}$ and $\mathbf{b}$ is defined as follows. Its magnitude equals $|\mathbf{a}||\mathbf{b}| \sin \theta$, and its direction is perpendicular to $\mathbf{a}$ and $\mathbf{b}$ such that $\mathbf{a}$, $\mathbf{b}$ and $\mathbf{a} \times \mathbf{b}$ form a right-handed system. So viewed from a position facing the direction of $\mathbf{a} \times \mathbf{b}$, the vector $\mathbf{a}$ has to be rotated clockwise through an angle of θ to have the direction of $\mathbf{b}$. If $\mathbf{a}$ is parallel to $\mathbf{b}$ or if one of them is the zero vector $\mathbf{0}$, then $\mathbf{a} \times \mathbf{b}$ is defined to be $\mathbf{0}$. The notation $\mathbf{a} \wedge \mathbf{b}$ is also used for $\mathbf{a} \times \mathbf{b}$. The following properties hold, for all vectors $\mathbf{a}$, $\mathbf{b}$ and $\mathbf{c}$:

  (i) $\mathbf{b} \times \mathbf{a} = -(\mathbf{a} \times \mathbf{b})$.
  (ii) $\mathbf{a} \times (k\mathbf{b}) = (k\mathbf{a}) \times \mathbf{b} = k(\mathbf{a} \times \mathbf{b})$.
  (iii) The magnitude $|\mathbf{a} \times \mathbf{b}|$ is equal to the area of the parallelogram with sides determined by $\mathbf{a}$ and $\mathbf{b}$.
  (iv) $\mathbf{a} \times (\mathbf{b} + \mathbf{c}) = \mathbf{a} \times \mathbf{b} + \mathbf{a} \times \mathbf{c}$, the distributive law.
  (v) If the vectors, in terms of their components (with respect to the standard vectors $\mathbf{i}, \mathbf{j}, \mathbf{k}$), are $\mathbf{a} = a_1\mathbf{i} + a_2\mathbf{j} + a_3\mathbf{k}$, $\mathbf{b} = b_1\mathbf{i} + b_2\mathbf{j} + b_3\mathbf{k}$, then $\mathbf{a} \times \mathbf{b} = (a_2b_3 - a_3b_2)\mathbf{i} + (a_3b_1 - a_1b_3)\mathbf{j} + (a_1b_2 - a_2b_1)\mathbf{k}$. This can be written, with an abuse of 3×3 determinant notation, as

$$\mathbf{a} \times \mathbf{b} = \begin{vmatrix} \mathbf{i} & \mathbf{j} & \mathbf{k} \\ a_1 & a_2 & a_3 \\ b_1 & b_2 & b_3 \end{vmatrix}.$$

vector projection (of a vector on a vector)   Given non-zero vectors $\mathbf{a}$ and $\mathbf{b}$, let $\overrightarrow{OA}$ and $\overrightarrow{OB}$ be *directed line-segments* representing $\mathbf{a}$ and $\mathbf{b}$, and let θ be the angle between them (θ in radians, with $0 \leq \theta \leq \pi$). Let C be the *projection* of B on the line OA. The **vector projection** of $\mathbf{b}$ on $\mathbf{a}$ is the vector represented by $\overrightarrow{OC}$. Since $|OC| = |OB| \cos \theta$, this vector projection is equal to $|\mathbf{b}| \cos \theta$ times the unit vector $\mathbf{a}/|\mathbf{a}|$. Thus the vector projection of $\mathbf{b}$ on $\mathbf{a}$ equals

$$\left(\frac{\mathbf{a} \cdot \mathbf{b}}{\mathbf{a} \cdot \mathbf{a}} \right) \mathbf{a}.$$

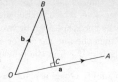

The **scalar projection** of **b** on **a** is equal to $(\mathbf{a}\cdot\mathbf{b})/|\mathbf{a}|$, which equals $|\mathbf{b}|\cos\theta$. It is positive when the vector projection of **b** on **a** is in the same direction as **a** and is negative when the vector projection is in the opposite direction to **a**; and its absolute value gives the length of the vector projection of **b** on **a**.

vector triple product For vectors **a**, **b** and **c**, the vector $\mathbf{a}\times(\mathbf{b}\times\mathbf{c})$, being the *vector product* of **a** with the vector $\mathbf{b}\times\mathbf{c}$, is called a **vector triple product**. The use of brackets here is essential, since $(\mathbf{a}\times\mathbf{b})\times\mathbf{c}$, another vector triple product, gives, in general, quite a different result. The vector $\mathbf{a}\times(\mathbf{b}\times\mathbf{c})$ is perpendicular to $\mathbf{b}\times\mathbf{c}$ and so lies in the plane determined by **b** and **c**. In fact, $\mathbf{a}\times(\mathbf{b}\times\mathbf{c})=(\mathbf{a}\cdot\mathbf{c})\mathbf{b}-(\mathbf{a}\cdot\mathbf{b})\mathbf{c}$.

velocity Suppose that a particle is moving in a straight line, with a point O on the line taken as origin and one direction taken as positive. Let x be the *displacement* of the particle at time t. The **velocity** of the particle is equal to $\dot{x}$ or dx/dt, the *rate of change* of x with respect to t. The velocity is positive when the particle is moving in the positive direction and negative when it is moving in the negative direction.

Venn diagram A **Venn diagram** is a particular method for displaying relations between subsets of some *universal set*. The universal set E is represented by the interior of a rectangle, say, and subsets of E are represented by regions inside this, bounded by simple closed curves. For instance, two sets A and B can be represented by the interiors of overlapping circles and then the sets $A\cup B$, $A\cap B$ and $A\setminus B$, for example, are represented by the shaded regions shown.

Given one set A, the universal set is divided into two disjoint subsets A and A', which can be clearly seen in a simple Venn diagram. Given two sets A and B, the universal set E is divided into four disjoint subsets $A\cap B$, $A'\cap B$, $A\cap B'$ and $A'\cap B'$. A Venn diagram drawn with two overlapping circles for A and B clearly shows the four corresponding regions. Given three sets A, B and C, the universal set E is divided into eight disjoint subsets $A\cap B\cap C$, $A'\cap B\cap C$, $A\cap B'\cap C$, $A\cap B\cap C'$, $A\cap B'\cap C'$, $A'\cap B\cap C'$, $A'\cap B'\cap C$ and $A'\cap B'\cap C'$, and these can be illustrated in a Venn diagram as shown.

Venn diagrams can be used with care to prove properties such as *de Morgan's laws*, but some authors prefer other proofs because a diagram may only illustrate a special case. Four general sets, for example, should not be represented by four overlapping circles because they cannot be drawn in such a way as to make apparent the 16 disjoint subsets into which E should be divided.

vertex　　See *ellipse*, *hyperbola* and *parabola*; and *cone*.

vertex (of a graph), **vertex-set**　　See *graph*.

volume of a solid of revolution　　Let $y = f(x)$ be the graph of a function f *continuous* on $[a, b]$ and such that $f(x) \geq 0$ for all x in $[a, b]$. The **volume V of the solid of revolution** obtained by rotating, through one revolution about the x-axis, the region bounded by the curve $y = f(x)$, the x-axis and the lines $x = a$ and $x = b$, is given by

$$V = \int_a^b \pi y^2 \, dx = \int_a^b \pi (f(x))^2 \, dx.$$

PARAMETRIC FORM.　For the curve $x = x(t)$, $y = y(t)$　$(t \in [\alpha, \beta])$, the volume V is given by

$$V = \int_\alpha^\beta \pi y^2 \frac{dx}{dt} \, dt = \int_\alpha^\beta \pi (y(t))^2 x'(t) \, dt.$$

Von Neumann, John (1903–1957)　　Von Neumann, 'Doctor Miracle', was born in Budapest but lived in America from 1930. Within pure mathematics, he is best known for his work in functional analysis, particularly in the area of Hilbert spaces. In applied mathematics, he was one of the founders of optimization theory and the theory of games. He wrote a fundamental text on mathematical economics. He had a lifelong interest in mechanical devices and was something of an inventor. This led to his being involved crucially in the initial development of the modern electronic computer and the important concept of the stored program. His most significant failure was his abortive attempt to introduce Viennese café life to Princeton, to his great regret.

W

Wallis's Product   See *pi*.

Weierstrass, Karl (1815–1897)   Nineteenth-century mathematical analysis developed out of the unruly cornucopia of eighteenth-century calculus. The process was started by people like Cauchy. It came to maturity in the work of Weierstrass. In the late eighteenth century, mathematicians had been rather vague about the difference between a function and a formula. By Weierstrass's time, things had developed to the point where he was able and concerned to give an example of a function that is everywhere continuous but nowhere differentiable. It was, in a sense, the point at which mathematical analysis departed from intuition and common sense, much to the annoyance of many of Weirstrass's detractors. Some of his work was done while he was a provincial school teacher, having little contact with the world of professional mathematicians. He must be one of the few people to have been promoted directly from school teacher to professor of mathematics at the late age of 40.

weighted mean   See *mean*.

Z

Z   See *integer*.

Z_n   See *residue class* (modulo n).

zero divisor   = *divisor of zero*.

zero element   An element z is a **zero element** for a *binary operation* ∘ on a set S if, for all a in S, $a \circ z = z \circ a = z$. Thus the real number 0 is a zero element for multiplication since, for all a, $a0 = 0a = 0$. The term 'zero element', also denoted by 0, may be used for an element such that $a + 0 = 0 + a = a$ for all a in S, when S is a set with a binary operation $+$ called addition. Strictly speaking, this is a *neutral element* for the operation $+$.

zero function   In real analysis, the **zero function** is the *real function* f such that $f(x) = 0$ for all x in $\mathbf{R}$.

zero matrix   The $m \times n$ **zero matrix O** is the $m \times n$ matrix with all its entries zero. A zero column matrix or row matrix may be denoted by $\mathbf{0}$.

zero (of a function)   See *root*.

zero vector   See *vector*.

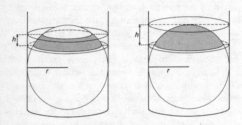

zone   A **zone** of a sphere is the part between two parallel planes. If the sphere has radius r and the distance between the planes is h, the area of the curved surface of the zone equals $2\pi rh$.

   A **circumscribing cylinder** of a sphere is a right-circular cylinder with the same radius as the sphere and with its axis passing through the centre of the sphere. Suppose that a zone is formed by two parallel planes. Take the circumscribing cylinder with its axis perpendicular to the two planes as shown. It is an interesting fact that the area of the curved surface of the zone is equal to the area of the part of the circumscribing cylinder between the same two planes. The special case when one of the planes touches the sphere gives the area of a **spherical cap** as $2\pi rh$.

Appendix 1

TABLE OF AREAS AND VOLUMES

(For unexplained notation, see under the relevant reference.)

Rectangle, length a, width b:
   Area $= ab$.

Parallelogram:
   Area $= bh = ab\sin\theta$.

Triangle:
   Area $= \frac{1}{2}$ base $\times$ height $= \frac{1}{2}bc\sin A$.

Trapezium:
   Area $= \frac{1}{2}h(a+b)$.

Circle, radius r:
   Area $= \pi r^2$,
   Length of circumference $= 2\pi r$.

Right-circular cylinder, radius r, height h:
   Volume $= \pi r^2 h$,
   Curved surface area $= 2\pi rh$.

Right-circular cone:
   Volume $= \frac{1}{3}\pi r^2 h$,
   Curved surface area $= \pi rl$.

Frustum of a cone:
   Volume $= \frac{1}{3}\pi h(a^2 + ab + b^2)$,
   Curved surface area $= \pi(a+b)l$.

Sphere, radius r:
   Volume $= \frac{4}{3}\pi r^3$,
   Surface area $= 4\pi r^2$.

Zone of a sphere:
   Curved surface area $= 2\pi rh$.

Appendix 2

TABLE OF DERIVATIVES

$f(x)$	$f'(x)$
k (constant)	0
x	1
x^k	kx^{k-1}
$\sin x$	$\cos x$
$\cos x$	$-\sin x$
$\tan x$	$\sec^2 x$
$\sec x$	$\sec x \tan x$
$\operatorname{cosec} x$	$-\operatorname{cosec} x \cot x$
$\cot x$	$-\operatorname{cosec}^2 x$
e^{kx}	ke^{kx}
$\ln x$	$1/x$
$a^x \quad (a > 0)$	$a^x \ln a$
$\sin^{-1} x$	$\dfrac{1}{\sqrt{1 - x^2}}$
$\cos^{-1} x$	$-\dfrac{1}{\sqrt{1 - x^2}}$
$\tan^{-1} x$	$\dfrac{1}{1 + x^2}$
$\sinh x$	$\cosh x$
$\cosh x$	$\sinh x$
$\tanh x$	$\operatorname{sech}^2 x$
$\coth x$	$-\operatorname{cosech}^2 x$
$\sinh^{-1} x$	$\dfrac{1}{\sqrt{x^2 + 1}}$
$\cosh^{-1} x$	$\dfrac{1}{\sqrt{x^2 - 1}}$
$\tanh^{-1} x$	$\dfrac{1}{1 - x^2}$

Appendix 3

TABLE OF INTEGRALS

Notes:

(i) The table gives, for each function f, an antiderivative ϕ. The function ϕ_1 given by $\phi_1(x) = \phi(x) + c$, where c is an arbitrary constant, is also an antiderivative of f.

(ii) In certain cases, for example when $f(x) = 1/x$, $\tan x$, $\cot x$, $\sec x$, $\operatorname{cosec} x$ and $\sqrt{x^2 - a^2}$, the function f is not continuous for all x. In these cases, a definite integral $\int_a^b f(x)\,dx$ can be evaluated as $\phi(b) - \phi(a)$ only if a and b both belong to an interval in which f is continuous.

$f(x)$	$\phi(x) = \displaystyle\int f(x)\,dx$
$x^k \quad (k \neq -1)$	$\dfrac{x^{k+1}}{k+1}$
$1/x$	$\ln|x|$
$\sin x$	$-\cos x$
$\cos x$	$\sin x$
$\tan x$	$-\ln|\cos x| = \ln|\sec x|$
$\sec x$	$\ln|\sec x + \tan x|$
$\operatorname{cosec} x$	$\ln|\operatorname{cosec} x - \cot x| = \ln|\tan \tfrac{1}{2}x|$
$\cot x$	$\ln|\sin x|$
$\sin^2 x$	$\tfrac{1}{2}(x - \tfrac{1}{2}\sin 2x)$
$\cos^2 x$	$\tfrac{1}{2}(x + \tfrac{1}{2}\sin 2x)$
$\sinh x$	$\cosh x$
$\cosh x$	$\sinh x$
$e^{kx} \quad (k \neq 0)$	e^{kx}/k
$e^{ax}\sin bx$	$\dfrac{e^{ax}}{a^2 + b^2}(a\sin bx - b\cos bx)$
$e^{ax}\cos bx$	$\dfrac{e^{ax}}{a^2 + b^2}(a\cos bx + b\sin bx)$

$f(x)$	$\phi(x) = \int f(x)\,dx$
$a^x \quad (a > 0, a \neq 1)$	$a^x / \ln a$
$\ln x$	$x \ln x - x$
$\dfrac{1}{\sqrt{a^2 - x^2}} \quad (a > 0)$	$\sin^{-1} \dfrac{x}{a}$
$\dfrac{1}{a^2 + x^2} \quad (a > 0)$	$\dfrac{1}{a} \tan^{-1} \dfrac{x}{a}$
$\dfrac{1}{x^2 - a^2} \quad (a > 0)$	$\dfrac{1}{2a} \ln \left| \dfrac{x - a}{x + a} \right|$
$\dfrac{1}{\sqrt{x^2 + a^2}} \quad (a > 0)$	$\sinh^{-1} \dfrac{x}{a} \quad \text{or} \quad \ln(x + \sqrt{x^2 + a^2})$
$\dfrac{1}{\sqrt{x^2 - a^2}} \quad (a > 0)$	$\cosh^{-1} \dfrac{x}{a} \quad \text{or} \quad \ln \left| x + \sqrt{x^2 - a^2} \right|$
$\sqrt{x^2 + a^2}$	$\frac{1}{2} x \sqrt{x^2 + a^2} + \frac{1}{2} a^2 \ln(x + \sqrt{x^2 + a^2})$
$\sqrt{x^2 - a^2}$	$\frac{1}{2} x \sqrt{x^2 - a^2} - \frac{1}{2} a^2 \ln \left| x + \sqrt{x^2 - a^2} \right|$
$\sqrt{a^2 - x^2} \quad (a > 0)$	$\frac{1}{2} x \sqrt{a^2 - x^2} + \frac{1}{2} a^2 \sin^{-1} \dfrac{x}{a}$

Appendix 4

TABLE OF SERIES

$$e^x = 1 + \frac{x}{1!} + \frac{x^2}{2!} + \cdots + \frac{x^n}{n!} + \cdots \quad \text{(for all } x\text{)},$$

$$\sin x = x - \frac{x^3}{3!} + \frac{x^5}{5!} - \frac{x^7}{7!} + \cdots + (-1)^n \frac{x^{2n+1}}{(2n+1)!} + \cdots \quad \text{(for all } x\text{)},$$

$$\cos x = 1 - \frac{x^2}{2!} + \frac{x^4}{4!} - \frac{x^6}{6!} + \cdots + (-1)^n \frac{x^{2n}}{(2n)!} + \cdots \quad \text{(for all } x\text{)},$$

$$\sinh x = x + \frac{x^3}{3!} + \frac{x^5}{5!} + \frac{x^7}{7!} + \cdots + \frac{x^{2n+1}}{(2n+1)!} + \cdots \quad \text{(for all } x\text{)},$$

$$\cosh x = 1 + \frac{x^2}{2!} + \frac{x^4}{4!} + \frac{x^6}{6!} + \cdots + \frac{x^{2n}}{(2n)!} + \cdots \quad \text{(for all } x\text{)},$$

$$\ln(1 + x) = x - \frac{x^2}{2} + \frac{x^3}{3} - \frac{x^4}{4} + \cdots + (-1)^{n-1}\frac{x^n}{n} + \cdots \quad (-1 < x \leq 1),$$

$$\tan^{-1} x = x - \frac{x^3}{3} + \frac{x^5}{5} - \frac{x^7}{7} + \cdots + (-1)^n \frac{x^{2n+1}}{2n+1} + \cdots \quad (-1 \leq x \leq 1),$$

$$\sin^{-1} x = x + \frac{1}{2}\frac{x^3}{3} + \frac{1.3}{2.4}\frac{x^5}{5} + \frac{1.3.5}{2.4.6}\frac{x^7}{7} + \cdots$$
$$+ \binom{2n}{n}\frac{x^{2n+1}}{2^{2n}(2n+1)} + \cdots \quad (-1 \leq x \leq 1),$$

$$(1 + x)^\alpha = 1 + \frac{\alpha}{1!}x + \frac{\alpha(\alpha - 1)}{2!}x^2 + \cdots$$
$$+ \frac{\alpha(\alpha - 1)\ldots(\alpha - n + 1)}{n!}x^n + \cdots \quad (-1 < x < 1).$$

(This is a binomial expansion; when α is a non-negative integer, the expansion is a finite series and is then valid for all x.)

TABLE OF TRIGONOMETRIC FORMULAE

$$\tan A = \frac{\sin A}{\cos A}, \qquad \cot A = \frac{\cos A}{\sin A} = \frac{1}{\tan A},$$

$$\sec A = \frac{1}{\cos A}, \qquad \operatorname{cosec} A = \frac{1}{\sin A},$$

$$\cos^2 A + \sin^2 A = 1, \quad \sec^2 A = 1 + \tan^2 A, \quad \operatorname{cosec}^2 A = 1 + \cot^2 A.$$

Addition formulae

$$\sin(A + B) = \sin A \cos B + \cos A \sin B,$$
$$\sin(A - B) = \sin A \cos B - \cos A \sin B,$$
$$\cos(A + B) = \cos A \cos B - \sin A \sin B,$$
$$\cos(A - B) = \cos A \cos B + \sin A \sin B,$$
$$\tan(A + B) = \frac{\tan A + \tan B}{1 - \tan A \tan B},$$
$$\tan(A - B) = \frac{\tan A - \tan B}{1 + \tan A \tan B}.$$

Double-angle formulae

$$\sin 2A = 2 \sin A \cos A,$$
$$\cos 2A = \cos^2 A - \sin^2 A,$$
$$\cos 2A = 1 - 2 \sin^2 A, \qquad \sin^2 A = \tfrac{1}{2}(1 - \cos 2A),$$
$$\cos 2A = 2 \cos^2 A - 1, \qquad \cos^2 A = \tfrac{1}{2}(1 + \cos 2A),$$
$$\tan 2A = \frac{2 \tan A}{1 - \tan^2 A}.$$

Tangent of half-angle formulae

Let $t = \tan \frac{1}{2}A$. Then

$$\sin A = \frac{2t}{1+t^2}, \qquad \cos A = \frac{1-t^2}{1+t^2}, \qquad \tan A = \frac{2t}{1-t^2}.$$

Product formulae

$$\sin A \cos B = \tfrac{1}{2}(\sin(A+B) + \sin(A-B)),$$
$$\cos A \sin B = \tfrac{1}{2}(\sin(A+B) - \sin(A-B)),$$
$$\cos A \cos B = \tfrac{1}{2}(\cos(A+B) + \cos(A-B)),$$
$$\sin A \sin B = \tfrac{1}{2}(\cos(A-B) - \cos(A+B)).$$

Sums and differences

$$\sin C + \sin D = 2 \sin \tfrac{1}{2}(C+D) \cos \tfrac{1}{2}(C-D),$$
$$\sin C - \sin D = 2 \cos \tfrac{1}{2}(C+D) \sin \tfrac{1}{2}(C-D),$$
$$\cos C + \cos D = 2 \cos \tfrac{1}{2}(C+D) \cos \tfrac{1}{2}(C-D),$$
$$\cos C - \cos D = -2 \sin \tfrac{1}{2}(C+D) \sin \tfrac{1}{2}(C-D).$$

TABLE OF SYMBOLS

Symbol	Reference
$\neg$	negation
$\wedge$	conjunction
$\vee$	disjunction
$\Rightarrow$, $\Leftrightarrow$	implication
$\sim$	equivalence relation
$\exists$, $\forall$	quantifier
$\in$, $\notin$	belongs to
$\subseteq$, $\supseteq$	subset
$\subset$, $\supset$	proper subset
$\cup$, $\bigcup$	union
$\cap$, $\bigcap$	intersection
A', $\overline{A}$	complement
$\emptyset$	empty set
$A \times B$	Cartesian product
$A \setminus B$, $A - B$	difference set
$A + B$, $A \triangle B$	symmetric difference
$n(A)$, $\#(A)$, $|A|$	cardinality
$\mathcal{P}(A)$	power set
$n!$	factorial
$[a, b]$	closed interval, least common multiple
(a, b)	open interval, greatest common divisor
$[a, b)$, $(a, b]$	interval
$\binom{n}{r}$	binomial coefficient
$[x]$	integer part
$\{x\}$	fractional part
$|x|$	absolute value
$|z|$	modulus
$\overline{z}$	conjugate
$\Re z$, $\operatorname{Re} z$	real part
$\Im z$, $\operatorname{Im} z$	imaginary part

Symbol	Reference
$\overrightarrow{AB}$	directed line-segment
$\|AB\|,\quad \|\overrightarrow{AB}\|$	length
$\|P\|$	norm
$\sqrt{}$	square root
$\approx$	approximation
$\equiv$	congruence
$\Sigma,\ \sum$	summation notation
$\Pi,\ \prod$	product notation
π	pi
$f: x \mapsto y$	function, mapping
$f: S \to T$	function, mapping
$\to$	limit
$\nearrow,\ \searrow$	limit from the left, and right
$f \circ g$	composition
f^{-1}	inverse function, inverse mapping
$f',\ \dfrac{df}{dx},\ y',\ \dfrac{dy}{dx}$	derivative, derived function
$f'',\ f''',\ \ldots,\ f^{(n)},\ \dfrac{d^2 f}{dx^2},\ \ldots,\ \dfrac{d^n f}{dx^n}$	higher derivative
$y'',\ y''',\ \ldots,\ y^{(n)},\ \dfrac{d^2 y}{dx^2},\ \ldots,\ \dfrac{d^n y}{dx^n}$	higher derivative
$f_x,\ f_y,\ f_1,\ f_2,\ \dfrac{\partial f}{\partial x},\ \dfrac{\partial f}{\partial y}$	partial derivative
$f_{xx},\ f_{xy},\ \ldots,\ f_{11},\ f_{12},\ \ldots$	higher-order partial derivative
$\dfrac{\partial^2 f}{\partial x^2},\ \dfrac{\partial^2 f}{\partial x \partial y},\ \ldots$	higher-order partial derivative
$\dot{x},\ \ddot{x}$	rate of change
$\displaystyle\int$	integral, antiderivative
$\mathbf{a} \cdot \mathbf{b}$	scalar product
$\mathbf{a} \times \mathbf{b},\quad \mathbf{a} \wedge \mathbf{b}$	vector product
$\mathbf{a} \cdot (\mathbf{b} \times \mathbf{c}),\quad [\mathbf{a}, \mathbf{b}, \mathbf{c}]$	scalar triple product
$\mathbf{a} \times (\mathbf{b} \times \mathbf{c})$	vector triple product
$\mathbf{A}^T,\quad \mathbf{A}^t,\quad \mathbf{A}'$	transpose
$\mathbf{A}^{-1}$	inverse matrix
$\|\mathbf{A}\|$	determinant
$\langle G, \circ \rangle$	group
$\langle R, +, \times \rangle$	ring

Appendix 7

TABLE OF GREEK LETTERS

Name	Lower Case	Capital
Alpha	α	A
Beta	β	B
Gamma	γ	Γ
Delta	δ	Δ
Epsilon	ϵ	E
Zeta	ζ	Z
Eta	η	H
Theta	θ	Θ
Iota	ι	I
Kappa	κ	K
Lambda	λ	Λ
Mu	μ	M
Nu	ν	N
Xi	ξ	Ξ
Omicron	o	O
Pi	π	Π
Rho	ρ	P
Sigma	σ	Σ
Tau	τ	T
Upsilon	υ	Υ
Phi	ϕ	Φ
Chi	χ	X
Psi	ψ	Ψ
Omega	ω	Ω